WEIRD SCENES INSIDE THE CANYON

LAUREL CANYON, COVERT OPS & THE DARK HEART OF THE HIPPIE DREAM

DAVID McGOWAN

HEADPRESS

TABLE OF CONTENTS

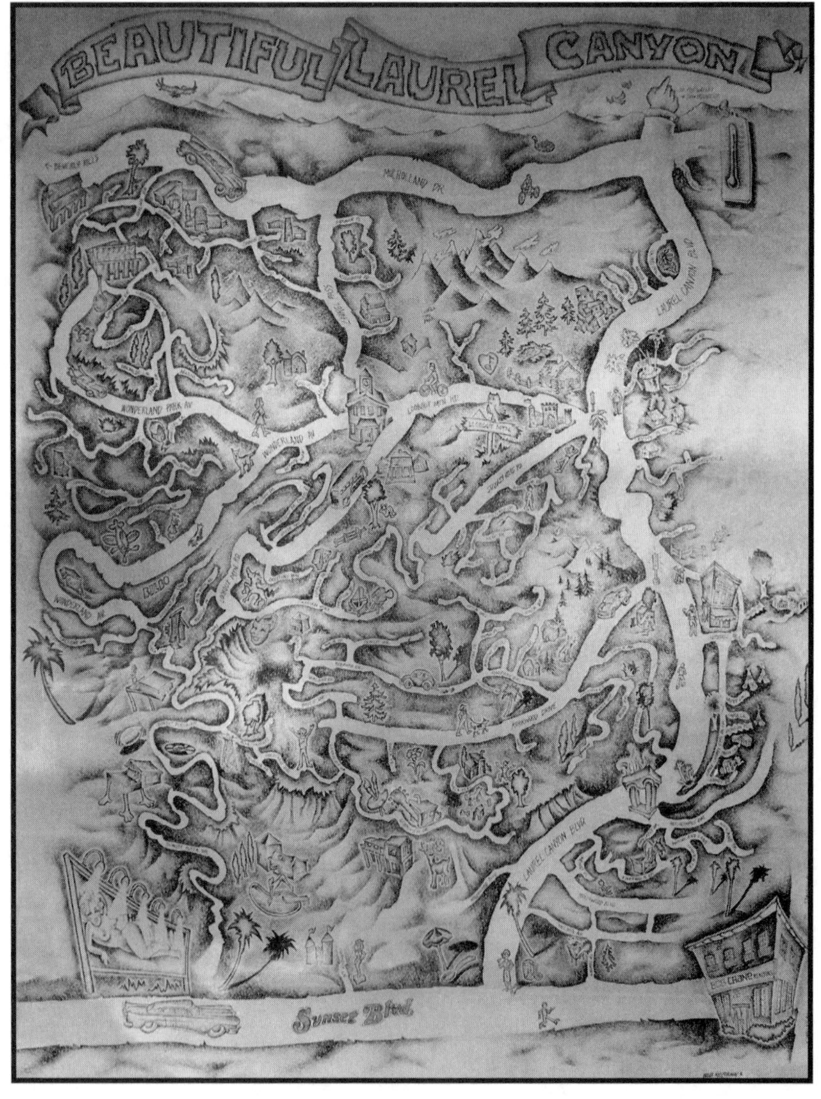
BEAUTIFUL LAUREL CANYON
MULHOLLAND DR.
LAUREL CANYON BLVD
WONDERLAND PARK AV
WONDERLAND AV
LOOKOUT MTN RD
WONDERLAND AV
LAUREL CANYON BLVD
Sunset Blvd.

FOREWORD

by Nick Bryant

Oscar Wilde said of art, "Those who go beneath the surface do so at their peril." And author David McGowan has found that Wilde's quote is quite prophetic for the rock'n'roll scene that thrived in Laurel Canyon in the 1960s and 1970s. *Weird Scenes Inside the Canyon* is McGowan taking a hammer to the icons and mythologies of 1960s counterculture, reducing them to dust, swept away by gusts of pomp, pretense, and even deceit. McGowan though isn't wielding his hammer with the zeal of an establishment conformist or neocon, but rather in the same forlorn spirit as Nietzsche declaring that "God is dead." As a homegrown product of Los Angeles with an encyclopedic knowledge of the southern California rock scene, McGowan appears to be essentially declaring that the gods of his youth are dead.

Laurel Canyon was the fountainhead for the peace, love, and brown rice vibes that overflowed America's airwaves as the Vietnam War raged, but lurking beneath its tie-dyed and florid veneer was an exquisite darkness of drugs, unbridled debauchery, full-tilt depravity, and shocking carnage. When readers of this book are delivered to Laurel Canyon's blood-drenched tapestry of murder and mayhem, they will have to decide whether or not those sinister synchronicities are uncanny coincidences, conspiracies—or perhaps a kaleidoscopic blending of both.

Sprinkled throughout these pages is the ominous specter of the military/intelligence complex, and perched quite literally atop Laurel Canyon was the top-secret Lookout Mountain Laboratory, which seems to be McGowan's grand metaphor for Dr. Strangelove having a bird's-eye view of the nascent hippie movement, treating it as though it were a petri dish brimming with a lethal biological weapon that could be unleashed in meticulously monitored increments. Indeed, many of Laurel Canyon's rock 'n' roll idols had former incarnations steeped in the world of military/intelligence operations. Jim Morrison, aka "the Lizard King," was one such example. Mr. Mojo Risin' didn't much like to talk about his parents and was even known to tell reporters that his parents were dead. But as it turns out, Lizard King, Sr. was not only alive and well, he just happened to be the commander of the US warships that allegedly came under attack by North Vietnamese torpedo boats in the Gulf of Tonkin, sparking America's napalm-fueled bloodbath in Vietnam.

Frank Zappa, another major mover and shaker of the Laurel Canyon scene, was certainly the raddest of the rad, so surely he couldn't have had any connections to the military/intelligence complex... right? Not exactly. According to various accounts collected by McGowan, Zappa was a pro-military autocrat who didn't really resonate with the counterculture's peace and love vibe. Like the Lizard King's dad, Zappa, Sr. was a cog in the intelligence community's dark machinations; Francis Zappa was a chemical warfare specialist with a top security clearance at Edgewood Arsenal near Baltimore, Maryland. Some readers might recognize Edgewood as the location of ominous mind control experiments conducted by the CIA under the rubric of MK-ULTRA.

Guilt by familial association has the potential to be an ill-fated formula for speculation, but McGowan relates accounts of Laurel Canyon luminaries whose own hands were possibly awash in the blood of the military/intelligence complex. Consider, for example, "Papa" John Phillips, who penned the smash hit San Francisco (Be Sure to Wear Flowers in Your Hair), imploring thousands of runaways to make bacchanal-laced pilgrimages to the City by the Bay. The son of a Marine Corps captain, Phillips was among the more prominent fixtures of Laurel Canyon who had a particularly interesting interrelationship with the military machine.

Rock superstar Stephen Stills was the cofounder of two Laurel Canyon dynamos—Buffalo Springfield, and, of course, Crosby, Stills, Nash & Young. Surely then hippie icon Stills couldn't possibly be enmeshed in the military-intelligence complex? Maybe, maybe not. The progeny of yet another military family, Stills spent chunks of his childhood in El Salvador, Costa Rica, and Panama, where the US has a history of spreading a genocidal form of "democracy." And McGowan has sifted through accounts of Stills actually confessing to running around the jungles of Vietnam in the early 1960s—anecdotes generally dismissed, as the author notes, as drug-fueled delusions.

Tales of drugs, unbridled debauchery and full-tilt depravity are often populated by ethical eunuchs whose elite deviance yields to particularly malignant appetites, and the people calling Laurel Canyon home were no exception. McGowan introduces us to aging beatnik Vito Paulekas and his "Freaks," a dance troupe of Dionysian goddesses who accompanied Vito to the LA nightclubs where the fledgling Laurel Canyon bands were playing their early gigs. In addition to saturating the dance floors with sultry young nubiles for emerging bands, Vito was also a purveyor of teenage girls for the up-and-coming rockers. McGowan also comments on Vito's swift exodus to Haiti, for reasons explained herein.

Vito Paulekas certainly isn't a household name, but he was far from being a fringe player on the Laurel Canyon scene, where he and his Freaks mingled freely with rock 'n' roll's burgeoning royalty. McGowan collects anecdotes suggesting that Vito may have played a key role in the formation and early success of the Byrds—though his name is conspicuously absent from the autobiographical tome of Byrds co-founder David Crosby. We also find Vito in a string of low-budget films, and in a cameo appearance on one of rock's first concept albums: Zappa's *Freak Out!* Vito's parental skills, however, left a lot to be desired, as evinced by the very mysterious and bizarre death of his young son, Godo.

Further excavating the idolatry of his youth, McGowan encounters Laurel Canyon fixture Billy Bryars, a male madam and gay porn entrepreneur. Bryers was investigated for trafficking child pornography in the 1970s, whereupon his stable of male hustlers began coughing up the names of frequent flyers at his bordello, the most notable among them being super freak G-man J. Edgar Hoover and partner Clyde Tolson.

The 1960s was a "revolutionary" epoch not only in music but also in Hollywood, and McGowan discusses the symbiosis between the Laurel Canyon music scene and Hollywood's "Young Turks," with the box office phenomenon *Easy Rider* providing a salient nexus between Laurel Canyon rockers and Hollywood upstarts. Many of those upstarts, including Warren Beatty, Peter and Jane Fonda, Jack Nicholson, Candice Bergen, Marlon Brando, Roman Polanski and Sharon Tate, Peter Lawford, Dennis Hopper, Ryan O'Neal, Mia Farrow, Peter Sellers, and Zsa Zsa Gabor, were among Papa John and Mama Michelle Phillips' circle of friends.

Also making the rounds in Laurel Canyon was America's favorite psychopath, Charles Manson. And Charlie and his "Family" weren't just a peripheral flock of crazed killers among the Laurel Canyon sovereigns; to the contrary, the Family mingled with many of the Canyon's rock stars. Manson even laid down tracks in Brian Wilson's home studio, stunning the likes of Neil Young. "He had this kind of music that nobody else was doing," said Neil of Charlie. "I thought he really had something crazy, something great. He was like a living poet." Charlie also impressed Terry Melcher, the Byrds' first producer and a major force in sculpting the Laurel Canyon music scene. Melcher also recorded Manson, finding him to be a much more amicable character than David Crosby.

Manson's homicidal lieutenant Bobby Beausoleil also had some impressive moves as a guitarist—and an occultist. Beausoleil played in a number of forgotten bands that had an occult topspin, one of which even opened for Buffalo Springfield. Bobby eventually landed a gig as a rhythm guitarist for the Grass Roots, which later transmuted into the Laurel Canyon band Love.

McGowan also touches on the grisly "Four on the Floor" or "Wonderland" murders, which left notorious drug dealer Ron Launius and three of his gang bludgeoned to death on the floor of a house on Laurel Canyon's Wonderland Avenue. Launius dealt drugs to Laurel Canyon's aristocracy, as well as to porn star John Holmes, then in the twilight of his career. Holmes also befriended LA crime boss/club owner Eddie Nash, who he then betrayed, with fatal consequences.

Truth be told, the Manson and Wonderland Murders were merely spatters on Laurel Canyon's blood-drenched tapestry. In the pages of this fascinating book, McGowan chronicles tale after tale of suicide and murder, while delivering readers to a web of sinister synchronicities. Ultimately, it is up to the reader to decide whether Laurel Canyon, in its heyday, was the counterculture haven portrayed by other chroniclers of the era, or whether it was the epicenter of intrigues whose ripple effects are like the aftershock of a nuclear bomb.

Nick Bryant
July 29, 2013

"I think these days, especially in the States, you have to be a politician or an assassin or something to really be a superstar." Jim Morrison

Before he was the Lizard King: US Navy Admiral George Stephen Morrison and his son, James Douglas Morrison, on the bridge of the USS Bon Homme Richard, *January 1964.*

This book is dedicated to all those whose blood still stains the canyon floor.

PREFACE

It began innocently enough.

In my normal, everyday life I spend a fair amount of time researching corruption and criminality in the realms of politics and law enforcement. Much of that research has taken me down some very dark and twisted paths. But this was going to be different. I was, after all, going to be vacationing in a lush, tropical paradise and I really just wanted to turn my brain off for a couple weeks and forget about all of that.

Not long before this much-anticipated break from reality, my eldest daughter had given me a copy of Michael Walker's *Laurel Canyon: The Inside Story of Rock-and-Roll's Legendary Neighborhood*, which chronicles the Los Angeles music scene of the late 1960s through the 1970s. It seemed like the ideal escapist entertainment that would undoubtedly conjure up many fond memories of the music that provided the soundtrack to my formative years. What could be further removed from my usual reading material?

As is often the case though, things didn't work out exactly as planned. Alarm bells started going off in my head soon after arriving at my destination and diving into the book. What was this about secret underground tunnels connecting some of the iconic Laurel Canyon properties? And what about all those mysterious fires that wiped away the homes of a number of prominent singers and musicians? And why were there so many violent deaths so closely associated with a scene that was supposed to be all about peace and love? And what of Walker's throwaway mention of a "secret fortified" military installation sitting right smack-dab in the middle of hippiedom? And why did at least a few of America's new minstrels seem to come from career military families and from the world of covert intelligence operations? And how exactly do the casual allusions to pedophilia fit into this increasingly curious scene?

While Walker had done a decent job of telling the Laurel Canyon story from a mainstream perspective, there seemed to be a much more intriguing story hidden in the details that he tended to cast aside as interesting but largely meaningless incongruities. Before I was even halfway through my sorely needed rest-and-relaxation time, I was champing at the bit to get back home and dig deeper into this story. And immediately upon my return, I began devouring everything I could find that had been written on the subject.

Although I am regarded by many people as a 'conspiracy theorist,' which is more often than not utilized as a pejorative term, I do all of my research through very mainstream channels. I am a big believer in the notion that 'the truth is out there,' but don't expect it to be delivered to you in a tidy package by any mainstream media outlets. Finding it involves assembling a jigsaw puzzle of sorts, with the goal being to gather up all the bits and pieces of information that other writers tend to present as throwaway facts and/or interesting anomalies. Sometimes those bits and pieces end up being no more than interesting anomalies, but past experience has taught me that if those divergent facts are properly assembled, a new picture often begins to emerge that is strikingly at odds with what is widely accepted as our consensus reality.

At the end of the day, it is really all about pattern recognition. If, for example, just a few prominent Laurel Canyon musicians happened to come from military/intelligence families, then we could probably safely write that off as an interesting but largely inconsequential aberration. But if an uncanny number of the leading lights of the Laurel Canyon scene grew up in such an environment, then that is clearly a meaningful pattern. And if a few of the new breed of stars happened to have violent death intrude upon their personal lives, then that would be a tragic but largely inconsequential fact. But when it becomes clear that violent death surrounded the entire scene, with whole families at times dying off under suspicious circumstances, then that again is a distinguishing pattern—and one that has been all but ignored by other chroniclers of the scene.

There is little doubt in my mind that this book will not be warmly received by all readers. In our celebrity-driven culture, calling into question the character and motivations of so many widely admired and respected figures from the entertainment community is never a good way to win popularity contests. And when those revered figures are overwhelmingly viewed as icons of various leftist causes, it is definitely not the way to win fans among those who consider themselves to be liberals, progressives or leftists. But while my sympathies lie solidly in the leftward flanks of the political spectrum, there are no sacred cows in either this book or in any of my past work.

I really have no agenda other than to seek out unspoken truths and better my own understanding of the world we live in. I have no political party affiliations and have never been associated in any way with any governmental or quasi-governmental entities. And for the record, I was not born into the world of military intelligence operations; my rather uneventful childhood was spent in a quiet slice of suburbia with two public school teachers as parents. I have never claimed to be in possession of any 'inside information' or to have access to any highly placed, confidential sources. My research and the views expressed in my work are very much my own.

While almost all of my past and present literary contributions are generally regarded as being quite controversial, the individual facts contained in this volume are not really controversial at all. All of them, as previously noted, have been mined from very respectable mainstream sources. It is only the way that I have presented those facts—in other words, the way that I have chosen to assemble the puzzle—that makes them controversial.

There will undoubtedly be those who will stridently claim that I have carefully cherry-picked my facts to paint an unnecessarily dark portrait of many of the iconic figures who make up the cast of this story. Anyone, so the argument goes, could be made to look bad through such a journalistic approach. I would strongly disagree with that assessment, however. Such criticisms, in my opinion, completely miss the point of the book—which is that when stripped of the usual spin that accompanies them, and when assembled so that they become part of overriding patterns, these 'anomalous' facts reveal truths that would not otherwise be visible.

Another criticism I anticipate is that I did not go out and attempt to speak directly to the people who made up the scene. True enough, but the primary reason for that is that there is very little chance that the aging rock stars and their handlers would have wanted anything to do with me. Other chroniclers of the era have gained access to those involved, but that access has come, or so it appears to me, with a steep price in journalistic integrity. The inevitable result is what amounts to puff pieces with a mind-numbing sameness, with the same tired anecdotal stories uncritically told over and over again in the very same way, even when those stories can't possibly be true.

I have no desire to serve as a publicist for the estates of Jim Morrison, John Phillips or Frank Zappa, nor do I have any interest in filling the pages of this book with the same apocryphal tales told by other scribes. There are any number of literary offerings listed in the bibliography that will provide that type of a reading experience. My goal here is to break new ground and open readers' minds to the possibility that other writers may have left out some of the most important elements of this underreported tale.

The story of the scene that played out in Laurel Canyon from the mid-1960s through the end of the 1970s is an endlessly fascinating one. It wasn't until fairly recently that the mainstream version of the tale was belatedly told, and even now it remains a story unknown by most of those who were not a part of it. Virtually everyone has heard of the Haight-Ashbury scene up north in San Francisco, but even most native Angelenos remain ignorant of the even larger music and counterculture scene that played out in the Hollywood Hills.

It seems a bit odd that, nearly a full half-century after the fact, the Haight is almost universally regarded as the birthplace of hippies and flower children, despite the fact that the Laurel Canyon scene preceded and largely inspired what became a parallel scene up north. Why is it that the Haight has been thrust into the spotlight for so long while so little attention has been paid to the scene that spawned it? Perhaps the Laurel Canyon scene was hiding so many dark secrets that it was better to just let it lie undisturbed.

And perhaps it is now time to shine a light into some of the darker corners of the canyon to see what kind of skeletons might be hiding there.

1

VILLAGE OF THE DAMNED
BY WAY OF AN INTRODUCTION

"There's something happening here /
What it is ain't exactly clear"

JOIN ME NOW, IF YOU HAVE THE TIME, AS WE TAKE A STROLL DOWN MEMORY lane to a time nearly five decades ago—a time when America last had uniformed ground troops fighting a sustained and bloody battle to impose some decidedly Orwellian 'democracy' on a sovereign nation.

It is the first week of August, 1964, and US warships under the command of US Navy Admiral George Stephen Morrison have allegedly come under attack while patrolling Vietnam's Tonkin Gulf. This event, subsequently dubbed the 'Tonkin Gulf Incident,' will result in the immediate passing by the US Congress of the obviously pre-drafted Tonkin Gulf Resolution, which will, in turn, quickly lead to America's deep immersion into the bloody Vietnam quagmire. Before it is over, well over 50,000 American bodies—along with literally millions of Southeast Asian bodies—will litter the battlefields of Vietnam, Laos and Cambodia.

For the record, the Tonkin Gulf Incident appears to differ somewhat from other alleged provocations that have driven this country to war. This was not, as we have seen so many times before, a 'false flag' operation (which is to say, an operation that involves Uncle Sam attacking himself and then pointing an accusatory finger at someone else). It was also not, as we have also seen on more than one occasion, an attack that was quite deliberately provoked. No, what the Tonkin Gulf Incident actually was, as it turns out, is an 'attack' that never took place at all. The entire incident, as has been all but officially acknowledged, was spun from whole cloth. (It is quite possible, however, that the *intent* was to provoke a defensive response, which could have then been cast as an unprovoked attack on U.S ships. The ships in question were on an intelligence mission and were operating in a decidedly provocative manner. It is quite possible that when Vietnamese forces failed to respond as anticipated, Uncle Sam decided to just pretend as though they had.)

Nevertheless, by early February 1965, the US will—without a declaration of war and with no valid reason to wage one—begin indiscriminately bombing North Vietnam. By March of that same year, the infamous Operation Rolling Thunder will commence. Over the course of the next three-and-a-half years, millions of tons of bombs, missiles, rockets, incendiary devices and chemical warfare agents will be dumped on the people of Vietnam in what can only be described as one of the worst crimes against humanity ever perpetrated on this planet.

Also in March of 1965, the first uniformed US soldier officially sets foot on Vietnamese soil (although Special Forces units masquerading as 'advisers' and 'trainers' have been there for at least four years, and likely much longer). By April 1965, fully 25,000 uniformed American kids, most still teenagers barely out of high school, are slogging through the rice paddies of Vietnam. By the end of the year, US troop strength will have surged to 200,000.

Meanwhile, elsewhere in the world in those early months of 1965, a new 'scene' is just beginning to take shape in the city of Los Angeles. In a geographically and socially isolated community known as Laurel Canyon—a heavily wooded, rustic, serene, yet vaguely ominous slice of LA nestled in the hills that separate the Los Angeles basin from the San Fernando Valley—musicians, singers and songwriters suddenly begin to gather as though summoned there by some unseen Pied Piper. Within months, the 'hippie/flower child' movement is begotten there, along with the new style of music that will provide the soundtrack for the tumultuous second half of the 1960s.

Beginning in the mid-1960s and carrying through the decade of the 1970s, an uncanny number of rock music superstars will emerge from

Laurel Canyon. The first to drop an album is the Byrds, whose biggest star will prove to be David Crosby. The band's debut effort, *Mr. Tambourine Man*, is released on the summer solstice of 1965. It will quickly be followed by releases from the John Phillips-led Mamas and the Papas (*If You Can Believe Your Eyes and Ears*, January 1966), Love with Arthur Lee (*Love*, May 1966), Frank Zappa and the Mothers of Invention (*Freak Out*, June 1966), Buffalo Springfield, featuring Stephen Stills and Neil Young (*Buffalo Springfield*, October 1966), and the Doors (*The Doors*, January 1967).

One of the earliest on the Laurel Canyon/Sunset Strip scene is Jim Morrison, the enigmatic lead singer of the Doors. Jim will quickly become one of the most iconic, controversial, critically acclaimed, and influential figures to take up residence in Laurel Canyon. Curiously enough though, the self-proclaimed "Lizard King" has another claim to fame as well, albeit one that none of his numerous chroniclers will feel is of much relevance to his career and possible untimely death: he is the son, as it happens, of the aforementioned Admiral George Stephen Morrison.

And so it is that, even while the father is actively conspiring to fabricate an incident that will be used to massively accelerate an illegal war, the son is positioning himself to become an icon of the 'hippie'/anti-war crowd. Nothing unusual about that, I suppose. It is, you know, a small world and all. And it is not as if Jim Morrison's story is in any way unique.

During the early years of its heyday, Laurel Canyon's father figure is the rather eccentric personality known as Frank Zappa. Though he and his various Mothers of Invention lineups will never attain the commercial success of the band headed by the admiral's son, Frank will be a hugely influential figure among his contemporaries. Ensconced in an abode dubbed the 'Log Cabin'—which sat right in the heart of Laurel Canyon, at the crossroads of Laurel Canyon Boulevard and Lookout Mountain Avenue—Zappa will play host to virtually every musician who passes through the canyon in the mid- to late-1960s. He will also discover and sign numerous acts to his various Laurel Canyon-based record labels. Many of these acts will be rather bizarre and somewhat obscure characters (think Captain Beefheart and Larry "Wild Man" Fischer), but some of them, such as psychedelic rocker cum shock-rocker

Alice Cooper, will go on to superstardom.

Zappa, along with certain members of his sizable entourage (the Log Cabin was run as an early commune, with numerous hangers-on occupying various rooms in the main house and the guest house, as well as the peculiar caves and tunnels lacing the grounds of the home; far from the quaint homestead the name seems to imply, the Log Cabin was a cavernous five-level home that featured a 2,000+ square-foot living room with three massive chandeliers and an enormous floor-to-ceiling stone fireplace), will also be instrumental in introducing the look and attitude that will define the 'hippie' counterculture—although the Zappa crew prefers the label 'freak'. Nevertheless, Zappa will never really make a secret of the fact that he has nothing but contempt for the hippie culture that he will help create and with which he will surround himself.

Given that Zappa is, by various accounts, a pro-military, rigidly authoritarian control-freak, it is perhaps unsurprising that he will not feel a kinship with the youth movement that he will help nurture. And it is probably safe to say that Frank's dad also would have had little regard for the youth culture of the 1960s, given that Francis Zappa was, in case you were wondering, a chemical warfare specialist assigned to—where else?—the Edgewood Arsenal near Baltimore, Maryland. Edgewood is, of course, the longtime home of America's chemical warfare program, as well as a facility frequently cited as being deeply enmeshed in MKULTRA operations. Curiously enough, Frank Zappa literally grew up at the Edgewood Arsenal, having lived the first seven years of his life in military housing on the grounds of the facility. The family later moved to Lancaster, California, near Edwards Air Force Base, where Francis Zappa continued to busy himself doing classified work for the military/intelligence complex. His son, meanwhile, prepped himself to become an icon of the peace and love crowd. Again, nothing unusual about that, I suppose.

Zappa's manager is a shadowy character by the name of Herb Cohen, who had come out to LA from the Bronx with his brother Mutt just before the music and club scene began heating up. Cohen, a former US Marine, had spent a few years traveling the world before his arrival on the Laurel Canyon scene. Those travels, curiously, had taken him to the Congo in 1961, at the very time that leftist Prime Minister Patrice

Lumumba was being tortured and killed by our very own CIA. Not to worry though; according to one of Zappa's biographers, Cohen wasn't in the Congo on some kind of nefarious intelligence mission. No, he was there, on the contrary, *to supply arms to Lumumba* "in defiance of the CIA." Because, you know, that is the kind of thing that globetrotting ex-Marines did in those days (as we'll see soon enough when we take a look at another Laurel Canyon luminary).

Making up the other half of Laurel Canyon's First Family is Frank's wife, Gail Zappa, known formerly as Adelaide Sloatman. Gail hails from a long line of career Naval officers, including her father, who spent his life working on classified nuclear weapons research for the US Navy. Gail herself once worked as a secretary for the Office of Naval Research and Development (she also once told an interviewer that she had "heard voices all [her] life"). Many years before their nearly simultaneous arrival in Laurel Canyon, Gail had attended a Naval kindergarten class with "Mr. Mojo Risin'" himself, Jim Morrison (it is claimed that, as children, Gail once hit Jim over the head with a hammer). The very same Jim Morrison had later attended the same Alexandria, Virginia, high school as two other future Laurel Canyon luminaries—John Phillips and Cass Elliot.

"Papa" John Phillips, more so than probably any of the other illustrious residents of Laurel Canyon, will play a major role in spreading the emerging youth 'counterculture' across America. His contribution will be twofold: first, he will co-organize the famed Monterey Pop Festival, which, through unprecedented media exposure, will give mainstream America its first real look at the music and fashions of the nascent hippie movement. Second, Phillips will pen an insipid song known as San Francisco (Be Sure To Wear Flowers In Your Hair), which will quickly rise to the top of the charts. Along with the Monterey Pop Festival, the song will be instrumental in luring the disenfranchised (a preponderance of whom will be underage runaways) to San Francisco to create the Haight-Ashbury phenomenon and the famed 1967 Summer of Love.

Before arriving in Laurel Canyon and opening the doors of his home to the soon-to-be famous, the already famous, and the infamous (such as Charlie Manson, whose 'Family' also spent time at the Log Cabin and at the Laurel Canyon home of "Mama" Cass Elliot, which, in case you didn't know, sat right across the road from the Laurel Canyon home of Abigail Folger and Voytek Frykowski, but let's not get ahead of ourselves here), John Edmund Andrew Phillips was, shockingly enough, yet another child of the military/intelligence complex. The son of US Marine Corp Captain Claude Andrew Phillips and a mother who claimed to have psychic and telekinetic powers, John attended a series of elite military prep schools in the Washington, DC area, culminating in an appointment to the prestigious US Naval Academy at Annapolis.

After leaving Annapolis, John married Susie Adams, a direct descendant of Founding Father John Adams. Susie's father, James Adams, Jr., had been involved in what Susie described as "cloak-and-dagger stuff with the Air Force in Vienna," or what others like to call covert intelligence operations. Susie herself would later find employment at the Pentagon, alongside John Phillips' older sister, Rosie, who dutifully reported to work at the complex for nearly thirty years. John's mother, "Dene" Phillips, also worked for most of her life for the federal government in some unspecified capacity. And John's older brother, Tommy, was a battle-scarred former US Marine who found work on the Alexandria police force as a cop, albeit one with a disciplinary record for exhibiting a violent streak when dealing with people of color.

John Phillips, of course—though surrounded throughout his life by military/intelligence personnel—did not involve himself in such matters. Or so we are to believe. Before succeeding in his musical career, however, John did seem to find himself, quite innocently of course, in some rather unusual places. One such place was Havana, Cuba, where Phillips arrived at the very height of the Cuban Revolution. For the record, Phillips has claimed that he went to Havana as nothing more than a concerned private citizen, with the intention of—you're going to love this one—"fighting for Castro." Because, as I mentioned earlier, a lot of folks in those days traveled abroad to thwart CIA operations before taking up residence in Laurel Canyon and joining the 'hippie' generation. During the two weeks or so that the Cuban Missile Crisis played out, a few years after Castro took power, Phillips found himself cooling his heels in Jacksonville, Florida—alongside the Mayport Naval Station.

Anyway, let's move on to yet another of Laurel Canyon's earliest and brightest stars, Mr. Stephen Stills. Stills will have the distinction of being a founding member of two of Laurel Canyon's most acclaimed and beloved bands: Buffalo Springfield, and, needless to say, Crosby, Stills

& Nash. In addition, Stills will pen perhaps the first, and certainly one of the most enduring anthems of the sixties generation, For What It's Worth, the opening lines of which appear at the top of this chapter (Stills' follow-up single will be entitled Bluebird, which, coincidentally or not, happens to be the original codename assigned to the CIA's MK-ULTRA program).

Before his arrival in Laurel Canyon, Stephen Stills was the product of yet another career military family. Raised partly in Texas, young Stephen spent large swaths of his childhood in El Salvador, Costa Rica, the Panama Canal Zone, and various other parts of Central America—alongside his father, who was, we can be fairly certain, helping to spread 'democracy' to the unwashed masses in that endearingly American way. As with the rest of our cast of characters, Stills was educated primarily at schools on military bases and at elite military academies. Among his contemporaries in Laurel Canyon, he was widely viewed as having an abrasive, authoritarian personality. Nothing unusual about any of that, of course, as we have already seen.

There is, however, an even more curious aspect to the Stephen Stills story: Stephen will later tell anyone who will sit and listen that he had served time for Uncle Sam in the jungles of Vietnam. These tales will be universally dismissed by chroniclers of the era as nothing more than drug-induced delusions. Such a thing couldn't possibly be true, it will be claimed, since Stills arrived on the Laurel Canyon scene at the very time that the first uniformed troops began shipping out and he remained in the public eye thereafter. And it will of course be quite true that Stephen Stills could not have served with uniformed ground troops in Vietnam, but what will be ignored is the undeniable fact that the US had thousands of 'advisers'—which is to say, CIA/Special Forces operatives—active in the country for a good many years before the arrival of the first official ground troops. What will also be ignored is that, given his background, his age, and the timeline of events, Stephen Stills not only could indeed have seen action in Vietnam, he would seem to have been a prime candidate for such an assignment. After which, of course, he could rather quickly become—stop me if you've heard this one before—an icon of the peace generation.

Another of those icons, and one of Laurel Canyon's most flamboyant residents, is a young man by the name of David Crosby, founding member of the seminal Laurel Canyon band the Byrds, as well as, of course, Crosby, Stills & Nash. Crosby is, not surprisingly, the son of an Annapolis graduate and WWII military intelligence officer, Major Floyd Delafield Crosby. Like others in this story, Floyd Crosby spent much of his post-service time traveling the world. Those travels landed him in places like Haiti, where he paid a visit in 1927, when the country just happened to be, coincidentally of course, under military occupation by the US Marines. One of the Marines doing that occupying was a guy that we met earlier by the name of Captain Claude Andrew Phillips.

But David Crosby is much more than just the son of Major Floyd Delafield Crosby. David Van Cortlandt Crosby, as it turns out, is a scion of the closely intertwined van Cortlandt, van Schuyler and van Rensselaer families. And while you're probably thinking, "the Van Who families?," I can assure you that if you plug those names in over at Wikipedia, you can spend a pretty fair amount of time reading up on the power wielded by this clan for the last, oh, two-and-a-quarter centuries or so. Suffice it to say that the Crosby family tree includes a truly dizzying array of US senators and congressmen, state senators and assemblymen, governors, mayors, judges, Supreme Court justices, Revolutionary and Civil War generals, signers of the Declaration of Independence, and members of the Continental Congress. It also includes, I should hasten to add—for those of you with a taste for such things—more than a few high-ranking Masons. Stephen van Rensselaer III, for example, reportedly served as Grand Master of Masons for New York. And if all that isn't impressive enough, according to the New England Genealogical Society, David Van Cortlandt Crosby is also a direct descendant of Founding Fathers and Federalist Papers authors Alexander Hamilton and John Jay.

If there is, as many believe, a network of elite families that has shaped national and world events for a very long time, then it is probably safe to say that David Crosby is a bloodline member of that clan (which may explain, come to think of it, why his semen seems to be in such demand in certain circles—because, if we're being honest here, it certainly can't be due to his looks or talent). If America had royalty, then David Crosby would probably be a Duke, or a Prince, or something similar. But other than that, he is just a normal, run-of-the-mill kind of guy who just happened to shine as one of Laurel Canyon's brightest stars. And who, I guess I should add, has a real fondness for guns, especially handguns, which he has maintained a sizable collection of for his entire life. According to those closest to him, it is a rare occasion when Mr. Crosby is not packing heat (John Phillips also owned and sometimes carried handguns). And according to Crosby himself, he has, on at least one occasion, discharged a firearm in anger at another human being. All of which made him, of course, an obvious choice for the Flower Children to rally around.

Another shining star on the Laurel Canyon scene, just a few years later, will be singer-songwriter Jackson Browne, who is—are you getting as bored with this as I am?—the product of a career military family. Browne's father was assigned to postwar reconstruction work in Germany, which very likely means that he was in the employ of the OSS, precursor to the CIA. As readers of my earlier work, *Understanding the F-Word*, may recall, US involvement in postwar reconstruction in Germany largely consisted of maintaining as much of the Nazi infrastructure as possible while shielding war criminals from capture and prosecution. Against that backdrop, Jackson Browne was born in a military hospital in Heidelberg, Germany. Some two decades later, he emerged as... oh, never mind.

Let's talk instead about three other Laurel Canyon vocalists who will rise to dizzying heights of fame and fortune: Gerry Beckley, Dan Peek and Dewey Bunnell. Individually, these three names are probably unknown to virtually all readers, but collectively, as the band America, the three will score huge hits in the early seventies with such songs as Ventura Highway, A Horse With No Name, and the Wizard of Oz-themed The Tin Man. I guess I probably don't need to add here that all three of these lads were products of the military/intelligence community. Beckley's dad was the commander of the now-defunct West Ruislip USAF base near London, England, a facility deeply immersed in intelligence operations. Bunnell's and Peek's fathers were both career Air Force officers serving under Beckley's dad at West Ruislip, which is where the three boys first met.

We could also, I suppose, discuss Mike Nesmith of the Monkees and Cory Wells of Three Dog Night (two more hugely successful Laurel Canyon bands), who both arrived in LA not long after serving time with the US Air Force. Nesmith also inherited a family fortune estimated at $25 million. Gram Parsons, who will briefly replace David Crosby in the

Byrds before fronting the Flying Burrito Brothers, was the son of Major Cecil Ingram "Coon Dog" Connor II, a decorated military officer and bomber pilot who reportedly flew over fifty combat missions. Parsons was also an heir, on his mother's side, to the formidable Snively family fortune. Said to be the wealthiest family in the exclusive enclave of Winter Haven, Florida, the Snively family was the proud owner of Snively Groves, Inc., which reportedly owned as much as one-third of all the citrus groves in the state of Florida.

And so it goes as one scrolls through the roster of Laurel Canyon superstars. What one finds, far more often than not, are the sons and daughters of the military/intelligence complex and the sons and daughters of extreme wealth and privilege—oftentimes, you'll find both rolled into one convenient package. Every once in a while, you will also stumble across a former child actor, like Brandon DeWilde, or Monkee Mickey Dolenz, or eccentric prodigy Van Dyke Parks. You might also encounter some former mental patients, such as James Taylor, who spent time in two different mental institutions in Massachusetts before hitting the Laurel Canyon scene, or Larry "Wild Man" Fischer, who was institutionalized repeatedly during his teen years, once for attacking his mother with a knife (an act that was gleefully mocked by Zappa on the cover of Fischer's first album). Finally, you might find the offspring of an organized crime figure, like Warren Zevon, the son of William "Stumpy" Zevon, a lieutenant for infamous LA crimelord Mickey Cohen.

All these folks gathered nearly simultaneously along the narrow, winding roads of Laurel Canyon. They came from across the country—although the Washington, DC area was noticeably over-represented—as well as from Canada and England, and, in at least one case, all the way from Nazi Germany. They came even though, at the time, there was no music industry in Los Angeles. They came even though, at the time, there was no live music scene to speak of. They came even though, in retrospect, there was no discernible reason for them to do so.

It would, of course, make sense these days for an aspiring musician to venture out to Los Angeles. But in those days, the centers of the music universe were Nashville, Memphis and New York. It wasn't the industry that drew the Laurel Canyon crowd, you see, but rather the Laurel Canyon crowd that transformed Los Angeles into the epicenter of the music industry. To what then do we attribute this unprecedented gathering of future musical superstars in the hills above Los Angeles? What was it that inspired them all to head out west? Perhaps Neil Young said it best when he told an interviewer that he couldn't really say why he headed out to LA circa 1966; he and others "were just going like Lemmings."

2

POWER TO THE PEOPLE CALL THIS A COUNTERCULTURE?

"Everyone there had at one time or another been into Satanism, or, like myself, had dabbled around the edges for sexual kicks." Sammy Davis, Jr., referring to the victims at 10050 Cielo Drive

IN THE PREVIOUS CHAPTER, WE MET A SAMPLING OF SOME OF THE MOST successful and influential rock music superstars who emerged from Laurel Canyon during its glory days. But these were, alas, more than just musicians and singers and songwriters who had come together in the canyon; they were destined to become the spokesmen and *de facto* leaders of a generation of disaffected youth (as Carl Gottlieb noted in David Crosby's co-written autobiography, "the unprecedented mass appeal of the new rock'n'roll gave the singers a voice in public affairs"). That, of course, makes it all the more curious that these icons were, to an overwhelming degree, the sons and daughters of the military/intelligence complex and the scions of families that have wielded vast wealth and power in this country for a very long time.

It could of course be argued that there was nothing necessarily nefarious in the fact that so many of these icons of a past generation hailed from military/intelligence families. Perhaps, it could be suggested, they had embarked on their chosen careers as a form of rebellion against the values of their parents. And that, I suppose, might be true in a couple of cases. But what are we to conclude from the fact that such an astonishing number of these folks (along with their girlfriends, wives, managers, etc.) hail from a similar background? Are we to believe that the *only* kids from that era who had musical talent were the sons and daughters of Navy admirals, chemical warfare engineers and Air Force intelligence officers? Or are they just the only ones who were signed to lucrative contracts and relentlessly promoted by their labels and the media?

If these artists were rebelling against, rather than subtly promoting, the values of their parents, then why didn't they ever speak out against the people they were allegedly rebelling against? Why did Jim Morrison never denounce, or even mention, his father's key role in escalating one of America's bloodiest illegal wars? And why did Frank Zappa never pen a song exploring the horrors of chemical warfare (though he did pen a charming little ditty entitled Ritual Dance Of The Child-Killer)? And which Mamas and the Papas song was it that laid waste to the values and actions of John Phillips' parents and in-laws? And in which interview, exactly, did David Crosby and Stephen Stills disown the family values that they were raised with?

We will be taking a much closer look at these performers, as well as at many of their contemporaries, as we endeavor to determine how and why the youth 'counterculture' of the 1960s was given birth. According to virtually all the accounts that I have read, this was essentially a spontaneous, organic response to the war in Southeast Asia and to the prevailing social conditions of the time. 'Conspiracy theorists,' of course, have frequently opined that what began as a legitimate movement was at some point co-opted and undermined by intelligence operations such as CointelPro. Entire books, for example, have been written examining how presumably virtuous musical artists were subjected to FBI harassment and/or whacked by the CIA.

Here we will, as you may have already ascertained, take a decidedly different approach. The question that we will be tackling is a more deeply troubling one: "what if *the musicians themselves* (and various other leaders and founders of the 'movement') were every bit as much a part of the intelligence community as the people who were supposedly harassing them?" What if, in other words, the entire youth culture of the 1960s was created not as a grass-roots challenge to the status quo, but as a cynical exercise in discrediting and marginalizing the budding anti-war movement and creating a fake opposition that could be easily controlled and led astray? And what if the harassment these folks were subjected to was largely a stage-managed show designed to give the leaders of the counterculture some much-needed 'street cred'? What if, in reality, they were pretty much all playing on the same team?

I should probably mention here that, contrary to popular opinion, the hippie/flower child movement was not synonymous with the anti-war movement. As time passed, there was, to be sure, a fair amount of overlap between the two 'movements.' And the mass media outlets, as is their wont, did their very best to portray the flower-power generation as the torch-bearers of the anti-war movement—after all, a ragtag band of unwashed, drug-fueled long-hairs sporting flowers and peace symbols was far easier to marginalize than, say, a bunch of respected college professors and their concerned students. The reality, however, is that the anti-war movement was already well underway before the first aspiring 'hippie' arrived in Laurel Canyon. The first Vietnam War 'teach-in' was held on the campus of the University of Michigan in March of 1965. The first organized walk on Washington occurred just a few weeks later. Needless to say, there were no hippies in attendance at either event. That 'problem' would soon be rectified. And the anti-war crowd—those who were serious about ending the bloodshed in Vietnam, anyway—would be none too appreciative.

As Barry Miles has written in his coffee-table book, *Hippie*, there were some hippies involved in anti-war protests, "particularly after the police riot in Chicago in 1968 when so many people got injured, but on the whole the movement activists looked on hippies with disdain." Peter Coyote, narrating the documentary *Hippies* on the History Channel, added that, "Some on the left even theorized that the hippies were the end result of a plot by the CIA to neutralize the anti-war movement with LSD, turning potential protestors into self-absorbed naval-gazers." An exasperated Abbie Hoffman once described the scene as he remembered it thusly: "There were all these activists, you know, Berkeley radicals, White Panthers... all trying to stop the war and change things for the better. Then we got flooded with all these 'flower children' who were into drugs and sex. *Where the hell did the hippies come from?!*"

As it turns out, they came, initially at least, from a rather private, isolated, largely self-contained neighborhood in Los Angeles known as

Laurel Canyon. In contrast to the other canyons slicing through the Hollywood Hills, Laurel Canyon has its own market, the semi-famous Laurel Canyon Country Store; its own deli and cleaners; its own elementary school, the Wonderland School; its own boutique shops and salons; and, in more recent years, its own celebrity rehab facility named, as you may have guessed, the Wonderland Center. During its heyday, the canyon even had its own management company, Lookout Management, to handle the talent. At one time, it even had its own newspaper.

One other thing that I should add here is that this has not been an easy line of research for me to conduct, primarily because I have been, for as long as I can remember, a huge fan of 1960s music and culture. Though I didn't come of age, so to speak, until the 1970s, I have always felt as though I was cheated by being denied the opportunity to experience firsthand the era that I was so obviously meant to inhabit. During my high school and college years, while my peers were mostly into faceless corporate rock (think Journey, Foreigner, Kansas, Boston, etc.) and, perhaps worse yet, the twin horrors of new wave and disco music, I was faithfully spinning my Hendrix, Joplin and Doors albums (which I still have, in the original vinyl versions) while my color organ (remember those?) competed with my black light and strobe light. I grew my hair long until well past the age when it should have been sheared off. I may have even strung beads across the doorway to my room... but it is possible that I am confusing my life with that of Greg Brady, who, as we all remember, once converted his dad's home office into a groovy bachelor pad.

Anyway, one of the most difficult aspects of this journey that I have been on for the last fifteen years or so has been watching so many of my former idols and mentors fall by the wayside as it became increasingly clear to me that people who I once thought were the good guys were, in reality, something entirely different. The first to fall, naturally enough, were the establishment figures—the politicians who I once, quite foolishly, looked up to as people who were fighting the good fight, within the confines of the system, to bring about real change. Though it now pains me to admit this, there was a time when I admired the likes of (egads!) George McGovern and Jimmy Carter, as well as California pols Tom Hayden and Jerry Brown. I even had high hopes, oh-so-many-years-ago, for (am I really admitting this in print?) Bill Clinton.

Since I mentioned Jerry "Governor Moonbeam" Brown, by the way, I must now digress just a bit. As luck would have it, Jerry Brown was, curiously enough, a longtime resident of a little place called Laurel Canyon. As readers of my previous work, *Programmed to Kill*, may recall, Brown lived on Wonderland Avenue, not too many doors down from 8763 Wonderland Avenue, the site of the infamous "Four on the Floor" murders, regarded by grizzled LA homicide detectives as the most bloody and brutal multiple murder in the city's very bloody history.

As it turns out, the most bloody mass murder in LA's history took place in one of the city's most serene, pastoral and exclusive neighborhoods. And strangely enough, the case usually cited as the runner-up for the title of bloodiest crime scene—the murders of Stephen Parent, Sharon Tate, Jay Sebring, Voytek Frykowski and Abigail Folger at 10050 Cielo Drive in Benedict Canyon, just a couple miles to the west of Laurel Canyon—had deep ties to the Laurel Canyon scene as well.

As previously mentioned, victims Folger and Frykowski lived in Laurel Canyon, at 2774 Woodstock Road, in a rented home right across the road from a favored gathering spot for Laurel Canyon royalty. Many of the regular visitors to Cass Elliot's home, including a number of shady drug dealers, were also regular visitors to the Folger/Frykowski home. (Frykowski's son, by the way, was stabbed to death on June 6, 1999, thirty years after his father met the same fate.) Victim Jay Sebring's acclaimed hair salon sat right at the mouth of Laurel Canyon, just below the Sunset Strip, and it was Sebring, alas, who was credited with sculpting Jim Morrison's famous mane. One of the investors in his Sebring International business venture was none other than Mr. John Phillips.

Sharon Tate was also well known in Laurel Canyon, where she was a frequent visitor to the homes of friends like John Phillips, Cass Elliot, and Abigail Folger. And when she wasn't in Laurel Canyon, many of the canyon regulars, both famous and infamous, made themselves at home at her place on Cielo Drive. Canyonite Van Dyke Parks, for example, dropped by for a visit on the very day of the murders. And Denny Doherty, the other "Papa" in the Mamas and the Papas, has claimed that he and John Phillips were invited to the Cielo Drive home on the night of the murders, but, as luck would have it, they never made it over. (Similarly, Chuck Negron of Three Dog Night, a regular visitor to the Wonderland death house, had set up a drug buy on the night of that mass murder, but he fell asleep and never made it over.)

Along with the victims, the alleged killers also lived in and/or were very much a part of the Laurel Canyon scene. Bobby "Cupid" Beausoleil, for example, lived in a Laurel Canyon apartment during the early months of 1969. Charles "Tex" Watson, who allegedly led the death squad responsible for the carnage at Cielo Drive, lived for a time in a home on—guess where?—Wonderland Avenue. During that time, curiously enough, Watson co-owned and worked in a wig shop in Beverly Hills, Crown Wig Creations, Ltd., that was located near the mouth of Benedict Canyon. Meanwhile, one of Jay Sebring's primary claims-to-fame was his expertise in crafting men's hairpieces, which he did in his shop near the mouth of Laurel Canyon. A typical day then in the late 1960s would find Watson crafting hairpieces for an upscale Hollywood clientele near Benedict Canyon, and then returning home to Laurel Canyon, while Sebring crafted hairpieces for an upscale Hollywood clientele near Laurel Canyon, and then returned home to Benedict Canyon. And then one crazy day, as we all know, one of them became a killer and the other his victim. But there's nothing odd about that, I suppose, so let's move on.

Oh, wait a minute... we can't quite move on just yet, as I forgot to mention that Sebring's Benedict Canyon home, at 9820 Easton Drive, was a rather infamous Hollywood death house that had once belonged to Jean Harlow and Paul Bern. The mismatched pair were wed on July 2, 1932, when Harlow, already a huge star of the silver screen, was just twenty-one years old. Just two months later, on September 5, Bern caught a bullet to the head in his wife's bedroom. He was found sprawled naked in a pool of his own blood, his corpse drenched with his wife's perfume. Upon discovering the body, Bern's butler promptly contacted MGM's head of security, Whitey Hendry, who in turn contacted Louis B. Mayer and Irving Thalberg. All three men descended upon the Benedict Canyon home to, you know, tidy up a bit. A couple hours later, they decided to contact the LAPD. This scene would be repeated years later when Sebring's friends would rush to the very same home to clean up before officers investigating the Tate murders arrived.

Bern's death was, as is so often the case, written off as a suicide. His newlywed wife, strangely enough, was never called as a witness at the inquest. Bern's *other* wife—which is to say, his common-law wife, Dorothy Millette—reportedly boarded a Sacramento riverboat on September 6, 1932, the day after Paul's death. She was next seen floating belly up in the Sacramento River. Her death, as would be expected, was also ruled a suicide. Less than five years later, Harlow herself dropped dead at the ripe old age of twenty-six. At the time, authorities opted not to divulge the cause of death, though it was later claimed that bad kidneys had done her in. During her brief stay on this planet, Harlow had cycled through three turbulent marriages and yet still found time to serve as godmother to Bugsy Siegel's daughter, Millicent.

Though Bern's was the most famous body to be hauled out of the Easton Drive house in a coroner's bag, it certainly wasn't the only one. Another man had reportedly committed suicide there as well, in some unspecified fashion. Yet another unfortunate soul drowned in the home's pool. And a maid was once found swinging from the end of a rope. Her death, needless to say, was ruled a suicide as well. That's a lot of blood for one home to absorb, but the house's morbid history, though a turn-off to many prospective residents, was reportedly exactly what attracted Jay Sebring to the property. His murder would further darken the black cloud hanging over the home.

As Laurel Canyon chronicler Michael Walker has noted, LA's two most notorious mass murders, one in August of 1969 and the other in July of 1981 (both involving five victims, though at Wonderland one of the five miraculously survived), provided rather morbid bookends for Laurel Canyon's glory years. Walker though, like others who have chronicled that time and place, treats these brutal crimes as though they were unfortunate aberrations. The reality, however, is that the nine bodies recovered from Cielo Drive and Wonderland Avenue constitute just the tip of a very large, and very bloody, iceberg.

To partially illustrate that point: Diane Linkletter (daughter of famed entertainer Art Linkletter), legendary comedian Lenny Bruce, screen idol Sal Mineo, starlet Inger Stevens, and silent film star Ramon Novarro, all have something in common—all were found dead in their homes, either in or at the mouth of Laurel Canyon, in the decade between 1966 and 1976. And all five were, in all likelihood, murdered in those Laurel Canyon homes.

Only two of them are officially listed as murder victims (Mineo, who was stabbed to death outside his home at 8563 Holloway Drive on February 12, 1976, and Novarro, who was killed near the Country

Store in a decidedly ritualistic fashion on the eve of Halloween, 1968). Inger Stevens' death in her home at 8000 Woodrow Wilson Drive, on April 30, 1970 (*Walpurgisnacht* on the occult calendar), was officially a suicide, though why she opted to propel herself through a decorative glass screen as part of that suicide remains a mystery. Perhaps she just wanted to leave behind a gruesome crime scene, and simple overdoses can be so, you know, bloodless and boring.

Diane Linkletter, according to legend, sailed out the window of her Shoreham Towers apartment because, in her LSD-addled state, she thought she could fly. We know this because Art himself told us that it was so, and because the story was retold throughout the 1970s as a cautionary tale about the dangers of drugs. What we weren't told, however, is that Diane (born, curiously enough, on Halloween day, 1948) wasn't alone when she plunged six stories to her death on the morning of October 4, 1969. *Au contraire*, she was with a gent by the name of Edward Durston, who, in a completely unexpected turn of events, accompanied actress Carol Wayne to Mexico some fifteen years later. Carol, alas, perhaps weighed down by her enormous breasts, managed to drown in barely a foot of water, while Mr. Durston promptly disappeared. As would be expected, he was never questioned by authorities about Wayne's curious death. After all, it is quite common for the same guy to be the sole witness to two separate 'accidental' deaths.

Art also neglected to mention that just weeks before Diane's curious death, another member of the Linkletter clan, Art's son-in-law, John Zwyer, caught a bullet to the head in the backyard of his Hollywood Hills home. But that, of course, was an 'unconnected' suicide.

I'm not even going to discuss here the circumstances of Lenny Bruce's death from acute morphine poisoning on August 3, 1966, because, to be perfectly honest, I don't know too many people who don't already assume that Lenny was whacked. I'll just note here that his funeral was well-attended by the Laurel Canyon rock icons, and control over his unreleased material fell into the hands of a guy by the name of Frank Zappa. And another unsavory character named Phil Spector, whose crack team of studio musicians, dubbed the Wrecking Crew, were the actual musicians playing on many studio recordings by such Laurel Canyon bands as the Monkees, the Byrds, the Beach Boys, and the Mamas and the Papas.

3

DIG! THE LAUREL CANYON DEATH LIST

"I mean, fuck, he auditioned for Neil [Young] for fuck's sake." Graham Nash, explaining to author Michael Walker how close Charles Manson was to the Laurel Canyon scene

DURING THE TEN-YEAR PERIOD DURING WHICH LENNY BRUCE, RAMON Novarro, Sal Mineo, Diane Linkletter, Inger Stevens, Sharon Tate, Jay Sebring, Voytek Frykowski and Abigail Folger all turned up dead, numerous other people connected to Laurel Canyon did as well, often under very questionable circumstances. The list includes, but is certainly not limited to, all of the following names:

☠ Marina Elizabeth Habe, whose body was carved up and tossed into the heavy brush along Mulholland Drive, just west of Bowmont Drive, on December 30, 1968. Habe, just seventeen at the time of her death, was the daughter of Hans Habe, who emigrated to the US from fascist Austria circa 1940. Shortly thereafter, Hans married a General Foods heiress and began studying psychological warfare at the Military Intelligence Training Center. After completing his training, he put his psychological warfare skills to use by creating eighteen newspapers in occupied Germany—under the direction, no doubt, of the OSS.

☠ Christine Hinton, who was killed in a head-on collision on September 30, 1969. At the time, Hinton was a girlfriend of David Crosby and the founder and head of the Byrds' fan club. She was also the daughter of a career Army officer stationed at the notorious Presidio military base in San Francisco. Another of Crosby's girlfriends from that same era was Shelley Roecker, who grew up on the Hamilton Air Force Base in Marin County.

☠ Jane Doe #59, found dumped into the heavy undergrowth of Laurel Canyon in November 1969, within sight of where Habe had been dumped less than a year earlier. The teenage girl, who was never identified, had been stabbed 157 times in the chest and throat.

☠ Alan "Blind Owl" Wilson, singer, songwriter and guitarist for the Laurel Canyon blues-rock band, Canned Heat, was found dead in his Topanga Canyon home on September 3, 1970. His death was written off as a suicide/OD. Wilson had moved to Topanga Canyon after the band's Laurel Canyon home—on Lookout Mountain Avenue, next door to Joni Mitchell and Graham Nash's home—burned to the ground. "Blind Owl" was just twenty-seven years old at the time of his death. A little more than a decade later, Wilson's former bandmate, Bob "The Bear" Hite, who had once acknowledged in an interview that he had partied in the canyons with various members of the Manson Family, died of a heart attack at the ripe old age of thirty-six.

☠ Jimi Hendrix, who reportedly briefly occupied the sprawling mansion just north of the Log Cabin after he moved to LA in 1968, died in London under seriously questionable circumstances on September 18, 1970. Though he rarely spoke of it, Jimi had served a stint in the US Army with the 101st Airborne Division at Fort Campbell. His official records indicate that he was forced into the service by the courts and then released after just one year when he purportedly proved to be a poor soldier. One wonders though why he was assigned to such an elite division if he was indeed such a failure. One also wonders why he wasn't subjected to disciplinary measures rather than being handed a free pass out of his ostensibly court-ordered service. In any event, Jimi himself once told reporters that he was given a medical discharge after breaking an ankle during a parachute jump. One biographer has claimed that Jimi faked being gay to earn an early release. The truth, alas, remains rather elusive. At the time of Jimi's death, the first person called by his girlfriend—Monika Danneman, last to see Hendrix alive—was Eric Burden of the Animals. Two years earlier, Burden had relocated to LA and taken over ringmaster duties from Frank Zappa after Zappa had vacated the Log Cabin and moved into a less high-profile Laurel Canyon home. Within a year of Jimi's death, a reported prostitute-turned-groupie named Devon Wilson, who had been with Jimi the day before his death, plunged from an eighth-floor window of New York's Chelsea Hotel. On March 5, 1973, a shadowy character named Michael Jeffery, who had managed both Hendrix and Burden, was killed in a midair plane collision. Jeffery was known to openly boast of having organized crime connections and of working for the CIA. After Jimi's death, it was discovered that Jeffery had been funneling most of Hendrix's gross earnings into offshore accounts in the Bahamas linked to international drug trafficking. Years later, on April 5, 1996, Danneman, the daughter of a wealthy German industrialist, was found dead near her home in a fume-filled Mercedes.

☠ Jim Morrison, who for a time lived in a home on Rothdell Trail, behind the Laurel Canyon Country Store, may or may not have died in Paris on July 3, 1971. The events of that day remain shrouded in mystery and rumor, and the details of the story, such as they are, have changed over the years. What is known is that, on that very same day, Admiral George Stephen Morrison delivered the keynote speech at a decommissioning ceremony for the aircraft carrier *USS Bon Homme Richard*, from where, seven years earlier, he had helped choreograph the Tonkin Gulf Incident. A few years after Jim's death, his common-law wife, Pamela Courson, dropped dead as well, officially of a heroin overdose. Like Hendrix, Morrison had been an avid student of the occult, with a particular fondness for the work of Aleister Crowley. According to super-groupie Pamela Des Barres, he had also "read all he could about incest and sadism." Also like Hendrix (and Wilson), Morrison was just twenty-seven at the time of his (possible) death.

☠ Brandon DeWilde, a good friend of David Crosby and Gram Parsons, was killed in a freak accident in Colorado on July 6, 1972, when his van plowed under a flatbed truck. In the 1950s, DeWilde had been an in-demand child actor since the age of eight. He had appeared on-screen with some of the biggest names in Hollywood, including Alan Ladd, Lee Marvin, Paul Newman, John Wayne, Kirk Douglas and Henry Fonda. Around 1965, DeWilde fell in with Hollywood's 'Young Turks,' through whom he met and befriended Crosby, Parsons, and various other members of the Laurel Canyon Club. DeWilde was just thirty at the time of his death.

☠ Christine Frka, a former governess for Moon Unit Zappa and the Zappa family's former housekeeper at the Log Cabin, died on November 5, 1972, of an alleged drug overdose, though friends suspected foul play. As "Miss Christine," Frka had been a member of the Zappa-created GTOs, a musical act, of sorts, composed entirely of very young groupies. She was also the inspiration for the song, Christine's Tune: Devil In Disguise by Gram Parsons' Flying Burrito Brothers. Frka may have been in her early twenties when she died, possibly even younger.

☠ Danny Whitten, a guitarist/vocalist/songwriter with Neil Young's sometime band, Crazy Horse, died of an overdose on November 18, 1972. According to rock'n'roll legend, Whitten had been fired by Young earlier that day during rehearsals in San Francisco. Young and Jack Nitzsche, Phil Spector's former top assistant, had given Whitten $50 and put him on a plane back to LA. Within hours, he was dead. Whitten was just twenty-nine.

☠ Bruce Berry, a roadie for Crosby, Stills, Nash & Young, died of a heroin overdose in June 1973. Berry had just flown out to Maui to deliver a shipment of cocaine to Stephen Stills, and was promptly sent back to LA by Crosby and Nash. Berry was a brother of Jan Berry, of Jan and Dean. (Dean Torrence, the "Dean" of Jan and Dean, had played a part in the fake kidnapping of Frank Sinatra, Jr., just a couple weeks after the JFK assassination. The staged event was a particularly transparent effort to divert attention away from the questions that were cropping up, after the initial shock had passed, about the events in Dealey Plaza.)

☠ Clarence White, a guitarist who had played with the Byrds, was run over by a drunk driver and killed on July 14, 1973. White had grown up near Lancaster, not far from where Frank Zappa spent his teen years. At least one member of White's immediate family was employed at Edwards Air Force Base. The driver who killed young Clarence, just twenty-nine years old at the time of his death, was given a one-year suspended sentence and served no time.

☠ Gram Parsons, formerly with the International Submarine Band, the Byrds and the Flying Burrito Brothers, allegedly overdosed on a speedball at the Joshua Tree Inn on September 19, 1973. Just two months before his death, Parsons' Topanga Canyon home had burnt to the ground. After his death, his body was stolen from LAX by the Burrito's road manager, Phil Kaufman, and then taken back out to Joshua Tree and ritually burned on the autumnal equinox. Kaufman had been a prison buddy of Charlie Manson's at Terminal Island; when Phil was released from Terminal Island in March of 1968, he quickly reunited with his old pal, who had been released a year earlier. By the time of Gram's death, his family had already experienced its share of questionable deaths. Just before Christmas 1958, Parsons' father had sent Gram, along with his mother and sister, off to stay with family in Florida. The next day, just after the winter solstice, Ingram Cecil Connor, Jr. caught a bullet to the head. His death was recorded as a suicide and it was claimed that he had sent his family away to spare them as much pain as possible. It seems just as likely, however, that Cecil knew his days were numbered and wanted to get his family out of the line of fire. The next year, 1959, Gram's mother married again, to Robert Ellis Parsons, who adopted Gram and his sister Avis. Six years later, in June of 1965, Gram's mother died the day after a sudden illness landed her in the hospital. According to witnesses, she died "almost immediately" after a visit from her husband, Robert Parsons. Many of those close to the situation believed that Parsons had a hand in her death (very shortly thereafter, Robert Parsons married his stepdaughter's teenage babysitter). Following his mother's death, Parsons briefly attended Harvard University and then launched his music career with the formation of the International Submarine Band, which quickly found its way to—where else?—Laurel Canyon. Gram's death in 1973 at the age of twenty-six left his younger sister Avis as the sole surviving member of the family. She was killed in 1993, reportedly in a boating accident, at the age of forty.

☠ "Mama" Cass Elliot, the Earth Mother of Laurel Canyon whose circle of friends included musicians, Mansonites, young Hollywood stars, the wealthy son of a State Department official, singer/songwriters, assorted drug dealers, and some particularly unsavory characters the LAPD once described as "some kind of hit squad," died in the London home of Harry Nilsson on July 29, 1974. (Nilsson had been a frequent drinking buddy of John Lennon in Laurel Canyon and on the Sunset Strip.) At thirty-two, Cass had lived a long and productive life, by Laurel Canyon standards. Four years later, in the very same room of the very same London flat, still owned by Harry Nilsson, Keith Moon of the Who also died at age thirty-two, on September 7, 1978. Though initial press reports held that Cass had choked to death on a ham sandwich, the official verdict was heart failure. Her actual cause of death could likely be filed under "knowing where too many of the bodies were buried." Moon reportedly died from a massive overdose of a drug used to treat alcohol withdrawal.

☠ Amy Gossage, Graham Nash's girlfriend, was murdered in her San Francisco home on February 13, 1975. Just twenty years old at the time, she had been stabbed nearly fifty times and was bludgeoned beyond recognition. Amy's father, a famed advertising/PR executive, had died of leukemia in 1969. Not long after, her half-sister had been killed in a car crash. In May of 1974, her mother, the daughter of a wealthy banking family, died as well, reportedly of cirrhosis of the liver. That left just Amy, age nineteen, and her brother Eben, age twenty, both of whom reportedly had serious drug dependencies. Amy's brutal murder, cleverly enough, was pinned on Eben. Police had conveniently found blood-stained clothes, along with a hammer and scissors, sitting on the porch of Eben's apartment, looking very much as though it had been planted. A friend of Eben's would later remark, perhaps quite tellingly, "If Eben did kill her, I'm convinced he doesn't know he did it."

☠ Tim Buckley, a singer/songwriter signed to Frank Zappa's record label and managed by Herb Cohen, died of a reported overdose on June 29, 1975. Buckley had once appeared on an episode of *The Monkees*, and, like Monkee Peter Tork (and so many others in this story), he hailed from Washington, DC. He was the son of a mentally unbalanced and occasionally violent WWII hero. Buckley was just twenty-eight at the time of his death, which reportedly shocked many of his friends and relatives. Despite having released nine albums during his short life, Buckley died in debt, which probably had nothing to do with his management by Cohen. His son, Jeff Buckley, also an accomplished musician, managed to remain on this planet two years longer than his dad did; he was thirty when he died in a bizarre drowning incident on May 29, 1997.

☠ Phyllis Major Browne, wife of singer/songwriter Jackson Browne, reportedly overdosed on barbiturates on March 25, 1976. Her death was—you all should know the words to this song by now—ruled a suicide. She was just thirty years old.

There are a few other curious deaths we could add here as well, though they were more indirectly related to the Laurel Canyon scene. Nevertheless, they deserve an honorable mention:

☠ Bobby Fuller, singer/songwriter/guitarist for the Bobby Fuller Four, was found dead in his car near Grauman's Chinese Theater on July 18, 1966, after being lured away from his home by a mysterious 2:00–3:00 AM phone call of unknown origin. Fuller is best known for penning the hit song I Fought the Law, which had just hit the charts when he supposedly committed suicide at the age of twenty-three. There were multiple cuts and bruises on his face, chest and shoulders, dried blood around his mouth, and a hairline fracture to his right hand. He had been thoroughly doused with gasoline, including in his mouth and throat. The inside of the car was doused as well, and an open book of matches lay on the seat. It was perfectly obvious that Fuller's killer (or killers) had planned to torch the car, destroying all evidence, but likely got scared away. The LAPD, nevertheless, ruled Fuller's death a suicide—despite the coroner's conclusion that the gas had been poured *after* Bobby's death. Police later decided that it wasn't a suicide after all, but rather an accident. They didn't bother to explain how Fuller had accidentally doused himself with gasoline after accidentally killing himself. At the time of his death, one of Fuller's closest confidants was a prostitute named Melody who worked at PJ's nightclub, where Bobby frequently played. The club was co-owned by Eddie Nash, who would, many years later, orchestrate the Wonderland massacre. A few years after Bobby's death, his brother and bass player, Randy Fuller, teamed up with drummer Dewey Martin, formerly of Buffalo Springfield.

☠ Gary Hinman, a musician, music teacher, and part-time chemist, was brutally murdered in his Topanga Canyon home on July 27, 1969. Convicted of his murder was Mansonite Bobby Beausoleil, who had played rhythm guitar in a Laurel Canyon band known as the Grass Roots, which later achieved a fair amount of fame under the name Love.

☠ Janis Joplin, vocalist extraordinaire, was found dead of a heroin overdose on October 4, 1970, at the Landmark Hotel, about a mile east of the mouth of Laurel Canyon, where she occasionally visited. Indications were that she had taken or been given a "hot shot," many times stronger than standard street heroin. Joplin's father, by the way, was a petroleum engineer for Texaco. And though it might normally seem an odd coupling, it somehow seems perfectly natural, in the context of this story, that Janis once dated that great crusader in the war on all things immoral, William Bennett. Like Morrison, Hendrix and Wilson, Joplin died at the age of twenty-seven.

☠ Duane Allman and Berry Oakley, lead guitarist and bass player for the Allman Brothers, were killed in freakishly similar motorcycle crashes on October 29, 1971, and November 11, 1972, respectively. Allman was the son of Willis Allman, a US Army Sergeant who had been murdered by another soldier near Norfolk, Virginia (home of the world's largest naval installation) on December 26, 1949. In 1967, Duane and his younger brother, Gregg, then billing themselves as the Allman Joys, ventured out to Los Angeles. While there, Gregg auditioned for and was almost signed by the Laurel Canyon band Poco, which featured Buffalo Springfield alumni Richie Furay and Jim Messina, as well as future Eagle Randy Meisner. Duane was killed when a truck turned in front of his motorcycle at an intersection and inexplicably stopped. Just over a year later, Oakley had a similar run-in with a bus, just three blocks from where Allman had been killed. Following the crash, Berry had dusted himself off and declined medical attention, insisting that he was okay. Three hours later, he was rushed to the hospital where he died. Both Oakley and Allman were just twenty-four years old.

☠ Gary Thain, bassist for the band Uriah Heep—yet another group with a keen interest in magick and the occult, with album titles such as *Demons and Wizards* and *Magician's Birthday*—was found dead on December 8, 1975, five years to the day before Nilsson sidekick John Lennon would be gunned down at the Dakota Apartments in New York City. Thain had once played with sometime Canyonite Jimi Hendrix and his first live appearance with Uriah Heep was at the Whisky-a-Go-Go on February 1, 1972. His death was, alas, attributed to a drug overdose. Thain is yet another member of the 'Twenty-Seven Club.'

☠ Tommy Bolin, best known as a guitarist for the band Deep Purple, was also found dead of a reported drug overdose almost exactly one year later, on December 4, 1976, though varying stories have surfaced concerning the circumstances of his death. Bolin had previously played for the James Gang, in the position once filled by Joe Walsh, who by the time of Bolin's death had become a member of Laurel Canyon's most commercially successful band, the Eagles. Bolin died a couple years shy of making the Twenty-Seven Club.

It wasn't only the musicians with ties to Laurel Canyon who died young and often under questionable, and sometimes quite violent, circumstances. The dark undercurrents pulsing through the canyons in the early 1970s that left such a trail of destruction extended well beyond the Hollywood Hills, as illustrated by the deaths of a handful of mostly forgotten figures in the rock community:

☠ Phil King, an early frontman for Blue Öyster Cult, a band whose album art and song lyrics suggested a keen interest in the occult, was shot three times in the back of the head in New York City on April 27, 1972, just three days shy of *Walpurgisnacht*. Three months later, on July 24, 1972, Bobby Ramirez, the drummer for an early formation featuring frontman Edgar Winter, was beaten and stabbed to death in a Chicago bar. He was twenty-three years old.

☠ Rory Storm, the founder and frontman for the UK's Rory Storm and the Hurricanes, was found dead on September 28, 1972. Born Alan Caldwell on the autumnal equinox of 1939 in Liverpool, England, Storm had close ties to that other, far more famous band from Liverpool. The Hurricanes' original drummer was none other than Ritchie Starkey, who left the band to join John, Paul and George, becoming Ringo Starr in the process. It is said that George Harrison, who dated Storm's younger sister, initially wanted to join the Hurricanes but had to settle for the Quarrymen when he was deemed too young. That same sister would later date a young Paul McCartney. Popular on the Liverpool/Hamburg club circuit, the Hurricanes at times shared the stage with the Beatles, both before and after Starr's defection. Rory's band though—which he initially wanted to name Dracula and the Werewolves—never caught fire the way the Beatles did and by the late 1960s/early 1970s, Storm had to find work as a DJ. In Amsterdam at the time of his father's death in 1972, Rory returned to Liverpool to be with his grieving mother. On September 28, 1972, just one week after Rory's thirty-third birthday, both mother and son turned up dead in the family home. In a rather unlikely turn of events, it was claimed that both had independently committed suicide on the same day in different rooms of the same house. Storm reportedly had sleeping pills in his system, but not in sufficient concentrations to have caused his demise, leaving the actual cause of death something of a mystery.

☠ Ronald "Pigpen" McKernan, a founding member of the Grateful Dead from its early incarnations as the Zodiacs and the Warlocks, died on March 8, 1973. A vocalist and multi-instrumentalist, McKernan had a short romantic relationship and a somewhat longer friendship with fellow death-list member Janis Joplin. Pigpen was found dead at his home, reportedly of a gastrointestinal hemorrhage. His death is primarily of interest because he was, like Joplin, twenty-seven years old at the time, qualifying him for membership in the Twenty-Seven Club alongside charter members Joplin, Brian Jones, Jimi Hendrix and Jim Morrison, and more recent hall-of-famers such as Kurt Cobain and Amy Winehouse.

☠ Graham Bond, who was widely considered to be a founding father of the 1960s British R&B boom, was killed on May 5, 1974, when he was reportedly run over by a train at London's Finsbury Park station. His death, to no one's surprise, was ruled a suicide. Bond, who was adopted and believed himself to be the biological son of occultist/spy Aleister Crowley, had a deep fascination with the occult. He also reportedly struggled with what the psychiatric community refers to as a manic depressive disorder, which was aggravated by chronic drug abuse. Bond was just thirty-six years old at the time of his death.

☠ Pete Ham, a singer/songwriter/guitarist and the leader of the British band Badfinger, another outfit with close ties to those lads from Liverpool, was found swinging from the end of a rope on April 23, 1975. Ham's band was first signed by the Beatles' own Apple label, and their first single, Come And Get It, was penned by Paul McCartney. According to rock lore, McCartney recorded the song himself and then insisted that Ham's band play and record it exactly the same way. Sir Paul also personally auditioned all four members of Badfinger to decide who would provide the lead vocal on the single. Ham's greatest claim to fame though was being the co-writer of the oft-recorded Without You, a song that became a monster hit around the world when it was committed to vinyl in 1972 by John Lennon's Sunset Strip/Laurel Canyon sidekick, Harry Nilsson—the very same Harry Nilsson whose London flat served as the death scene for both Mama Cass and Keith Moon. The song received numerous awards and Ham and his band moved over to Warner Bros. Records with the expectation that Badfinger was soon to become quite a sensation. It wasn't meant to be. Within a few years, Pete Ham was unemployed and turned up dead in his garage. Ham is yet another member of the Twenty-Seven Club, though not by much; his death came just three days before his twenty-eighth birthday. His passing was barely reported on, due in part to the fact that neither Warner Bros. nor the Beatles organization bothered to make an announcement or issue any public comment. Just one month later, his girlfriend gave birth to a daughter that Ham was never to know. Eight-and-a-half years later, on November 18, 1983, Tom Evans, Ham's former bandmate and the co-writer of Without You, was also found swinging from the end of a rope.

Shit happens, it appears.

4

RELATED LIVES AND RELATIVE DEATHS

"No one here gets out alive."
Jim Morrison

BEFORE MOVING ON FROM THE LAUREL CANYON DEATH LIST, THERE ARE A few more celebrity deaths that demand a closer inspection. The first is a truly tragic tale of a rising star in Laurel Canyon, who, by the time of her death, had been completely forgotten. The second is the story of a man who had only tangential ties to Laurel Canyon, but whose life and death may provide one of the keys to understanding the canyon scene. And the third is the story of a guy who had no real connections to Laurel Canyon, but whose life arc has been so illuminatingly bizarre that it merits inclusion here.

Judee Lynn Sill was born in Studio City, California, not far from the northern entrance to Laurel Canyon, on October 7, 1944. Almost a quarter-century later, she would be favorably compared to such other Laurel Canyon singer/songwriters as Joni Mitchell, Judi Collins and Carole King. When she died though, on November 23, 1979, not a single obituary was published to note her passing.

Judee's father, Milford "Bud" Sill, was reportedly a cameraman for Paramount Studios with numerous Hollywood connections. When Judee was still quite young, however, Bud moved the family to Oakland and opened a bar known as Bud's Bar. He also operated a side business as an importer of rare animals, which required him to spend a considerable amount of time traveling in Central and South America. Such a business, it should be noted, would provide an ideal cover for covert intelligence work. In any event, Bud Sill was dead by 1952, when Judee was just seven or eight years old. Depending on who is telling the story, Bud died either from pneumonia or a heart attack.

Following Bud's death, the family relocated back to Southern California and Judee's older brother Dennis, though still in his teens, took over the family importing business. That career didn't last long though as Dennis soon turned up dead down in Central America, either from a liver infection or a car accident. The animal importing business, I guess, is a rather dangerous one.

Following Bud's death, Judee's mother, Oneta, met and married Ken Muse, an Academy Award-winning animator for Hanna-Barbera who was described by Judee as an abusive, violent alcoholic. At fifteen, Judee fled her violent home life and lived with an older man with whom she pulled off a series of armed robberies in the San Fernando Valley. Those activities landed her in reform school, which did little to curb her appetite for drugs, crime and alcohol. She spent the next few years with a serious heroin addiction, which she financed by dealing drugs and turning tricks in some of LA's seedier neighborhoods.

By 1963, Judee had cleaned herself up enough to enroll in junior college. In the early winter of 1965, however, Judee's mom, her last surviving family member, died either of cancer or of complications arising from her chronic alcoholism (take your pick; the details of this story will likely remain forever elusive). Barely an adult, Judee was left all alone in the world, and thus began another downward spiral into drugs and crime, which culminated in her being arrested and possibly serving time on forgery and drug charges.

In the late 1960s, with her addictions apparently temporarily curbed, Sill joined the Laurel Canyon scene, where she attempted to forge a career as a singer/songwriter. Her first big break came when she sold the song Lady O to the Turtles (yet another Laurel Canyon band to hit it big in the mid-1960s; best known for the hit single Happy Together, the Turtles were led by lead vocalist/songwriter Howard Kaylan, who happened to be, small world that it is, a cousin of Frank Zappa's manager and business partner, Herb Cohen). The band released the song, which featured Judee's guitar work, in 1969. The next year, Sill became the first artist signed to David Geffen's fledgling Asylum record label. The year after that, her self-titled debut album became Asylum's first official release. The first single from the album, Jesus Was A Crossmaker, was produced by Graham Nash, whom she opened for on tour following the album's release.

Though critically well-received, the album's sales were disappointing, in part because the record was overshadowed by the debut albums of Jackson Browne and the Eagles, both released by Asylum shortly after the release of Judee's album. Sill's second album, 1973's *Heart Food*, was even more of a commercial disappointment. Nevertheless, in 1974, she began work on a third album in Monkee Mike Nesmith's recording studio. Prior to completion, however, she abandoned the project and promptly disappeared without a trace. What became of her between that time and her death some five years later remains largely a mystery. It is assumed that she once again descended into a life of drugs and prostitution, but no one seems to know for sure.

It is alleged that she was seriously injured when her car was rear-ended by actor Danny Kaye, causing her to suffer from chronic back pain thereafter, thus contributing to her drug addictions. According to a friend of hers, she lived in a home that featured an enormous photo of Bela Lugosi above the fireplace, a large ebony cross above her bed, and racks of candles. She is said to have read extensively from Rosicrucian manuscripts and from the writings of Aleister Crowley, to have possessed a complete collection of the work of Helena Blavatsky, and to have been a gifted tarot card reader.

What is known for sure is that, on the day after Thanksgiving, 1979, Judee Sill, the last surviving member of her family, was found dead in a North Hollywood apartment. The cause of death was listed as "acute cocaine and codeine intoxication." It was claimed that a suicide note was found, but friends insisted that the supposed note was either a portion of a diary entry or an unfinished song. One of her friends would later note that, at some point in her life, Judee began to realize that "there was a part of her that wasn't under her conscious control." I'm guessing that the guy up for review next could relate to that...

Phil Ochs, a folk singer/songwriter and political activist, was found hanged in his sister's home in Far Rockaway, New York, on April 9, 1976.

Throughout his life, Ochs was one of the most overtly political of the 1960s rock and folk music stars. A regular attendee at anti-war, civil rights, and labor rallies, Ochs appeared to be, at all times, an unwavering political leftist (he named his first band the Singing Socialists). That all changed, however, and rather dramatically, in the months before his death.

Born in El Paso, Texas, on December 19, 1940, Phil and his family moved frequently during the first few years of his life. His father, Dr. Jacob Ochs, had been drafted by the US Army and assigned to various military hospitals in New York, New Mexico and Texas. In 1943, Dr. Ochs was shipped overseas, returning two years later with a medical discharge. Upon his return, he was immediately institutionalized and didn't return to his family for another two years. During that time, he was subjected to every psychiatric 'treatment' imaginable, including electroshock 'therapy.' When he finally returned to his family, in 1947, he was but a shell of his former self, described by Phil's sister as "almost like a phantom."

Beginning in the fall of 1956, Phil Ochs began attending Staunton Military Academy, the very same institution that future serial killer/cult leader Gary Heidnik would attend just one year after Ochs graduated. During Phil's two years there, a friend and fellow band member was found swinging from the end of a rope. (I probably don't need to add here that the death was ruled a suicide.) Following graduation, Phil enrolled at Ohio State University, but not before, oddly enough, having a little plastic surgery done to alter his appearance (doing such things, needless to say, was rather uncommon in 1958).

In early 1962, just months before his scheduled graduation, Ochs dropped out of college to pursue a career in music. By 1966, he had released three albums. In 1967, under the management of his brother, Michael Ochs, Phil moved out to Los Angeles. Michael had begun working the previous year as an assistant to Billy James, who maintained a party house at 8504 Ridpath in—you guessed it—Laurel Canyon. As the 1970s rolled around, and with his career beginning to fade, Phil Ochs began to travel internationally, usually accompanied by vast quantities of booze and pills. Those travels included a visit to Chile not long before the US-sponsored coup that toppled Salvador Allende.

In the summer of 1975, Phil Ochs' public persona abruptly changed.

Adopting the name John Butler Train, Ochs proclaimed himself a CIA operative and presented himself as a belligerent, right-wing thug. He told an interviewer that, "on the first day of summer 1975, Phil Ochs was murdered in the Chelsea Hotel by John Train... For the good of societies, public and secret, he needed to be gotten rid of." That symbolic assassination, on the summer solstice, took place at the same hotel that Devon Wilson had flown out of a few years earlier. One of Ochs' biographers would later write that Phil/John "actually believed he was a member of the CIA." Also in those final months of his life, Ochs began compiling curious lists, with entries that apparently reference US biological warfare research: "shellfish toxin, Fort Dietrich, cobra venom, Chantilly Race Track, hollow silver dollars, New York Cornell Hospital..."

Many years before Ochs' metamorphosis, in an interesting bit of foreshadowing, psychological warfare operative George Estabrooks explained, in his book *Hypnotism*, how US intelligence agencies had been working to create the perfect spy: "We start with an excellent subject... we need a man or woman who is highly intelligent and physically tough. Then we start to develop a case of multiple personality through hypnotism. In his normal waking state, which we will call Personality A, or PA, this individual will become a rabid communist. He will join the party, follow the party line and make himself as objectionable as possible to the authorities. Note that he will be acting in good faith. He is a communist, or rather his PA is a communist and will behave as such. Then we develop Personality B (PB), the secondary personality, the unconscious personality, if you wish, although this is somewhat of a contradiction in terms. This personality is rabidly American and anti-communist. It has all the information possessed by PA, the normal personality, whereas PA does not have this advantage... My super spy plays his role as a communist in his waking state, aggressively, consistently, fearlessly. But his PB is a loyal American, and PB has all the memories of PA. As a loyal American, he will not hesitate to divulge those memories."

Estabrooks never explained what would happen if the programming were to go haywire and Personality B were to emerge and become the conscious personality, but my guess is that such a person would be considered a severe liability and would be treated accordingly. They might even find themselves swinging from the end of a rope. Phil Ochs was thirty-five at the time of his death.

Stacy Sutherland, the lead guitarist and a founding member of the 13th Floor Elevators, was shot to death on August 24, 1978. Despite considerable critical acclaim, the Elevators had only lasted a few years, from late 1965 through early 1968. Sutherland was imprisoned in 1969 on drug charges and reportedly drank heavily after that. He was just thirty-two when he was shot and killed by his wife Bunny during a domestic dispute. The shooting, curiously enough, was determined to be accidental, which I suppose means that Bunny accidentally picked up the gun, accidentally disengaged the safety, accidentally pointed it at her husband, accidentally put her finger on the trigger, and then accidentally pulled that trigger.

Even more interesting is the story of the band's frontman. During the group's brief period of existence, Sutherland was overshadowed by the enigmatic Roky Erickson. Born Roger Kynard Erickson on July 15, 1947, Roky was a musical prodigy who took up the piano at age five and the guitar at age ten. He was also, according to the 2005 documentary feature *You're Gonna Miss Me*, a severely abused child; there are strong indications, according to the filmmakers, that architect father Roger, who rarely spoke to the family, sexually abused Roky and his four younger brothers.

Though all but forgotten now, Erickson was a hugely influential figure in the mid- to late 1960s. Before there was a San Francisco scene, Texan Roky had coined the term 'psychedelic rock' and was the first to use feedback and distortion. His distinctive vocals were a major influence on fellow Texan Janis Joplin, who considered joining the Elevators before being shuffled off to San Francisco and superstardom. Erickson was also considered to be very good looking and was an immensely charismatic figure who was well liked by all who met him, men and women alike.

Roky began his music career at a young age, after making the curious decision to drop out of high school just a few weeks shy of graduating. By December 1965, he had formed the Elevators with Sutherland and a psychology student by the name of Tommy Hall, who was not a musician but who appears to have nevertheless been the driving force behind the concept of creating a psychedelic band. Hall was a very outspoken, Learyesque advocate of hallucinogenic drugs like LSD and magic mushrooms. He later became a devout follower of Scientology.

The band's first album, *The Psychedelic Sounds of the 13th Floor Elevators*, was released in November 1966, when singer/songwriter Roky was just nineteen. The band's sophomore effort, *Easter Everywhere*, was released the following November. Just months later though, the group's run would effectively end, though two more albums were subsequently released by the band's label.

The Elevators' final performance was at a world's fair in San Antonio, Texas, on, of all days, April 20, 1968. It was there, it is said, that Roky suffered a complete breakdown and began "speaking gibberish." He was still just twenty years old. Erickson was diagnosed as being a 'paranoid schizophrenic' and was forced to endure involuntary electro-convulsive 'therapy.' While hospitalized, he began hearing voices telling him "horrible things." A doctor treating him at the time claimed that Roky would not recover and would be a vegetable for the rest of his life.

After reportedly escaping with the help of a friend, Erickson headed to San Francisco where he started doing heroin and other hard drugs and soon developed hepatitis. Returning to Austin, Roky was busted with a single marijuana 'joint.' An attorney convinced him to plead 'not guilty by reason of insanity,' a ridiculous defense given the charge, and Erickson was quickly hustled off to Austin State Hospital. He was still just twenty years old at the time of his arrest.

Supposedly due to escape attempts, Roky was transferred to Rusk State Hospital, a stark, barren, maximum-security facility for the criminally insane. While there, Erickson was subjected to more forced ECT treatments and the forced administration of Thorazine. For three-and-a-half years. Also while confined there, he put together a prison band known as the Missing Links. One member of the band had killed two kids and raped and stabbed his own mother. Another had been involved in the rape and murder of a young boy in Houston. A third had killed his own parents and a sibling. And then there was Roky, who had been in possession of an insignificant amount of marijuana.

As 1972 came to a close, it was determined that Roky's sanity had been "restored" and he was released soon after. He was, however, just a shell of his former self.

In the mid-seventies, Erickson formed a new band, Roky Erickson and the Aliens, whose albums *I Think of Demons* (1980) and *The Evil One* (1981) revealed the frontman's then-current obsessions. At about that same time, he told an interviewer that, "the devil, you see, he's my friend." He also told an interviewer that an alien had taken possession of his body, a belief that he still claimed to hold as recently as 2005.

During the 1980s, Erickson withdrew from public view and continued his descent into madness. It is said that he developed a bizarre obsession with the US mail, particularly junk mail solicitations, and that he indulged that obsession for years, poring for hours over his and other people's mail. That chapter of his life reached a peak when he was arrested on mail theft charges after it was discovered that he had taken mail from neighbors and had it displayed in his home. He was, alas, once again institutionalized.

Throughout the 1990s, Roky appears to have continued to live a bizarre and troubled life. A reporter for *Rolling Stone* who attempted to interview him in 1995 described a heartbreaking scene: the formerly charismatic singer looked nothing like his younger self, with his teeth reduced to rotting stumps and his hair wild and matted. Multiple televisions, stereos and police scanners blared at maximum volume throughout his home, creating a cacophony of noise apparently intended to drown out the ever-present voices in his head.

Roky's fortunes began to change in the following decade, after his younger brother Sumner was awarded legal custody of the troubled icon in 2001. In fact, it could be argued that Erickson deserves a special place of honor on this list in that he appears to have pulled off the unlikely feat of returning from the dead. *Rolling Stone*, after all, wrote an obituary for Roky and the band way back in December 1968. But more than forty years later, in 2010, Erickson released an album of new material entitled *True Love Cast Out All Evil*. That disc was released, naturally enough, on April 20. And in March of 2012, Roky completed his first ever tour of Australia and New Zealand.

One final note on Erickson: In 1990, a tribute album containing covers of Roky's songs by such artists as REM and ZZ Top was released. The title of that collection, *Where The Pyramid Meets The Eye: A Tribute to Roky Erickson*, was an obvious reference to the Masonic symbol that graces the back of the US dollar bill and that plays such a key role in various one-world conspiracy theories. The title was derived from a comment made by Erickson.

And with that, I think we can move on now from the Laurel Canyon

Death List, at least temporarily. The list is not yet complete, mind you, since we have only covered the years 1966–1976. Rest assured then that we will continue to add names as we follow the various threads of this story. Lots of names. It is, as it turns out, an inordinately long list.

5

DESIRABLE PEOPLE
THE CANYON'S PECULIAR PAST

"Charles R. 'Chuck' Heath was born in March of 1938... The family lived on Farmdale Avenue, near the base of Laurel Canyon, close to where Studio City is located today." Geoffrey Dunn, writing in The Lies of Sarah Palin (Chuck Heath is Sarah Palin's father)

UNTIL AROUND 1913, LAUREL CANYON REMAINED AN UNDEVELOPED SLICE of LA, a pristine wilderness area rich in native flora and fauna. That all began to change when Charles Spencer Mann and his partners began buying up land along what would become Laurel Canyon Boulevard, as well as on Lookout Mountain. A narrow road leading up to the crest of Lookout Mountain was carved out, and upon that crest was constructed a lavish seventy-room inn with sweeping views of the city below and the Pacific Ocean beyond. The Lookout Inn featured a large ballroom, riding stables, tennis courts and a golf course, among other amenities. But the inn, alas, would only stand for a decade; in 1923, it burned down, as tends to happen rather frequently in Laurel Canyon.

In 1913, Mann began operating what was billed as the nation's first trackless trolley, to ferry tourists and prospective buyers from Sunset Boulevard up to what would become the corner of Laurel Canyon Boulevard and Lookout Mountain Avenue. Around that same time, he built a massive tavern/roadhouse on that very same corner. Dubbed the Laurel Tavern, the structure boasted a 2,000+ square-foot formal dining room, guest rooms, and a bowling alley on the basement level. The Laurel Tavern, of course, would later be acquired by Tom Mix, after which it would be affectionately known as the Log Cabin.

Shortly after the Log Cabin was built, a department store mogul (or a wealthy furniture manufacturer; there is more than one version of the story, or perhaps the man owned more than one business) built an imposing, castle-like mansion across the road, at the corner of Laurel Canyon Boulevard and what would become Willow Glen Road. The home featured rather creepy towers and parapets, and the foundation is said to have been riddled with secret passageways, tunnels, and hidden chambers. The grounds of the estate were laced with trails leading to grottoes, elaborate stone benches, and hidden caves and tunnels.

Across Laurel Canyon Boulevard, the grounds of the Laurel Tavern/Log Cabin were also laced with odd caves and tunnels. As Michael Walker notes in *Laurel Canyon*, "Running up the hillside, behind the house, was a collection of man-made caves built out of stucco, with electric wiring and light bulbs inside." According to various accounts, one secret tunnel running under what is now Laurel Canyon Boulevard connected the Log Cabin, or its guesthouse, to the Houdini estate. This claim is frequently denounced as an urban legend, but given that both properties are known to possess unusual geological features, it's not hard to believe that the tunnel system on one property was connected at one time to the tunnel system on the other. The Tavern itself, as Gail Zappa would later describe it, was "huge and vault-like and cavernous."

With these two rather unusual structures anchoring an otherwise undeveloped canyon, and the Lookout Inn sitting atop uninhabited Lookout Mountain, Mann set about marketing the canyon as a vacation and leisure destination. The land that he carved up into subdivisions with names like "Bungalow Land" and "Wonderland Park" was presented as the ideal location to build vacation homes. But the new inn and roadhouse, and the new parcels of land for sale, definitely weren't for everyone. The roadhouse was essentially a country club, or what Jack Boulware of *Mojo* described as "a masculine retreat for wealthy men." And Bungalow Land was openly advertised as "a high class restricted park for desirable people only."

"Desirable people," of course, tended to be wealthy people without a great deal of skin pigmentation.

As the website of the current Laurel Canyon Association notes, "restrictive covenants were attached to the new parcel deeds. These were thinly veiled attempts to limit ownership to white males of a certain class. While there are many references to the bigotry of the developers in our area, it would appear that some residents were also prone to bias and lawlessness. This article was published in a local paper in 1925:

"Frank Sanceri, the man who was flogged by self-styled 'white knights' on Lookout Mountain in Hollywood several months ago, was found not guilty by a jury in Superior Judge Shea's courtroom of having unlawfully attacked Astrea Jolley, aged eleven.

"Wealthier residents were also attracted to Laurel Canyon: With the creation of the Hollywood film industry in 1910, the canyon attracted a host of 'photoplayers,' including Wally Reid, Tom Mix, Clara Bow, Richard Dix, Norman Kerry, Ramon Navarro, Harry Houdini and Bessie Love."

The author of this little slice of Laurel Canyon history would clearly like us to believe that the "wealthier residents" were a group quite separate from the violent vigilantes roaming the canyon. The history of such groups in Los Angeles, however, clearly suggests otherwise. Paul Young, for example, has written in *LA Exposed* of Los Angeles' early "vigilance committees, which stepped in to take care of outlaws on their own, often with the complete absolution of the mayor himself. Judge Lynch, for example, formed the Los Angeles Rangers in 1854 with some of the city's top judges, lawyers, and businessmen including tycoon Phineas Banning of the Banning Railroad. And there was the Los Angeles Home Guard, another bloodthirsty paramilitary organization, made up of notable citizens, and the much-feared El Monte Rangers, a group of Texas wranglers that specialized in killing Mexicans. As one would expect, there was no regard for the victim's rights in such kangaroo courts. Victims were often dragged from their homes, jail cells, even churches, and beaten, horse-whipped, tortured, mutilated, or castrated before being strung up on the nearest tree."

Before moving on, I need to mention here that, of the eight celebrity residents of Laurel Canyon listed by the Association, fully half died under questionable circumstances, and three of the four did so on days with occult significance. While Bessie Love, Norman Kerry, Richard Dix and Clara Bow all lived long and healthy lives, Ramon Navarro, as we have already seen, was ritually murdered in his home on Laurel Canyon Boulevard on the eve of Halloween, 1968. On January 18, 1923, matinée idol Wallace Reid was found dead in a padded cell at the mental institution to which he had been confined. Just thirty-one years old, Reid's death was attributed to his morphine addiction, though it was never explained how he would have fed that habit while confined to a cell in a mental hospital.

Tom Mix died on a lonely stretch of Arizona highway in the proverbial single-car crash on October 12, 1940 (the birthday of notorious occultist Aleister Crowley), when he quite unexpectedly encountered some temporary construction barricades that had been set up alongside a reportedly washed-out bridge. Although he wasn't speeding (by most accounts), Mix was nevertheless allegedly unable to stop in time and veered off the road, while a crew of what were described as "workmen" reportedly looked on. It wasn't the impact that killed Mix though, but rather a severe blow to the back of the head and neck, purportedly delivered during the crash by an aluminum case he had been carrying in the back seat of his car. There is now a roadside marker at the spot where Mix died. If you should happen to stop by to have a look, you may as well pay a visit to the Florence Military Reservation as well, since it's just a stone's throw away.

Harry Houdini died on Halloween day, 1926, purportedly of an attack of appendicitis precipitated by a blow to the stomach. The problem with that story, however, is that medical science now recognizes it to be an impossibility. According to a recent book about the famed illusionist—*The Secret Life of Houdini*, by William Kalush and Larry Sloman—Houdini was likely murdered by poisoning. Questions have been raised, the book notes, by the curious lack of an autopsy, an "experimental serum" that Houdini was apparently given in the hospital, and indications that his wife, Bess, may have been poisoned as well, though she survived. On March 23, 2007, an exhumation of Houdini's remains was formally requested by his surviving family members. It is unclear at this time when, or even if, that will happen.

Houdini's death, on October 31, 1926, came exactly eight years after the first death to occur in what would become known as the "Houdini house." In 1918, not long after the home was built, a lovers' quarrel arose on one of the home's balconies during a Halloween/birthday party. The gay lover of the original owner's son reportedly ended up splattered on the ground below. According to legend, the businessman succeeded in getting his son off the hook, but only after paying off everyone he could find to pay off, including the trial judge. The aftermath of the party proved to be financially devastating for the family, and the home was apparently put up for sale.

Not long after that, as fate would have it, Harry Houdini was looking for a place to stay in the Hollywood area, as he had decided to break into the motion picture business. He found the perfect home in Laurel Canyon—the home that would, forever after, carry his name. By most accounts, he lived there from about 1919 through the early 1920s, during a brief movie career in which he starred in a handful of Hollywood films. A key scene in one of those films, *The Grim Game*, was reportedly shot at the top of Lookout Mountain, very near where the Lookout Inn then stood.

On October 31, 1959, precisely thirty-three years after Houdini's death, and forty-one years after the unnamed party guest's death, the distinctive mansion on the corner of Laurel Canyon Boulevard and Willow Glen Road burned to the ground in a fire of mysterious origin. (The ruins of the estate remain today, undisturbed for nearly fifty years.) On October 31, 1981, exactly twenty-two years after the fire across the road, the legendary Log Cabin on the other side of Laurel Canyon Boulevard also burned to the ground, in yet another fire of mysterious origin. (Some reports speculated that it was a drug lab explosion.) And twenty-five years after that, on October 31, 2006, *The Secret Life of Houdini* was published, challenging the conventional wisdom on Houdini's death.

Far more compelling than the revelations about Houdini's death, however, was something else about the illusionist that the book revealed for the first time: Harry Houdini was engaged in doing intelligence work for both the US Secret Service and Scotland Yard. And his traveling escape act, as it turns out, was pretty much a cover for those activities—in very much the same way that an actor by the name of John Wilkes Booth appears to have used his career as a traveling stage performer as a cover for intelligence operations. It is a time-honored tradition that seems to remain largely unchanged to this day.

The Sloman book, of course, doesn't make such reckless allegations about any performers other than Houdini. What the book does do, however, is compellingly document that Houdini was, in fact, an intelligence asset who used his magic act as a cover. Not only did the authors obtain corroborating documentation from Scotland Yard, they also received an endorsement of their claim from no less an authority than John McLaughlin, former Acting Director of the Central Intelligence Agency.

It appears then, that, of the eight celebrity residents of Laurel Canyon listed on the Laurel Canyon Association website, at least two (Novarro and Houdini), and quite possibly as many as four, were murdered. That seems like a rather high homicide rate given that, statistically speaking, a white person in this country has about a one-in-345,000 chance of being murdered. Non-white persons, of course, have a far greater chance of becoming the victims of a homicide, but nowhere near the one-in-four to one-in-two odds that a white celebrity living in Laurel Canyon faced.

Statistically speaking, if you were a famous actor in the 1920s, you would have been better off playing a round of Russian Roulette than living in Laurel Canyon.

Anyway... two ambitious projects in the 1940s brought significant changes to Laurel Canyon. First, Laurel Canyon Boulevard was extended into the San Fernando Valley, providing access to the canyon from both the north and the south. The boulevard became a winding thoroughfare, providing direct access to the Westside from the Valley. Traffic, needless to say, increased considerably, which probably worked out well for the planners of the other project, because it meant that the increased traffic brought about by that other project probably wasn't noticed at all. And that's good, you see, because the other project was a secret one.

What would become known as Lookout Mountain Laboratory was originally envisioned as a fortified air defense center. Built in 1941 and nestled in two-and-a-half secluded acres off what is now Wonderland Park Avenue, the installation was hidden from view and surrounded by an electrified fence. By 1947, the facility featured a fully operational movie studio. In fact, it is claimed that it was the world's only completely self-contained movie studio. With 100,000 square feet of floor space, the covert studio included sound stages, screening rooms, film processing labs, editing facilities, an animation department, and seventeen climate-controlled film vaults. It also had a helicopter pad and a bomb shelter.

Over its lifetime, the studio produced some 19,000 classified motion pictures—more than all the Hollywood studios combined (which I guess makes Laurel Canyon the real 'motion picture capital of the world'). Officially, the facility was run by the US Air Force and did nothing more nefarious than process AEC footage of atomic and nuclear bomb tests. The studio, however, was clearly equipped to do far more than just process film. There are indications that Lookout Mountain Laboratory had an advanced research and development department that was on the cutting edge of new film technologies. Such technological advances as 3-D effects were apparently first developed at the Laurel Canyon site. And Hollywood luminaries like John Ford, Jimmy Stewart, Howard Hawks, Ronald Reagan, Bing Crosby, Walt Disney, Hedda Hopper and Marilyn Monroe were given clearance to work at the facility on undisclosed projects. There is no indication that any of them ever spoke of their work at the clandestine studio.

The facility retained as many as 250 producers, directors, technicians, editors, animators, etc., both civilian and military, all with top security clearances—and all reporting to work in a secluded corner of Laurel Canyon. Accounts vary as to when the facility ceased operations. Some claim it was in 1969, while others say the facility remained in operation longer. In any event, by all accounts the secret bunker had been up and running for more than twenty years before Laurel Canyon's rebellious teen years, and it remained operational for the most turbulent of those years.

The existence of the facility remained unknown to the general public until the early 1990s, though it had long been rumored that the CIA operated a secret movie studio somewhere in or near Hollywood. Filmmaker Peter Kuran was the first to learn of its existence, through classified documents he obtained while researching his 1995 documentary *Trinity and Beyond*. And yet even today, nearly twenty years after its limited public disclosure, one would have trouble finding even a single mention of this secret military/intelligence facility anywhere in the 'conspiracy' literature.

I think we can all agree though that there is nothing the least bit suspicious about a covert military facility operating in the epicenter of hippie culture, so let's move on.

In the 1950s, as Barney Hoskyns has written in *Hotel California*, Laurel Canyon was home to all "the hippest young actors," including, according to Hoskyns, Marlon Brando, James Dean, James Coburn and Dennis Hopper. It was home to Natalie Wood as well. In fact, Natalie lived in the very home that Cass Elliot would later turn into a Laurel Canyon party house. And like the home's later occupant, Wood died young under rather mysterious circumstances. As did, to a lesser extent, Canyonite James Dean. And as did, come to think of it, a few other people with very close ties to Canyonite Dennis Hopper.

Dean, Hopper's close friend and co-star, died in a near head-on collision on September 30, 1955, at the tender age of twenty-four. Then there was Nick Adams, who had formerly roomed with Hopper. Like Hopper, Adams had worked alongside James Dean in *Rebel Without a Cause*. According to Dean himself, Adams had worked alongside Dean even earlier than that, when both were young male prostitutes working the mean streets of Hollywood. Adams died on February 6, 1968, at the age of thirty-six, in his home at 2126 El Roble Lane in Coldwater Canyon (one canyon west of Laurel Canyon, thus narrowly sparing Adams from a spot on the Laurel Canyon Death List).

Adams' official cause of death was listed as suicide, of course, but no one really seems to believe that. Actor Forrest Tucker has bluntly declared that, "All of Hollywood knows Nick Adams was knocked off." Nick's relatives reportedly received numerous hang-up calls on the day of his death, and his tape recorder, journals and various other papers and personal effects were conspicuously missing from his home. His lifeless body, sitting upright in a chair, was discovered by his attorney, Ervin "Tip" Roeder. On June 10, 1981, Roeder and his wife, actress Jenny Maxwell (best known for being spanked by Elvis in *Blue Hawaii*), were gunned down outside their Beverly Hills condo.

Next to fall was Sal Mineo, who, like Dean and Adams, had worked with Hopper on *Rebel Without a Cause* and remained a friend thereafter. Like Hopper, Mineo was a regular in the Sunset Strip clubs where the Doors, Love, the Byrds and the Mothers played. He had been alongside Hopper and Peter Fonda during the infamous 'riot' on the Sunset Strip in November 1966. And as has already been discussed, Mineo was stabbed to death in close proximity to those very same clubs on February 12, 1976.

Last to fall was Natalie Wood, who also appeared in *Rebel Without a Cause* and who had at various times dated both Dennis Hopper and Nick Adams. Wood died on November 29, 1981, in a drowning incident off Catalina Island that has never been adequately explained. At the time, she was in the company of actors Robert Wagner and Christopher Walken. Natalie was forty-three when she was laid to rest.

Of the four actors stricken with what has been dubbed the "*Rebel Without a Cause* Curse," two were former residents of Laurel Canyon, another lived at—and was killed at—the mouth of the canyon, and the fourth lived just a mile away, as the crow flies, in neighboring Coldwater Canyon. As I may have mentioned previously, Laurel Canyon seems to be a rather dangerous place to live.

The list of famous former residents of Laurel Canyon also includes the names W.C. Fields, Mary Astor, Roscoe "Fatty" Arbuckle, Errol Flynn, Orson Welles, and Robert Mitchum, who was infamously arrested on marijuana charges in 1948 at 8334 Ridpath Drive, the same street that would later be home to rockers Roger McGuinn, Don Henley and Glen Frey, as well as Paul Rothchild, producer of both the Doors and Love. Mitchum's arrest, by the way, appears to have been a thoroughly staged affair that cemented his 'Hollywood bad boy' image and gave his career quite a boost, but I guess that's not really relevant here.

Another famous resident of Laurel Canyon was science-fiction writer Robert Heinlein, who resided at 8775 Lookout Mountain Avenue. Like so many other characters in this story, Heinlein was a graduate of the US Naval Academy at Annapolis and he had served as a naval officer. After that, he embarked on a successful writing career. And despite the fact that he was, by any objective measure, a rabid right-winger, his work was warmly embraced by the flower-power generation.

If that capsule biography sounds vaguely familiar, by the way, it is probably because it is virtually identical to the biography of a guy named L. Ron Hubbard, whom you may have heard of.

Heinlein's best-known work is the novel *Stranger in a Strange Land*, which many in the Laurel Canyon scene found to be hugely influential. Ed Sanders has written, in *The Family*, that the book "helped provide a theoretical basis for Manson's Family." Charlie frequently used *Strange*

Land terminology when addressing his flock, and he named his first Family-born son Valentine Michael Manson in honor of the book's lead character.

David Crosby was a big Heinlein fan as well. In his autobiography, he references Heinlein on more than one occasion, and proclaims that, "In a society where people can go armed, it makes everybody a little more polite, as Robert Heinlein says in his books." Frank Zappa was also a member of the Robert Heinlein fan club. Barry Miles notes in his biography of the rock icon that his home contained "a copy of Saint-Exupery's *The Little Prince* and other essential sixties reading, including Robert Heinlein's sci-fi classic, *Stranger in a Strange Land*, from which Zappa borrowed the word 'discorporate' for [the song] Absolutely Free."

And that, fearless readers, brings us to the Laurel Canyon era that we are primarily concerned with, the wild and wooly 1960s. But before returning to that era, what conclusions can be drawn from this brief look at early canyon history? For one, it appears that murder and random acts of violence have been a part of the culture of the canyon since the earliest days of its development. It also appears that intelligence operatives posing as entertainers have likewise been a part of the canyon scene since the earliest days. And, finally, it seems that intelligence operatives who didn't even bother to pose as entertainers were streaming into the canyon to report to work at Lookout Mountain Laboratory for at least twenty years before the first rock star set foot there.

We are supposed to believe that all of the musical icons who settled in Laurel Canyon in the 1960s and 1970s just sort of spontaneously came together (one finds the word "serendipitous" sprinkled freely throughout the literature). But how many peculiar coincidences do we have to overlook in order to believe that this was just a chance gathering?

Let's suppose, hypothetically speaking, that you happen to be Jim Morrison and have recently arrived in Laurel Canyon and now find yourself fronting a band that is on the verge of taking the country by storm. Just a mile or so down Laurel Canyon Boulevard from you lives another guy who also recently arrived in Laurel Canyon, and who also happens to front a band on the verge of stardom. He happens to be married to a girl that you attended kindergarten with, and her dad, like yours, was involved in atomic weapons research and testing (Admiral George Morrison for a time did classified work at White Sands). Her husband's dad, meanwhile, is involved in another type of WMD research: chemical warfare.

This other guy's business partner/manager is a spooky ex-Marine who just happens to have a cousin who, bizarrely enough, also fronts a rock band on the verge of superstardom. And this third rock-star-on-the-rise also happens to live in Laurel Canyon, just a mile or two from your house. Just down a couple of other streets, also within walking distance of your home, live two other kids who—wouldn't you know it?—also happen to front a new rock'n'roll band. These two kids happened to attend the same Alexandria, Virginia, high school that you attended, and one of them also attended Annapolis, just like your dad did, and just like your kindergarten friend's dad did.

Though almost all of you hail from the Washington, DC area, you now find yourselves on the opposite side of the country, in an isolated canyon high above the city of Los Angeles, where you are all clustered around a secret military installation. Given his background in research on atomic weapons, your father is probably familiar to some extent with the existence and operations of Lookout Mountain Laboratory, as is the father of your kindergarten friend.

The question that naturally arises here, I suppose, is this: What do you suppose the odds are that all of that just came together purely by chance?

When early installments of this story were posted online, I received a fair amount of negative feedback. Among other things, I was accused of inferring "guilt by association" and of engaging in "character assassination." One rather strident respondent complained that it was unfair to take a few isolated facts about an individual and use them to paint a sinister picture.

To some extent, these are valid complaints. And yes, it is fairly easy to gather together a few *different* isolated facts and use them to paint a much different portrait of these artists and pen an impassioned defense of any of them. (Jim Morrison and Frank Zappa seem to have the most rabid fans, by the way, in case anyone was wondering.) But what I ask is that you try to stand back and take in the big picture, and then ask yourself the following question: Exactly how many coincidences does it take to make a conspiracy?

And yes, by the way, I am very much aware of the fact that Jim Morrison was fond of telling interviewers that his parents were dead, and that, according to legend, he did so because they were, in essence, dead to him. But as one photograph reveals, Jim's dad wasn't dead to him just months before his emergence as a rock star. The photo, reproduced at the front of this book, shows the two Morrisons on the bridge of the *USS Bon Homme Richard* in January 1964. It seems rather obvious to me that telling people that your parents are dead could be a very effective way of avoiding talking about who your father really is. It was such an effective strategy, in fact, that it took over four decades for the truth to finally come out.

6

VITO AND HIS FREAKERS
THE SINISTER ROOTS OF HIPPIE CULTURE

"Call them freaks, the underground, the counterculture, flower children or hippies—they are all loose labels for the youth culture of the sixties." Barry Miles, author of Hippie

"Vito was in his fifties, but he had four-way sex with goddesses... He held these clay-sculpting classes on Laurel Avenue, teaching rich Beverly Hills dowagers how to sculpt. And that was the Byrds' rehearsal room. Then Jim Dickson had the idea to put them on at Ciro's, on the basis that all the freaks would show up and the Byrds would be their Beatles." Kim Fowley

"THIS IS HOW I REMEMBER MY LIFE. OTHER FOLKS MAY NOT HAVE THE SAME memories, even though we might have shared some of the same experiences."

So begins David Crosby's autobiography, *Long Time Gone* (co-written by Carl Gottlieb). As it turns out, quite a few other folks seem to remember some people in Crosby's life who are all but ignored in the lengthy book. The names are casually dropped only once, and not by Crosby but rather in a quote from Byrds' manager Jim Dickson in which he describes the scene at the Sunset Strip clubs when the Byrds were playing: "We had them all. We had Jack Nicholson dancing, we had Peter Fonda dancing with Odetta, we had Vito and his Freakers."

Following that brief mention by Dickson, Gottlieb briefly explains to readers that, "Vito and his Freakers were an acid-drenched extended family of brain-damaged cohabitants." And that, in an incredibly self-indulgent 489-page tome, is the only mention you will find of "Vito and his Freakers"—despite the fact that, by just about all other accounts, the group dismissed as "brain-damaged cohabitants" played a crucial role in the early success of Crosby's band. And in the early success of Arthur Lee's band. And in the early success of Frank Zappa's band. And in the early success of Jim Morrison's band. But especially in the early success of David Crosby's band.

As Barry Miles noted in his biography of Frank Zappa, "The Byrds were closely associated with Vito and the Freaks: Vito Paulekas, his wife Szou and Carl Franzoni, the leaders of a group of about thirty-five dancers whose antics enlivened the Byrds early gigs." In *Waiting for the Sun*, Barney Hoskyns wrote that the early success of the Byrds and other bands was due in no small part to "the roving troupe of self-styled 'freaks' led by ancient beatnik Vito Paulekas and his trusty, lusty sidekick Carl Franzoni." Alban "Snoopy" Pfisterer, former drummer and keyboardist for the band Love, went further still, claiming that Vito actually "got the Byrds together, as I remember—they did a lot of rehearsing at his pad."

According to various other accounts, the Byrds did indeed utilize Vito's 'pad' as a rehearsal studio, as did Arthur Lee's band. More importantly, the freaks drew the crowds into the clubs to see the fledgling bands perform. But as important as their contribution was to helping launch the careers of the Laurel Canyon bands, "Vito and his Freakers" were notable for something else as well; according to Barry Miles, writing in his book *Hippie*, "The first hippies in Hollywood, perhaps the first hippies anywhere, were Vito, his wife Szou, Captain Fuck and their group of about thirty-five dancers. Calling themselves Freaks, they lived a semi-communal life and engaged in sex orgies and free-form dancing whenever they could."

Some of those who were on the scene at the time agree with Miles' assessment that Vito and his troupe were indeed the very first hippies. Arthur Lee, for example, boasted that they "started the whole hippie thing: Vito, Carl, Szou, Beatle Bob, Bryan and me." One of David Crosby's fellow Byrds, Chris Hillman, also credited the strange group with being at the forefront of the hippie movement: "Carl and all those guys were way ahead of everyone on hippiedom fashion." Ray Manzarek of the Doors remembered them as well: "There were these guys named Carl and Vito who had a dance troupe of gypsy freaks. They were let in for free, because they were these quintessential hippies, which was great for tourists."

If these rather colorful people really were the very first hippies, the very first riders of that 'countercultural' wave, then we should probably try to get to know them. As it turns out, however, that is not such an easy thing to do. Most accounts—and there aren't all that many—offer little more than a few first names, with no consensus agreement on how those first names are even spelled ("Karl" and "Carl" appear interchangeably, as do "Szou" and "Zsou," and "Godot" and "Godo"). But for you, dear readers—because I am a giver—I have gone the extra mile and sifted through the detritus to dig up at least some of the sordid details.

By all accounts the troupe was led by one Vito Paulekas, whose full name was Vitautus Alphonso Paulekas. Born the son of a Lithuanian sausage-maker on May 20, 1913, Vito hailed from Lawrence, Massachusetts (though some accounts claim it was Lowell, Massachusetts). Parents John and Rose Paulekas had three other kids, giving Vito an older sister named Albena and two younger brothers, Bronislo and John.

Some accounts claim that from a young age, Vito developed a habit of running afoul of the law. According to Miles, for example, Vito spent a year-and-a-half in a reformatory as a teenager and "was busted several times after that." A family member though disputes those claims. What isn't disputed is that, in 1938, he was convicted of armed robbery and handed a twenty-five year sentence following a botched attempt at holding up a movie theater. In 1932, at the height of the Great Depression, he had won a marathon dance competition held at Revere Beach. His winnings had given him a taste of the good life that he was thereafter unable to sustain, leading to the robbery attempt.

In 1942, just four years after his conviction, Vito was released into the custody, so to speak, of the US Merchant Marines (a branch of the US Navy during wartime), ostensibly to escort ships running lend-lease missions. Following his release from the service, circa 1946, he arrived in Los Angeles. Two years later, a curious event played out in another part of the country, as documented in the February 23, 1948, edition of *Time* magazine:

"One morning last week, bespectacled Bryant Bowden, editor of the weekly Okeechobee (Fla.) News, sauntered into the Okeechobee courthouse and stopped to eye the bulletin board in the main hall. Among the marriage-license applications, which, by Florida law, must be publicly posted for three days before a ceremony, he saw something which made him goggle. Winthrop Rockefeller, thirty-five, of New York—the fourth of John D. Rockefeller Jr.'s five sons and one of the most eligible bachelors in the world—had stated his intention of marrying one Eva Sears, also of New York. Editor Bowden had a bitter moment—his paper would not be published for two days. Then he remembered that he was the Okeechobee correspondent for the Associated Press. He telephoned the AP office in Jacksonville. A few hours later, the whole US journalistic horizon glowed a bright pink with the fireworks he had touched off. While the first headlines blazed (and while Manhattan gossip columnists scrambled to assure their readers that they had known all about the romance for months), herds of reporters were dispatched to find an answer to the question: Who is Eva Sears? Hearst's Cholly Knickerbocker (Ghighi Cassini) haughtily announced that she was Mrs. Barbara Paul Sears of the fine old Philadelphia Pauls and thus a society girl of impeccable pedigree. He was wrong."

Indeed he was. So who was this mystery woman—this woman who, as it turns out, had once had a brief career in Hollywood before moving to Paris and taking a job as a secretary at the US embassy? She appears to have gone by many names at different times in her life, including Eva Paul, Eva Paul Sears, Barbara Paul, Barbara Paul Sears, and "Bobo" Rockefeller. None of them, however, was the name she was given at the time of her birth. As *Time* noted, "Her parents were Lithuanian immigrants and she was born Jievute Paulekiute in a coal patch near Noblestown, Pa." Even that, however, was not her real name—at least not by American custom and tradition.

In her parents' homeland, "Paulekiute" is the feminine version of "Paulekas." Eva Paul's father, as it turns out, just happened to be the brother of Vito Paulekas' father. (A fact verified by—and brought to my attention by—a member of the Paulekas family.) I'm no genealogist, but I'm pretty sure that that means that the self-styled "King of the Hippies" was, improbably enough, a first cousin of Bobo Rockefeller and a cousin-in-law (for lack of a better term) of Winthrop Rockefeller himself. Vito was also a cousin of the couple's only child, Winthrop Paul Rockefeller, who would later serve as the lieutenant governor of the state of Arkansas.

The Paulekas family, alas, missed Winthrop and Bobo's day of celebration. According to *Time*, "Bobo's mother and stepfather... were unable to attend the ceremony because they were making a batch of Lithuanian cheese on their Indiana farm." I guess we all have our priorities. Truth be told though, the Paulekas clan has a somewhat different explanation: they were deliberately excluded from the ceremony as it was felt they were a bit too uncultured to break bread with the likes of the Duke and Duchess of Windsor and the Marquess of Blandford.

As for Vito, he appears to have rather quickly established himself in Los Angeles as a respected artist/sculptor. As early as August of 1949, the *Los Angeles Times* announced that an art exhibit at the Biltmore Hotel was to feature his work. In May of 1956, another announcement held that there would be an exhibit by "Vito and his students" to be held at the Vito Clay Studios on Laurel Avenue. Another announcement, in February of 1958, alerted readers that a gallery on La Cienega Boulevard would be featuring the work of sculptor "Vito Bouleka." And the next year, in May 1959, a gallery on Beverly Boulevard was scheduled to host an exhibit featuring works from "Vito Clay Studios."

Also during the decade of the 1950s, Vito married and fathered two children, though that marriage had melted down by the time the 1960s rolled around. It was Vito's second marriage, his first having been to a teen bride back in his marathon dancing days, before his prison stint. On July 7, 1961, he married yet again, to the aforementioned Szou, whose real name was Susan Cynthia Shaffer. Vito was forty-eight at the time and Szou was just eighteen. She had been only sixteen when they met.

Vito and Szou made their home in an unassuming building at the corner of Laurel Avenue and Beverly Boulevard, just below the mouth of Laurel Canyon and practically within spitting distance of Jay Sebring's hair salon. At street level was Szou's clothing boutique, which has been credited by some scenesters with being the very first to introduce hippie fashions. Upstairs were living quarters for Vito, Szou and their first-born son, Godo. Downstairs was what was known as the Vito Clay Studio, where, according to Miles and various others, Paulekas "made a living of sorts by giving clay modeling lessons to Beverly Hills matrons who found the atmosphere in his studio exciting." According to most accounts, it wasn't really the Mayan-tomb decor of the studio that many of the matrons found so exciting, but rather Vito's reportedly insatiable sexual appetite and John Holmesian physique. In any event, Vito's students also apparently included such Hollywood luminaries as Jonathan Winters, Mickey Rooney and Steve Allen.

As for his erstwhile sidekick, Carl Orestes Franzoni, he has claimed in interviews that his "mother was a countess" and his father "was a stone carver from Rutland, Vermont. The family was brought from Italy, from the quarries in the northern part of Italy, to cut the stone for the monuments of the United States." That would make his ancestors, it stands to reason, of considerable importance in the Masonic community. And there were in fact a couple of brothers named Franzoni who were brought over from Italy in the early 1800s to carve the Masonic monuments of Washington. According to Ihna Thayer Frary's *They Built the Capitol*, Guiseppe Franzoni, who came over with his brother Carlo, "had especially good family connections in Italy, he being a nephew of Cardinal Franzoni and son of the President of the Academy of Fine Arts at Carrara." Also making their way to the New World were Francisco Iardella, a cousin of the Franzoni brothers, and Giovanni Andrei, a brother-in-law of Guiseppe Franzoni.

By Carl Franzoni's own account, he himself grew up as something of a young hoodlum in Cincinnati, Ohio, and later went into business with some shady Sicilian characters selling mail-order breast and penis pumps out of an address on LA's fabled Melrose Avenue. As Franzoni remembered it, his business "partner's name was Scallacci, Joe Scallacci—the same name as the famous murderer Scallacci. Probably from the same family." Probably so.

Franzoni, born circa 1934, hooked up with the older Paulekas sometime around 1963 and soon after became his constant sidekick. Also in the troupe was a young Rory Flynn (Canyonite Errol Flynn's statuesque daughter), a bizarre character named Ricky Applebaum who had half a moustache on one side of his face and half a beard on the other, most of the young girls who would later become part of Frank Zappa's GTO project, and a lot of other colorful characters who donned pseudonyms like Linda Bopp, Butchie, Beatle Bob, Emerald, and Karen Yum Yum.

Also flitting about the periphery of the dance troupe were Navy brat Gail Sloatman and a curious character on the LA music scene by the name of Kim Fowley. Sloatman and Fowley were, for a time, closely allied and even cut a record together, America's Sweethearts, that Fowley produced. In 1966, Fowley produced a record for Vito as well, billed as Vito and the Hands. The seven-inch single, Where It's At, which featured the musicianship of some of Frank Zappa's Mothers of Invention cohorts, came no closer to entering the charts than did Fowley and Sloatman's effort. Sloatman though soon found work as an assistant to, and booking agent for, Elmer Valentine, whom we will meet shortly.

Fowley, as with so many other characters in this story, has a rather interesting history. He was born in 1939, the son of actor Douglas Fowley, a WWII Navy veteran and attendee of St. Francis Xavier Military Academy. According to the younger Fowley's account, he was initially abandoned to a foster home but later taken back and raised by his father. He grew up in upscale Malibu, California, where he shared his childhood home with "a bunch of actors and guys from the Navy." At the age of six-and-a-half, Fowley had an unusual experience that he later shared with author Michael Walker: dressed up in a sailor suit by his dad and his Navy buddies, he was taken "to a photographer named William, who took a picture of me in the sailor suit. His studio was next door to the Canyon [Country] Store." Right after that, he was driven down Laurel Canyon Boulevard to the near-mythical Schwab's Drugstore, where "everybody cheered and two chorus girls grabbed my six-year-old cock and balls and stuck a candy cigarette in my mouth."

It's probably safe to assume that childhood experiences such as that helped to prepare Fowley for his later employment as a young male street hustler, a profession that he practiced on the seedy streets of the City of Angels (by Fowley's own account, I should add, just as it was James Dean himself who claimed to have worked those same streets with Nick Adams). Following that, Fowley spent some time serving with the Army National Guard, after which he devoted his life to working in the LA music industry as a musician, writer and producer—as well as, according to some accounts, a master manipulator.

Around 1957, Fowley played in a band known as the Sleepwalkers, alongside future Beach Boy Bruce Johnston. At times, a diminutive young guitarist named Phil Spector—who had moved out to LA with his mother not too many years earlier, following the suicide of his father when Phil was just nine—sat in with the group. During the 1960s, Fowley was best known for producing such ridiculous yet beloved novelty songs as the Hollywood Argyles' Alley Oop and the Rivingtons' Papa Oom-Mow-Mow, though he also did more respectable work such as collaborating on some Byrds' tracks and having some of his original songs covered by both the Beach Boys and the Flying Burrito Brothers.

In 1975, Fowley would have perhaps his greatest success when he created the Runaways, further lowering the bar that Frank Zappa had already set rather low some years earlier when he had created and recorded the GTOs. The Runaways featured underage versions of Joan Jett and Lita Ford, whom Fowley tastefully attired in leather and lingerie. As he would later boast, "Everyone loved the idea of sixteen-year-old girls playing guitars and singing about fucking." Some of the young girls in the band, including Cherie Curry, would later accuse Fowley of requiring them to perform sexual services for him and his associates as a prerequisite for membership in the group.

Prior to assembling the Runaways, one of Fowley's proudest accomplishments was producing the 1969 album *I'm Back and I'm Proud* by rockabilly pioneer Gene Vincent, featuring backing vocals by Canyonite Linda Ronstadt. Just two years later, Vincent—a Navy veteran raised in that penultimate Navy town, Norfolk, Virginia—died unexpectedly on October 12, 1971, due reportedly to a ruptured stomach ulcer. Not long before his death, Vincent had been on tour in the UK but he had hastily returned to the US due to pressure from, among others, promoter Don Arden. Known none-too-affectionately as the "Al Capone of Pop," Arden had a penchant for guns and violence and he was known to openly boast of his affiliation with powerful organized crime figures. In addition to being a business partner of the equally nefarious Michael Jeffery, Arden was also the father of Sharon Osbourne and the former manager of her husband's band, Black Sabbath... but here I have surely digressed, so let's try to bring this back around to where we left off.

At least as early as 1962, not long before Carl Franzoni joined the group, the freak troupe was already hitting the clubs a couple nights each week to refine their unique style of dance (perhaps best described as an epileptic seizure set to music) and show off their distinctively unappealing, though soon to be quite popular, fashion sense. In those early days, they danced to local black R&B bands and to a band out of Fresno known as the Gauchos, in dives far removed from the fabled Sunset Strip—because, Franzoni has said, "There were no white bands [in LA] yet," and "There were no clubs on Sunset Boulevard."

That, of course, was all about to quickly change. As if by magic, new clubs began to spring up along the legendary Sunset Strip beginning around 1964, and old clubs considered to be long past their prime miraculously reemerged. In January 1964, a young Chicago vice cop named Elmer Valentine opened the doors to the now world-famous Whisky-a-Go-Go nightclub. Just over a year later, in spring of 1965, he opened a second soon-to-be-wildly-popular club, the Trip. Not long before that, near the end of 1964, the legendary Ciro's nightclub began undergoing extensive renovations. Opened in 1940 by Billy Wilkerson, an associate of Bugsy Siegel, the upscale club had flourished for the first twenty years of its existence, with a clientele that regularly included Hollywood royalty and organized crime figures. By the early 1960s, though, the Strip was dead, and the once prestigious club had gone to seed.

Ciro's reopened in early 1965, just before the Trip opened its doors and just in time, as it turns out, to host the very first club appearance by the musical act that was about to become the first Laurel Canyon band to commit a song to vinyl: The Byrds. By 1967, Gazzari's had opened up on the Strip as well, and in the early 1970s Valentine would open yet another club that endures to this day, the Roxy. Smaller clubs like the London Fog, where the Doors got their first booking as the house band in early 1966, opened their doors to the public in the mid-1960s as well.

The timing of the opening of Valentine's first two clubs, and the reopening of Ciro's, could not have been any more fortuitous. The paint was barely dry on the walls of the new clubs when bands like Love and the Doors and the Byrds and Buffalo Springfield and the Turtles and the Mothers of Invention and the Mamas and the Papas and the Lovin' Spoonful came knocking. The problem, however, was that the new clubs were not yet known to the general public, Ciro's had been long left for dead, and nobody had the slightest idea who any of these newfangled bands were. What was needed then was a way to create a buzz around the clubs that would draw people in and kick-start the Strip back to life, as well as, of course, launch the careers of the new bands.

The bands themselves could not be expected to fill the new clubs, since, besides being unknown, they also—and yeah, I know that you don't really want to hear this and I will undoubtedly be deluged with letters of complaint, but I'm going to say it anyway—weren't very good, at least not in their live incarnations. To be sure, they sounded great on vinyl, but that was largely due to the fact that the band members themselves didn't actually play on their records (at least not in the early days), and the rich vocal harmonies that were a trademark of the 'Laurel Canyon sound' were created in the studio with a good deal of multitracking and overdubs. On stage, it was another matter entirely.

Enter then the wildly flamboyant and colorful freak squad, who were one key component of the strategy that was devised to lure patrons into the clubs. Vito and Carl's dancers were a fixture on the Sunset Strip scene from the very moment that the new clubs opened their doors to the public, and they were, by all accounts, treated like royalty by the club owners. As John Hartmann, proprietor of the Kaleidoscope Club and brother of comedian Phil Hartman, acknowledged, he "would let Vito and his dancers into the Kaleidoscope free every week because they attracted people. They were really hippies, and so we had to have them. They got in free pretty much everywhere they went. They blessed your joint. They validated you. If they're the essence of hippiedom and you're trying to be a hippie nightclub, you need hippies."

As the aforementioned Kim Fowley put it, with characteristic bluntness, "A band didn't have to be good, as long as the dancers were there." Indeed, the band was largely irrelevant, other than to provide some semblance of a soundtrack for the real show, which was taking place on the dance floor. Gail Zappa once candidly admitted that, even at her husband's shows, the real attraction was not on the stage: "The customers came to see the freaks dance. Nobody ever talks about that, but that was the case." Frank Zappa added, "As soon as they arrived they would make things happen, because they were dancing in a way nobody had seen before, screaming and yelling out on the floor and doing all kinds of weird things. They were dressed in a way that nobody could believe, and they gave life to everything that was going on."

For reasons that clearly had more to do with boosting attendance at the clubs than with the dancing abilities displayed by the group, Vito and Carl seem to have become minor media darlings over the course of the 1960s and into the 1970s. The two can be seen, separately and together, in a string of cheap exploitation films, including *Mondo Bizarro* from 1966, *Something's Happening (aka The Hippie Revolt)* from 1967, the notorious *Mondo Hollywood*, also released in 1967, and *You Are What You Eat*, with David Crosby, Frank Zappa and Tiny Tim, which hit theaters in 1968. In 1972, Vito made his acting debut in a non-documentary film, *The White Horse Gang*.

Paulekas reportedly also popped up on Groucho Marx's *You Bet Your Life*, and Franzoni made an appearance on a 1968 Dick Clark TV special. The golden child, Godo Paulekas, was featured in a photo in *Life* magazine circa 1966, and the whole troupe showed up for an appearance on the *Tonight Show*. According to Barry Miles, Vito also "appeared regularly on the *Joe Pyne Show* and in between the bare-breasted girls in the late fifties and early sixties men's magazines."

Joe Pyne, for those of you too young to remember, is the guy we have to thank for paving the way for the likes of Bill O'Reilly, Rush Limbaugh, Sean Hannity, Michael Savage, Don Imus, Morton Downey, Jr., Jerry Springer and Wally George. For Mr. Pyne, you see, was the guy who pioneered the confrontational interview style favored by so many today. The decorated Marine Corps veteran debuted as a talk-radio host in 1950 and quickly became known for insulting and demeaning anyone who dared to disagree with him, guests and listeners alike. In 1957, he moved his show to LA and by 1965, he was nationally syndicated both on the radio and on television. His favored targets, as you may have guessed, included hippies, feminists, gays, and anti-war activists, and his interviews frequently ended with his guest either walking off or being thrown off the stage. Nearing the peak of his popularity, Pyne died on March 23, 1970, at the age of forty-five, reportedly of lung cancer. His ideological offspring, however, live on.

7

THE DEATH OF GODO PAULEKAS
ANGER'S INFANT LUCIFER

"Vito would come in every night with an entourage—mostly four or five really great-looking girls. It's a weird parallel, but it was like a nonviolent Manson situation, a little cult." Lou Adler, manager/producer of the Mamas and the Papas, co-organizer of the Monterey Pop Festival, investor in Jay Sebring's hair salon, and business partner of mobster/club owner Elmer Valentine

"I have said for years that there are some similarities between Vito and Manson... Vito was sort of like a pimp. He was welcome as a VIP with the emerging rock crowd because he always showed up with these free thinking fourteen- and fifteen-year-old girls that would be happy to satisfy their needs." A member of the Paulekas family, in e-mail correspondence with the author

RECRUITS FOR VITO AND CARL'S DANCE TROUPE WEREN'T LIKELY HARD TO come by, given that, according to Miles, Vito operated "the first crash pad in LA, an open house to countless runaways where everyone was welcome for a night, particularly young women." By the mid-1960s, the group had expanded into a second communal location in addition to the basement studio at 303 Laurel Avenue: the ubiquitous Log Cabin. According to Jack Boulware, writing in *Mojo*, architect Robert Byrd and his son built a new guesthouse (aka 'the treehouse') on the property in the early 1960s, and the "following year, a communal family of weirdos moved into the cabin and treehouse, centered around two underground hipsters named Vito Paulekas and Carl Franzoni, organizers of freeform dance troupes at clubs along the Sunset Strip." By 1967, the dancers were splitting "their rent with staff from the hippie publication *The Oracle*. Retired journalist John Bilby recalls at least thirty-six people living and partying at the Log Cabin and treehouse, including the band Fraternity of Man. 'Tim Leary was definitely there, George Harrison and Ravi Shankar were there,' Bilby says."

For the record, Fraternity of Man was a one-hit-wonder band best known for the ever-popular novelty song Don't Bogart Me. Tim Leary was, in this writer's humble opinion, best known for being a painfully obvious CIA asset. And *The Oracle* was a San Francisco-based publication with intelligence ties that specialized in pitching psychedelic occultism to impressionable youth. Leary, it probably should be noted, also had a home of his own in Laurel Canyon.

According to Barry Miles, "Franzoni's commune ended in May 1968," as that was when *The Oracle* moved out and our old friend Frank Zappa moved in. The lead Mother "had visited Carl at the Log Cabin on a previous trip and realized it was perfect for his needs." And it was an easy move for Frank, since he was already living in Laurel Canyon at the home of Pamela Zarubica (aka Suzy Creamcheese) at 8404 Kirkwood Drive, where Zappa had met his new wife, Gail, and where Gail's old kindergarten pal, Jim Morrison, was known to occasionally pass the time. Ms. Zarubica/Creamcheese was yet another member of Vito's dance troupe.

As multiple sources remember it, Miles is mistaken in his contention that Franzoni's commune came to an end; Frank Zappa took over as ringmaster, to be sure, but Franzoni and all his cohorts stayed on. Carl had a room in the basement, where he was known to bowl in the middle of the night, usually naked and intoxicated. The doomed Christine Frka had a room down there as well, as did other future GTOs. Various other members of the dance troupe occupied other nooks and crannies in both the main house and the guesthouse/treehouse. Indeed, as Miles noted correctly, the freak dancers became so closely associated with the Mothers of Invention that "they got dubbed as 'the Mothers Auxiliary' and Carl Franzoni, in particular, was included in a lot of group photographs." Vito and Carl also received vocal credits on the band's debut album (as did none other than Bobby Beausoleil).

And that, in a nutshell, is the story of Vito and his freak dancers—or at least a sanitized version. Because there is, as it turns out, a very dark underbelly to this story. And much of it is centered around that angelic hippie child that the readers of *Life* magazine met in 1966, and who we now must sadly add to the Laurel Canyon Death List. For young Godo Paulekas, you see, never made it past the age of three. The specifics of the tragedy are difficult to determine, unfortunately, as there is little agreement in the various accounts of the event.

According to Barry Miles, "Vito and Szou's three-year-old son Godo had fallen through a trapdoor on the roof of the building and died." Michael Walker tells of a "two or three" year old Godo "fall[ing] to his death from a scaffold at the studio." An article in the *San Francisco Weekly* had it as "a five-year-old boy" who died when he "fell through a skylight." Super-groupie and former freak dancer Pamela Des Barres agreed with the skylight scenario, but not the age: "Vito's exquisite little puppet child, Godot, fell through a skylight during a wacky photo session on the roof and died at age three-and-a-half." Alban Pfisterer of the band Love recalled a much darker scenario: "[Vito] got married, had a baby, gave it acid, and it fell off the roof and died."

When Robert Carl Cohen digitally remastered his notorious *Mondo Hollywood* for DVD release, he added postscripts for all the famous and infamous people who were featured in his film. For "Godo" Paulekas, he inserted the following caption: "Died age two—victim of medical malpractice." Thus we appear to have a further muddying of the waters. So muddy in fact that in addition to there being various competing 'fell from some scaffolding/fell through a trapdoor/crashed through a skylight' accounts, there are also at least two medical malpractice stories!

Before reviewing those though, it would perhaps be instructive to examine the context in which this tragedy played out. We know, for example, that a musician and writer named Raphael told writer Michael

Walker that he had been present one evening at Vito's place when Godo was brought out: "They passed that little boy around, naked, in a circle with their mouths. That was their thing about 'introducing him to sensuality.'" We also know that Vito and Szou had a rather odd reaction to the death of their firstborn son and only child, as recounted by Des Barres: "I was beside myself with sorrow, but Vito and Szou insisted on continuing our plans for the evening. We went out dancing, and when people asked where little Godot was, Vito said, 'He died today.' It was weird, really weird."

Barry Miles, who was also close to the scene, had a similar recollection, though he attempted to put a more positive spin on the reaction of the parents: "Vito and Szou's three-year-old son Godo had fallen through a trapdoor on the roof of their building and died. That evening Vito, Szou and the gang went out as usual, dancing with an even fiercer intensity to assuage their grief." Godo died at 7:30 PM on December 23, 1966, some thirty-six hours before Christmas morning. On the side of reality that I live on, the death of a child at any time would deter most parents from going out and partying the night away—that it occurred virtually on the eve of Christmas makes Vito and Szou's actions that much more incomprehensible.

Adding to the weirdness factor is the full text of the quote from the *San Francisco Weekly* that I previously presented an edited version of: "[Kenneth Anger's] first candidate to play Lucifer, a five-year-old boy whose hippie parents had been fixtures on the Los Angeles counterculture scene, fell through a skylight to his death. By 1967, Anger had relocated to San Francisco and was searching for a new Lucifer." As some readers may be aware, he soon found his new Lucifer in the form of Mansonite and former Grass Roots guitarist Bobby Beausoleil.

And so it was that the soon-to-be convicted murderer replaced the cherubic hippie child as the face of Lucifer. But what was it, one wonders, that drew Anger's twisted eye to the young boy? Beausoleil has said that some of Anger's film projects were for private collectors: "every once in a while he'd do a little thing that wouldn't be for distribution." Biographer Bill Landis has written that projects such as those led at one time to Anger being investigated by the police on suspicion that he had been producing snuff films.

Pamela Des Barres has shed further light on the dark edges of the freak troupe with this description of a scene that Vito had staged one evening in his studio: "two tenderly young girls were tonguing each other... everyone was silently observing the scene as if it were part of their necessary training by the headmaster, Vito... One of the girls on the four-poster was only twelve-years-old, and a few months later Vito was deported to Tahiti for this very situation, and many more just like it."

It was actually Haiti that Vito appears to have fled to, and then to Jamaica (which at the time had no extradition treaty with the United States), accompanied by his wife Szou and their new baby daughter Gruvi Nipples Paulekas, born on June 23, 1967. The couple would have several more offspring, each given an increasingly ridiculous name: Bp Paulekas, born on December 29, 1969; Sky Paulekas, born, bizarrely enough, on what would have been Godo's eighth birthday, December 1, 1971; and Phreekus Mageekus Paulekas, born on January 28, 1974, just a little more than a year before the couple divorced in March of 1975 in Northern California.

According to Miles, Vito's flight from justice occurred in December of 1968, though other accounts vary. Carl Franzoni, meanwhile, became embroiled in some unspecified legal troubles of his own and went into hiding, later resurfacing in Canada by some reports. At around that same time, Frank Zappa moved on to yet another location in Laurel Canyon, a high-security home on Woodrow Wilson Drive.

Also at around that same time, according to author Ed Sanders, the Manson Family came calling at the Log Cabin: "One former Manson family associate claims that a group of four to six family members lived on Laurel Canyon Boulevard in the log cabin house once owned by cowboy-actor Tom Mix. They lived there for a few weeks, in late 1968, in a cave-like hollow in back of the residence." According to Franzoni, Manson also came calling at the Vito Clay Studio on Laurel Avenue: "Applebaum took over Vito's place when Vito vacated at Beverly and Laurel. So he inherited all the people that came after that... he was the beginning of the Manson clan. Manson came there because he had heard about Vito but Vito was gone."

It makes perfect sense, in retrospect, that Charles Manson and his Family came calling just as Vito fled the scene, and that a Mansonite replaced the freak child as the embodiment of Lucifer. For the truth, you see, is that in many significant ways, Charles Manson was little more than a younger version of Vito Paulekas. Consider, if you will, all of the following Mansonesque qualities that Paulekas (and to some extent, Franzoni) seemed to share:

■ Vito considered himself to be a gifted artist and poet, as did our old friend Charlie Manson.

■ Vito, according to Miles, "was something of a guru," as was, quite obviously, Chuck Manson.

■ Vito surrounded himself with a flock of very young (often underage) women, as did Manson.

■ Vito was considerably older than his followers, and so too was Charlie.

■ When Vito addressed his flock, they listened with rapt attention as though they were being delivered the word of God, as was true with Manson as well.

■ Carl Franzoni was known to wear a black cape and refer to himself as "Captain Fuck," while Manson was also partial to black capes and would at times declare himself to be "the God of Fuck."

■ Vito is said to have had a virtually insatiable libido, as did, by numerous reports, Chuck Manson.

■ Vito's flock adopted nicknames to aid in the depersonalization process, as did Charlie's.

■ Vito's troupe included a Beverly Hills hairstylist named Sheldon Jaman, while Charlie's included a Beverly Hills hairpiece stylist named Charles Watson.

■ Vito believed in introducing children to sexuality at a very young age, while in the Manson Family, as Sanders has noted, "Infant sexuality was encouraged."

■ Vito apparently liked to stage live sex shows for his followers involving underage participants, which was also a specialty of Charles Milles Manson.

■ Finally, Vito encouraged his followers to drug themselves while he himself largely abstained, thus enabling him to at all times maintain control, while Manson limited his own drug intake for the very same reason.

Franzoni and Manson were not, by the way, the only folks on the Laurel Canyon/Sunset Strip scene who developed a fondness for black capes in the latter half of the 1960s. As Michael Walker noted in *Laurel Canyon*, during that same period of time David Crosby had "taken to wearing an Oscar Wilde/Frank Lloyd Wright-ish cape wherever he went."

In unrelated news, Ed Sanders notes in his controversial *The Family* that, "Around March 10, 1968, a convoy of seven Process automobiles containing thirty people and fourteen Alsatian dogs journeyed toward Los Angeles." Vincent Bugliosi added, in his best-selling *Helter Skelter*, that in "1968 and 1969, the Process launched a major recruiting drive in the United States. They were in Los Angeles in May and June of 1968 and for at least several months in the fall of 1969."

As Gary Lachman wrote in *Fortean Times* in May 2000, the Process Church of the Final Judgement, often referred to as just "the Process," was "one of the most controversial cults of the Sixties." Formed in 1963 in London as an offshoot of Scientology, the group was the brainchild of Robert Moore, a former cavalry officer who would soon adopt the name Robert DeGrimston, and Mary Ann MacLean, the proprietor of an elite prostitution ring with ties to the UK's so-called Profumo Affair. According to various reports, MacLean was at one time married to famed pugilist and freemason Sugar Ray Robinson, who, as we will see in a later chapter, lived right around the corner from future Love frontman Arthur Lee during that time.

The group arrived in the States in 1968, establishing footholds in Los Angeles, San Francisco, New Orleans, New York and Boston. The organization soon began producing a magazine that, as Lachmann says, had an "editorial policy [that] favoured Hitler, Satan and gore." Singer/songwriter Marianne Faithfull, who appeared in an issue of the magazine, later distanced herself from the group, saying that "There was something almost like fascism about the Process." The cult's fascist mindset was amply illustrated by their choice of a symbol, which Lachman accurately describes as bearing "an uncanny resemblance to the Nazi swastika."

In *The Family*, Sanders describes the Process as a "death-worshiping church" composed of "hooded snuffoids" who were directly connected to the Manson murders. Maury Terry likewise fleshed out connections between the Process and New York's Son of Sam murders in his equally controversial *The Ultimate Evil*. Spokespersons for the cult, not surprisingly, vehemently denied any involvement in any such murderous activities. One thing is certain though: Processians were instantly recognizable on the streets of LA due to their curious habit of donning black capes wherever they went.

In other news, it appears as though Frank Zappa also displayed some of the same less-than-admirable qualities shared by Manson and Paulekas. As Des Barres observed, "Vito was just like Frank, he never got high either. They were both ringmasters who always wanted to be in control." And as Barry Miles noted in his Zappa biography, Frank's daughter Moon "recalls men with straggling beards, body odour and bad posture who crouched naked near her playthings..." Also, the "Zappa children watched porn with their parents and were encouraged in their own sexuality as soon as they reached puberty. When they became teenagers, Gail insisted they shower with their overnight guests in order to conserve water." Apparently the Zappas were having a hard time paying their DWP bill.

By the early 1970s, Vito Paulekas had resurfaced up north in Cotati, California, with Carl Franzoni once again at his side. The two were, by all accounts, treated like rock stars in the funky little town, and they are to this day proudly and prominently featured on the city's official website. By some accounts, Vito even served as mayor of the town, with Franzoni assisting as his Director of Parks and Recreation. Paulekas also taught dance classes at Sonoma State College. Szou went to work for an attorney, leaving the hippie life behind.

Franzoni, meanwhile, turned up now and then on that early version of *America's Got Talent* known as *The Gong Show* (apparently as one of the 'Worm Dancers'). *The Gong Show*, of course, was the brainchild of Chuck Barris, who famously claimed that during the days when he appeared to be working as a mild-mannered game show producer, he was actually on the payroll of the CIA, and that while he was ostensibly serving as a chaperone to the couples who had won trips on *The Dating Game*, what he was really doing was carrying out assassinations. Possibly like that Harry Houdini guy, who we'll discuss in a later chapter.

Anyway, during the 1970s, the "cabin and treehouse scene," according to Jack Boulware, "grew creepy." Actually, it had always been pretty creepy; it likely just became a little more openly creepy. Eric Burden of the Animals moved in after Zappa vacated and the property continued to be communally occupied. In fact, it appears to have remained something of a commune throughout the 1970s, quite possibly right up until the time that it burned to the ground on October 31, 1981. Who paid the rent is anybody's guess—as is why such a prestigious property seems to have been made readily available to pretty much any "communal family of weirdos" who wanted to move in.

Vito Paulekas and Carl Franzoni appear to have remained in Northern California throughout the 1980s and into the 1990s. Vito married once again, for the fourth time, while he was in his sixties. Franzoni was still milling about the Santa Rosa area as of early 2013. In February of 2008, the aging freak, then reportedly seventy-four, rode along on a tour of 1960s hotspots offered by a local tour company and delighted the crowd by reenacting his distinctive dance style in front of Vito's former studio. The tour operator billed Franzoni as "the King of the Freaks," a title formerly held by his mentor, Vito Paulekas. The original king, alas, had died in October of 1992. His memorial service was held, appropriately enough, on October 31, 1992—All Hallows' Eve.

Returning now to the death of young Godo Paulekas, filmmaker Robert Carl Cohen, in an emailed defense of his medical malpractice claim, provided a detailed account of the incident—one that he said was told to him by Carl Franzoni on the evening of the tragedy and retold later by Vito himself: "Godo, two-and-a-half years of age at the time, was with his parents on the roof of 333 Laurel Ave. during a *LA Free Press* photo shoot. Two older children were holding his hands as they ran about. They led him onto a white-painted glass skylight, which collapsed. Godo fell through, sustaining a cut to his head and bruises. His parents took him to Hollywood Emergency Hospital, where the doctors stitched the cut on his head, and recommended he be taken to LA County General Hospital for observation overnight in case he'd sustained a concussion. A few hours later Vito received a phone call from LA County General that Godo had died. LA County DA [Evelle] Younger, convinced that Godo had been given drugs, ordered two separate autopsies by LA County Coroner Noguchi. The two autopsies both revealed that Godo had no drugs in his system, and that the cause of death had been strangulation due to the child's breathing his own vomit.

"Vito sued LA County for wrongful death due to medical malpractice. The charge was that, in contradiction to standard medical practice, Godo had been restrained by being strapped down on his back—something which is not normally done following a head injury (due to the possibility of the victim strangling on their own vomit). The reason this was done in Godo's case was probably because the child was offending the hospital staff by repeating some of the first words he'd learned, ie: 'Fuck you!' The LA authorities offered Vito a $20,000 pre-trial settlement, which he refused. I suggested to Vito that, since the case would be tried by a jury of mostly conservative people, usually retired civil servants, he get his long hair cut short, shave his beard and goatee, and wear a business suit and tie. Vito declined changing his appearance. The jury ruled in favor of the hospital."

A member of the Paulekas family heard a much different account, this one also coming directly from Vito: "He [Vito] and Sue told me that Godo fell from the roof through the skylight, as often told, but died when, in the hospital, the District Attorney's office insisted on testing Godot for drugs to prove Vito was drugging his own child. The best way [to test] was with a spinal tap that killed him because he was so young. That was his story to me and he elaborated about his screaming child being tied down in his presence for the spinal tap and then suddenly becoming lifeless."

It is perfectly obvious that both versions of events cannot possibly be true. In one version, Vito was present when Godo died, while in the other he received notification over the phone. One version of reality holds that the boy was tested for drugs after his death, while the other version claims that the drug test was what killed him. Godo was restrained in both versions of events, but in one it's so that he could be administered the spinal tap that killed him, while in the other it is the restraints that killed him—restraints utilized because for some reason he was yelling "fuck you!" at the hospital staff and no one knew of a nonviolent way to deal with an injured three-year-old!

If the medical malpractice story is true, then why did Vito tell more than one version of it? This is clearly not a situation where memories could have faded over time—no parent could confuse such particulars as if they actually watched their child die... before, of course, donning their dancing shoes and heading out to the Whisky.

There are, to be sure, a number of questions raised by the malpractice scenario, particularly with Cohen's account. For one thing, as if the reaction of the parents was not already difficult to understand, we are now being asked to believe that they went out dancing immediately after Godo was essentially murdered. Also, why is it that no one else who was making the scene in those days seems to remember a malpractice trial? And why were kids being allowed to play unsupervised on a roof? And would a toddler who crashed through a skylight and then fell a considerable distance among shards of broken glass really sustain only a minor cut and a few bruises? And would a hospital really be so callous as to inform parents of the death of a child by telephone? And if Vito was so quick to file suit against the city, why didn't he also sue his landlord for allowing such a dangerous condition to exist?

As it turns out, Godo's LA County Certificate of Death provides some insight into his short life and curious death. Clearly indicated is that the coroner found the cause of death to be "shock" due to "hemorrhage into deep cervical and superior mediastinal areas." The death was deemed to be an "accident" that occurred when Godo "fell through skylight while playing." He did, though, die at Los Angeles General Hospital, at 7:30 PM, precisely five hours after the accident occurred at 2:30 PM (though the times seem oddly approximate).

The timeline offered up by the document certainly seems a bit odd. Despite the fact that Godo died on December 23, his autopsy was not completed until April 13, a delay of nearly four months. Was that delay caused by the fabled second autopsy? Even if that were the case, four months seems like an inordinately long time to hold up the release of the body for burial. To further add to the mystery, even after the body was released, it was almost another full month before it was buried, on

May 9, 1967. Why did it take some four-and-a-half months to lay the child to rest?

The tragedy was reported not by the parents, but by a "Mr. Marvin Cahn, Attorney." After a child has suffered a serious accident, do parents with nothing to hide generally delay the arrival of help by calling an attorney and having him contact the proper authorities? It appears that there are, and probably always will be, unanswered questions surrounding the short life and curious death of the angelic hippie child who missed his big-screen debut as Lucifer.

I'll let a member of the Paulekas family provide the final words on the King of the Freaks. Asked by the author if he believed that Vito was a possible pedophile, he answered, "Probably. But I believe you have to go deeper into the libido and drives of so many rock stars and famous people who had an unhealthy relationship with sex and drugs. Any biography of the rockers of that time and probably any time just skirts [around] the reality that their greatest secret and shame includes the sex they had and have with very young girls and boys. Roman Polanski just got caught... I love hearing from people who tell me Vito saved their soul or protected them from danger when they were young and at risk... I am sure some became survivors and others fell deeper into the abyss. So it goes."

Indeed.

8

ALL THE YOUNG TURKS
HOLLYWOOD TRIPPING

"As all halfway-decent managers in the rock era have done, [Jim] Dickson worked on seducing the in-crowd and creating a buzz around [the Byrds]... The timing was perfect... LA's baby-boomers were mobile, getting around, looking for action. And now they were joined by the hip elite of Hollywood itself, from Sal Mineo and Peter Fonda to junkie comic Lenny Bruce." Barney Hoskyns, writing in Waiting for the Sun

AS IMPORTANT AS THE FREAKS WERE TO BUILDING AN AUDIENCE FOR THE new Laurel Canyon bands, there was another group that played a key role as well: Hollywood's so-called Young Turks. Like the freaks, the Turks became an immediate and constant presence on the newly emerging Sunset Strip scene. And as with the freaks, their presence on the Strip was heavily promoted by the media. Locals and tourists alike knew where to go to gawk at the freaks and, as an added bonus, quite possibly rub shoulders with the likes of Peter Fonda, Jack Nicholson, Bruce Dern, Dennis Hopper and Warren Beatty, along with their female counterparts—such as Jane Fonda, Nancy Sinatra and Sharon Tate.

And as with the freaks, the Turks were also instrumental in distracting attention away from the less than stellar musicianship on the stage. After all, young men offered the chance to see Jayne Mansfield in the flesh probably didn't even notice whether there was a band on the stage at all! Mansfield, by the way, like Mansonites Susan Atkins and Bobby Beausoleil, had direct ties to Anton LaVey and his Church of Satan.

Many of these young and glamorous Hollywood stars forged very close bonds with the Laurel Canyon musicians. Some of them, including Peter Fonda, found homes in the canyon so that they could live, work and party among the rock stars (and, in their free time, pass around John Phillips' wife Michelle to just about every swinging dick in the canyon, including Jack Nicholson, Dennis Hopper, Warren Beatty, Roman Polanski, and Gene Clark of the Byrds). Some of them never left; Jack Nicholson to this day lives in a spacious estate just off the portion of Mulholland Drive that lies between Laurel Canyon and Coldwater Canyon. Not far west of Nicholson's property (which now includes the neighboring estate formerly owned by Marlon Brando) sits the longtime home of Warren Beatty.

From the symbiotic relationship between Laurel Canyon actors and Laurel Canyon musicians arose a series of feature films that are now considered countercultural classics. One such film was *The Trip* (1967), an unintentionally hilarious attempt to create a cinematic facsimile of an LSD trip. Written by, of all people, Jack Nicholson, the movie starred fellow Turks Peter Fonda, Dennis Hopper and Bruce Dern. Seated in the director's chair was Roger Corman, who, throughout his career, worked side-by-side with David Crosby's dad on no less than twenty-three feature films. Recruited to supply the soundtrack for the film was Gram Parsons' International Submarine Band (Parsons' music, however, was ultimately not used, though the band does make a brief onscreen appearance). The house where most of the film was shot, at the top of Kirkwood Drive in Laurel Canyon, became the home of Love's Arthur Lee.

Another 'psychedelic' cult film of the late 1960s with deep roots in Laurel Canyon was the Monkees' 1968 big-screen offering, *Head*. Also scripted by Nicholson (with assistance from Bob Rafelson), the movie included cameo appearances by canyon dwellers Dennis Hopper, Jack Nicholson and Frank Zappa. The music—performed, of course, by the Monkees—was a mix of songs written by the band and contributions from Canyon songwriters like Carole King and Harry Nilsson. Shockingly, some of that music is actually pretty good. Even more shockingly, the movie overall is arguably the most watchable of the 1960s cult films. It is certainly a vast improvement over, for example, 1968's wretched *Psych Out* (starring Nicholson and Dern).

I do realize, by the way, that some of you out there in readerland cringe every time that I mention the Monkees as though they were a 'real' band. The reality though is that they were every bit as 'real' as most of their contemporaries. And while the made-for-TV Beatles replicants were looked down upon by music critics and fans alike, they were fully accepted as members of the musical fraternity by the other Laurel Canyon bands. The homes of both Mickey Dolenz and Peter Tork were popular canyon hangouts in the late sixties for a number of 'real' musicians. Also regularly dropping by Dolenz's party house were Dennis Hopper and Jack Nicholson.

The difference in perception between their peers and the public was attributable to the fact that the other bands knew something that the fans did not: the very same studio musicians who appeared without credit on the Monkees' albums also appeared without credit on their albums. And then, of course, there was the fact that so many of Laurel Canyon's 'real' musicians had taken a stab at being a part of the Monkees, including Stephen Stills, Love's Bryan MacLean, and Three Dog Night's Danny Hutton—all of whom answered the Monkees' casting call and were rejected.

There were undoubtedly other future stars who auditioned for the show as well, though most would probably prefer not to discuss such things. Despite persistent rumors, however, there was one local musician who we can safely conclude *did not* read for a part: Charles Manson. Given that the show was cast in 1965 and began its brief television run in 1966, while Charlie was still imprisoned at Terminal Island awaiting his release in March of 1967, there doesn't appear to be any way that Manson could have been considered for a part on the show. And that's kind of a shame when you think about it, because if he had been, we might today remember Charlie Manson not as one of America's most notorious criminals, but rather as the guy who made Marcia Brady swoon.

Returning to the countercultural films of the 1960s, the most critically acclaimed of the lot, and the one with the deepest roots in Laurel Canyon, was *Easy Rider*. Directed by Dennis Hopper, from a script co-written by he and Peter Fonda, the film starred Fonda and Hopper along with Jack Nicholson. Hopper's walrus-mustachioed character in the film was based on David Crosby, who was regularly seen racing his motorcycle up and down the winding streets of Laurel Canyon. (That motorcycle, by the way, had been a gift from Crosby's good buddy, Peter Fonda.) Fonda's absurd 'Captain America' character was inspired either by John Phillips' riding partner, Gram Parsons, or by Crosby's former bandmate in the Byrds, Roger McGuinn (depending upon who is telling the story). That very same Roger McGuinn scored the original music for the film. His contributions were joined on the soundtrack by offerings from fellow Canyonite musicians Steppenwolf, the Byrds, Fraternity of Man and Jimi Hendrix. And the movie's hippie commune was reportedly created and filmed in the canyons, near Mulholland Drive.

Since *Easy Rider* had such deep roots in the Laurel Canyon scene, we need to briefly focus our attention here on one other individual who worked on the film, art director Jeremy Kay, aka Jerry Kay. Before *Easy Rider*, Kay had worked on such cinematic abominations as *Angels from Hell*, *Hells Angels on Wheels* (with Jack Nicholson), and *Scorpio Rising* (Kenneth Anger's occult-tinged homage to gay biker culture). In the mid-1970s, Kay would write, direct and produce a charming little film entitled *Satan's Children*. Of far more interest here than his film credits though is his membership in the 1960s in a group known as the Solar Lodge of the Ordo Templi Orientis (or OTO), which found itself in the news, and not in a good way, just after *Easy Rider* opened on theater screens across America.

Two weeks after *Easy Rider* premiered on July 14, 1969, police acting on a phone tip raided the Solar Lodge's compound near Blythe, California, and found a six-year-old boy locked outdoors in a 6' x 6' wooden crate in the sweltering desert heat. The young boy, whose father was a Los Angeles County probation officer, had been chained to a steel plate for nearly two months in temperatures reaching as high as 117° F. According to an FBI report, the box also contained a can "partially filled with human waste and swarming with flies... The stench was nauseating." Before being put in the box, the child had been burned with matches and beaten with bamboo poles by cult members. The leader of the cult, Georgina Brayton, had reportedly told cult members that "when it was convenient, she was going to give [the boy] LSD and set fire to the structure in which he was chained and give him just enough chain to get out of reach of the fire." Killing the child had also been discussed (and apparently condoned by the boy's mind-fucked mother).

Eleven adult members of the sect were charged with felony child abuse, the majority of them young white men in their early twenties. All were brought to trial and convicted. In a curious bit of timing, the raid that resulted in the arrests and convictions coincided with the torture and murder of musician Gary Hinman by a trio of Manson acolytes. Though it is, not surprisingly, vehemently denied by concerned parties, various sources have claimed that Manson had ties to the group, which also maintained a home near the USC campus in Los Angeles. There is no doubt that Charlie preached the same dogma, including the notion of an apocalyptic race war looming on the horizon. The massacre at the Tate residence occurred less than two weeks after the raid on the OTO compound. Manson's Barker Ranch hideout would be raided a few months later, on October 12, 1969—the birthday, as I may have already mentioned, of Aleister Crowley, the Grand Poobah of the OTO until his death in 1947.

Anyway, sorry about that little digression, folks. I'm not entirely sure how we ended up at the Barker Ranch when the focus of this chapter was supposed to be on the Young Turks. So having now established that those Turks were a fully integrated part of the Laurel Canyon/Sunset Strip scene, and also that they played an important role in luring the public out to the new clubs to check out the new bands, our next task is to get to know a little bit about who these folks were and where they came from. Let's begin with Mr. Bruce Dern, who has some of the most provocative connections of any of the characters in this story.

It is probably safe to say that Dern's parents had rather impressive political connections, given that baby Bruce's godparents were sitting First Lady Eleanor Roosevelt and future two-time Democratic presidential nominee Adlai Stevenson (he lost both times, in 1952 and 1956, to Eisenhower). Bruce's paternal grandfather was a guy by the name of George Dern, who served as Secretary of War under President Franklin Roosevelt (for the youngsters in the crowd, Secretary of War is what we used to call the Secretary of Defense in a slightly less Orwellian era).

George had also served as Governor of Utah and Chairman of the National Governors' Association. Bruce's mother was born Jean MacLeish, and she happened to be the sister of Archibald MacLeish, who also served under Franklin Roosevelt, as the Director of the War Department's Office of Facts and Figures and as the Assistant Director of the Office of War Information. In other words, Archibald MacLeish was essentially America's Minister of War Propaganda. He also served at various times as an Assistant Secretary of State and as the Librarian of Congress. Perhaps the most impressive item on his résumé, however, was his membership in everyone's favorite secret society, Skull and Bones (class of 1915, one year before Prescott Bush was tapped in 1916).

It would appear then, that, even by Laurel Canyon standards, Mr. Dern has friends in very high places. Let's turn our attention next to the guy who shared the screen with Dern in *The Trip*, Mr. Peter Fonda. Of course, we all know that Fonda is the son of good ol' Hank Fonda, lovable Hollywood liberal and all-around nice guy. And certainly even a contrarian such as myself would not be so bold as to suggest that Henry Fonda might have some skeletons in his closet... right? Just for the hell of it, though, there are a few chapters of the Hank Fonda saga that we should probably review here.

We can begin, I suppose, by noting that Hank served as a decorated US Naval Intelligence officer during WWII, thus sparing Peter the stigma of being the only member of the Laurel Canyon in-crowd to have not been spawned by a member of the military/intelligence community. Not too many years after the war, Hank's wife, Francis Ford Seymour—who claimed to be a direct descendant of Jane Seymour, third wife of King Henry VIII—was found with her throat slashed open with a straight razor. Peter was just ten years old at the time of his mother's alleged suicide on April 14, 1950. When Seymour had met and married Hank, she was the widow of George Brokaw, who had, curiously enough, previously been married to prominent CIA operative Claire Booth Luce.

Fonda rebounded quickly from Seymour's unusual death and within eight months he was married once again, to Susan Blanchard, to whom he remained married until 1956. In 1957, Hank married yet again, this time to Italian Countess Afdera Franchetti (who followed up her four-year marriage to Fonda with a rumored affair with newly-sworn-in President John Kennedy). Franchetti, as it turns out, is the daughter of

Baron Raimondo Franchetti, who was a consultant to fascist dictator Benito Mussolini. The countess is also the great-granddaughter of Louise Sarah Rothschild, of the Rothschild banking family (perhaps you've heard of them?).

Before moving on, I should probably mention that Hank's first wife, Margaret Sullavan—who was yet another child of Norfolk, Virginia—also allegedly committed suicide, on New Year's Day, 1960. Nine months later, her daughter Bridget followed suit. In 1961, very soon after the deaths of first her mother and then her sister, Sullavan's other daughter, Brook Hayward, walked down the aisle with the next Young Turk on our list, Dennis Hopper. For those who may be unfamiliar with Hopper's body of work, he is the guy who was once found wandering naked and bewildered in a Mexican forest. And the guy who, after divorcing Hayward in 1969, married Michelle Phillips on Halloween day, 1970, only to have her file for divorce just eight days later claiming that Hopper had kept her handcuffed and imprisoned for a week while making "unnatural sexual demands."

Without passing judgment here, I think it's fair to say that Michelle Phillips has been around the block a time or two, if you catch my drift, so if even *she* thought Hopper's demands were a bit over the top, then one can only wonder just how "unnatural" they might have been. For what it's worth, Hopper once told a journalist that he "didn't handcuff her, [he] just punched her out!" In his mind, apparently, that made him somewhat less of a troglodyte.

Most official biographies of Hopper would lead one to believe that he was the son of a simple farmer. Dennis recently acknowledged, however, that that was clearly not the case: "My mother's father was a wheat farmer and I was raised on their farm. But my father was not a farmer." To the contrary, Hopper's dad was "a working person in intelligence" who during WWII "was in the OSS. He was in China, Burma, India." Hopper has proudly proclaimed that his father "was one of the 100 guys that liberated General Wainright out of prison in Korea," which might be a little more impressive were it not for the fact that it was actually the Red Army that freed Wainright and other prisoners; the US intel team just came to pick them up, debrief them and transport them home... but that, I suppose, isn't really relevant.

After the war, according to Hopper, his dad routinely carried a gun, which I suppose is what most lay ministers in the Methodist Church do. The family also left the farm in Kansas and relocated to San Diego, California, home of the Imperial Beach Naval Air Station, the United States Naval Radio Station, the United States Naval Amphibious Base, the North Island Naval Air Station, Fort Rosecrans Military Reservation, the United States Naval Training Center, the United States Marine Corps Recruit Depot, and the Miramar Marine Corps Air Station. And just north of the city sits the massive Camp Pendleton Marine Corps Base. Other than that, though, San Diego is just a sleepy little beach town where Hopper's dad ostensibly worked for the Post Office.

The more recent incarnation of Dennis Hopper, by the way, was wildly at odds with the hippie image that he had at one time tried very hard to cultivate. Before his death on May 29, 2010, Hopper was an unapologetic cheerleader for right-wing causes, who proudly boasted of having voted a straight Republican ticket for over thirty years.

To briefly recap then, we have thus far met three of the 'Young Turks' and we have found that one of them is the nephew of a Bonesman, another is the son of a Naval Intelligence officer who was once married to a Rothschild descendent, and the third was the slightly deranged son of an OSS officer. Come to think of it, we have actually covered one of the 'Turkettes' as well, since Jane Fonda obviously came from the same family background as her younger brother, Peter. As for the other female members of the posse, Sharon Tate was the daughter of Lt. Col. Paul Tate, a career US Army intelligence officer, and Nancy Sinatra is, of course, the daughter of Francis Albert Sinatra, whose known associates included Lucky Luciano, Meyer Lansky, Sam Giancana, Carlo Gambino, Goetano Luchese and Joseph Fishetti (a cousin of Al Capone).

Frank Sinatra was also a client of hairdresser-to-the-stars Jay Sebring, as was Henry Fonda, who at one time, strangely enough, lived in the guesthouse at 10050 Cielo Drive. Yet another client of Sebring's was the next Young Turk on our list, Warren Beatty, whose father, Ira Owens Beaty, was ostensibly a professor of psychology. Young Warren, however, spent all of his early years living in various spooky suburbs of Washington, DC. He was born in Richmond, Virginia, in 1937, after which his father moved the family to Norfolk, Virginia, which I think I may have mentioned is home to the world's largest Naval facility (the reason for that, by the way, is that Norfolk is the gateway to the nation's capital). The family later relocated to Arlington, Virginia, home of the Pentagon, where Warren attended high school and where he was known on the football field as—recalls John Phillips, who attended a rival school—"Mad Dog" Beaty.

Ira Beaty's relatively frequent relocations, and the fact that those relocations always seemed to land the family in DC suburbs that are of considerable significance to the military/intelligence community, would tend to indicate that Warren's dad was something other than what he appeared to be—though that is, of course, a speculative assessment. But if Ira Beaty was on the payroll of some government entity, working within the psychology departments of various DC-area universities, then it wouldn't require a huge leap of faith to further speculate about what type of work he was doing, given the wholesale co-opting of the field of psychology by the MK-ULTRA program and affiliated projects.

The next Young Turk up for review is the one who went on to become arguably the most acclaimed actor of his generation, Mr. Jack Nicholson. Before getting to him though, let's take a look at a biographical sketch of serial killer Ted Bundy as presented by Wikipedia: "Bundy was born at the Elizabeth Lund Home for Unwed Mothers in Burlington, Vermont. The identity of his father remains a mystery... To avoid social stigma, Bundy's grandparents Samuel and Eleanor Cowell claimed him as their son; in taking their last name, he became Theodore Robert Cowell. He grew up believing his mother Eleanor Louise Cowell to be his older sister. Bundy biographers Stephen Michaud and Hugh Aynesworth state that he learned Louise was actually his mother while he was in high school. True crime writer Ann Rule states that it was around 1969, shortly following a traumatic breakup with his college girlfriend."

Now if we just change a few names here and there, we come up with an accurate bio of Jack Nicholson, which goes something like this: Nicholson was born at some indeterminate location to an underage, unwed showgirl. The identity of his father remains a mystery... To avoid social stigma, Nicholson's grandparents John Joseph and Ethel Nicholson claimed him as their son; in taking their last name, he became John Joseph Nicholson, Jr. He grew up believing his mother June Francis Nicholson to be his older sister. Reporters state that he learned June was actually his mother in 1974, when he was thirty-seven years old. By then, June had been dead for just over a decade, having only lived to the age of forty-four.

It is said that Nicholson was born at St. Vincent's Hospital in New York City, but there is no record of such a birth either at the hospital or in the city's archives. As it turns out, Jack Nicholson has no birth certificate. Until 1954, by which time he was nearly an adult, he did not officially exist. Even today, the closest thing he has to a birth certificate is a 'Certificate of a Delayed Report of Birth' that was filed on May 24, 1954. The document lists John and Ethel Nicholson as the parents and identifies the location of the birth as the Nicholsons' home address in Neptune, New Jersey.

It appears then that there is no way to determine who Jack Nicholson really is. He has told journalists that he has no interest in identifying who his father was, nor, it would appear, in verifying his mother's identity. What we do know is that the nucleus of the 1960s clique known as the Young Turks (and Turkettes) was composed of the following individuals: the nephew of a Bonesman; the son of an OSS officer; the son of a Naval intelligence officer; the daughter of that same Naval intelligence officer; the daughter of an Army intelligence officer; the daughter of a guy who openly associated with prominent gangsters throughout his life; the son of a possible spychologist; and a guy whose early years are so shrouded in mystery that he may or may not actually exist.

I should probably also mention here that Henry Fonda scored his first acting gig through Dorothy "Dody" Brando, the director of a local theater and the mother of Jack Nicholson's future neighbor, Marlon Brando. Being the small world that it is, Marlon's mom happened to be a good friend of Hank's mom, Elma Fonda. Truth be told, the families had likely had close ties for a long time. *A very long time*. The ancestors of both Marlon Brando and Henry Fonda, you see, arrived in New York at nearly the same time, roughly three-and-a-half centuries ago.

Marlon Brando is in a direct line of descent from French Huguenot colonists Louis DuBois and Catharine Blanchan DuBois (and no, I'm not making that up), who arrived in New York from Mannheim, Germany, circa 1660 and promptly founded New Rochelle. Other descendents of DuBois include former US Senator Leverett Saltonstall, former Massachusetts Governor and Council on Foreign Relations member William Weld, former California First Lady Maria Shriver, and quite likely US

Presidents Jimmy Carter and Zachary Taylor.

Henry Fonda, on the other hand, is a direct descendent of Jellis Douw Fonda and Hester Jans Fonda, Dutch colonists who arrived in New York circa 1650 and settled near what would become Albany. The Fondas had sailed out of Friesland, Netherlands, on a ship dubbed the *Valckenier*, which happened to be co-owned by a very wealthy Dutchman by the name of Jan-Baptist van Rensselaer. And Mr. van Rensselaer, as those who have been paying attention in class will recall, happened to be from the bloodline that would one day produce a guy by the name of David van Cortland Crosby.

It would appear then that Peter Fonda kind of owed Crosby that Triumph motorcycle that he gave him back in the sixties, what with David's ancestors having been cool enough to give Peter's ancestors a lift over to the New World and all.

Let's wrap up this chapter with a quick review of what we have learned about the people populating Laurel Canyon in the mid-to-late 1960s. We know that one subset of residents was a large group of musicians who all decided, nearly simultaneously, to flood into the canyon. The most prominent members of this group were, to an overwhelming degree, the sons and daughters of the military/intelligence community. We also know that mingled in with them were the young stars of Hollywood, who also were, to an astonishing degree, the sons and daughters of the military/intelligence community. And, finally, we know that also in the mix were scores of military/intelligence personnel who operated out of the facility known as Lookout Mountain Laboratory.

I've got to say that, given the relatively small size of Laurel Canyon, I'm beginning to wonder if there was any room left over for any normal folks who might have wanted to live the rock'n'roll lifestyle.

9

WEIRD SCENES INSIDE THE CANYON

"There were a lot of weird people around. There was one guy who had a parrot called Captain Blood, and he was always scrawling real cryptic things on the inside walls of my house—Neil Young's too." Joni Mitchell, describing the Laurel Canyon scene toward the end of the 1960s

AS IT TURNS OUT, LAUREL CANYON WAS LARGE ENOUGH TO ACCOMMODATE at least a few more strange characters. Two of them were guys named Jerry Brown and Mike Curb. Actually, it's unclear whether Curb ever lived there, but he was very much a part of the scene in the 1960s and 1970s.

Edmund G. "Jerry" Brown, Jr. had a decidedly conservative upbringing. Born into a politically well-connected Republican family, Jerry devoted his early years to pursuing a career in the Jesuit priesthood. His father, a very active Republican Party operative, was an aspiring politician who initially had no luck in getting himself elected to public office. He ultimately succeeded though in capturing the coveted California Governor's seat in 1959, and he did it by employing a simple gimmick: he changed the "R" after his name to a "D" and was reborn as a Democrat. He held the seat for two terms, through to 1967, and then was replaced by a guy who had employed the exact same trick in reverse: he had replaced the "D" after his name with an "R."

That gentleman, of course, was Ronald Wilson Reagan, and he would govern the state through 1975, after which he handed the reins back over to the Brown family, this time to the younger Edmund Brown, who, like his dad, had decided that he was a liberal Democrat. In fact, according to the consensus opinion of the media at the time, Jerry was an ultraliberal extremist whose politics fell somewhere to the left of Fidel Castro and Che Guevara.

During Laurel Canyon's glory years, Jerry Brown resided in a home on Wonderland Avenue, within easy walking distance of the Wonderland death house and the homes of numerous singers, songwriters and musicians. His circle of friends in those days, as was widely reported, included the elite of Laurel Canyon's country-rock stars, including Linda Ronstadt (with whom he was long rumored to be romantically involved), Jackson Browne and the Eagles.

Another figure making the rounds in Laurel Canyon during the same period of time was Mike Curb. At various times, Curb worked as a musician, composer, recording artist, film producer and record company executive. He also had the notable distinction of serving as the musical director on the notorious documentary feature *Mondo Hollywood*, which ostensibly chronicled the emerging Laurel Canyon/Sunset Strip scene. Filmed from 1965 through 1967, the film featured representatives from the Manson Family (Bobby Beausoleil), the Manson Family's victims (Jay Sebring), the freak troupe (Vito, Carl, Szou and Godo), and Laurel Canyon's musical fraternity (Frank Zappa, along with his future wife, Gail Sloatman). It also featured acid guru Richard Alpert, Jerry Brown's father, Pat Brown, and Princess Margaret, a good friend to John Phillips and a rumored lover of Mick Jagger.

As noted, *Mondo Hollywood* was the creation of filmmaker Robert Carl Cohen. It turns out he, too, had an interesting background for a guy destined to capture on film the emerging 1960s countercultural scene. In 1954, Cohen served in the US Army Signal Corps. The following year, he was on assignment to NATO. Following that, he served in Special Services in Germany. The very next year, he produced, directed, edited and narrated a documentary short entitled *Inside Red China*. Two years later, he wore all the same hats for a documentary entitled *Inside East*

Germany. A few years later, he put together another documentary entitled *Three Cubans*, a decidedly unsympathetic take on the Cuban revolution.

Cohen has proudly proclaimed that he was the first (or at least among the first) Western journalists/filmmakers allowed to enter and shoot footage in each of those ostensibly communist countries. In the case of Cuba (and likely the others as well), he did so under the direct sponsorship of the US State Department. Mr. Cohen would like us to believe that he undertook those projects as nothing more than what he outwardly appeared to be—an independent filmmaker—but a great deal of naiveté is required to believe that a private citizen not working for the intelligence community could land such assignments.

The *Los Angeles Times*, in a lengthy critique of Cohen's counterculture film published on October 1, 1967, offered up some curious and long-forgotten facts about the documentary feature: "I cannot presume to guess how much real life pokes through *Mondo Hollywood*. In violent, sudden ways, real death did intrude during the eighteen months of picture making. Three people were killed in automobile crashes. One of them was Jayne Mansfield, whose brief appearance—as a celebrity in a montage of premieres—remains in the final movie. The other two, including a bona fide philosopher, were scheduled to appear but died before filming. A writer who was to play himself died of drugs. A three-year-old child died of a fall through a trap door, although he and his parents are still in the picture. A pilot, who had agreed to fly in the film, died of a midair crash. In all, six people—none of them old, none of them in bed—died before *Mondo Hollywood* was released. Several buildings were also destroyed in this impermanent place. And the Goodyear blimp, which provided the platform for some spectacular aerials in the finished movie, crashed one day after its chores were done."

It appears then, that, just as in the real Laurel Canyon, Cohen's celluloid version masked a backdrop of violence, destruction and death.

As for Mike Curb, in addition to his work on *Mondo Hollywood*, he also served as 'song producer' on another key countercultural film of the era, *Riot on the Sunset Strip* (which, despite its title, had little to do with the actual event). In addition, Curb scored a slew of cheaply produced biker flicks, including *The Wild Angels*, *Devil's Angels*, *Born Losers*, *The Savage Seven* and *The Glory Stompers*. Along the way, he worked alongside many of Laurel Canyon's 'Young Turks,' including Peter Fonda and Dennis Hopper.

It is unclear whether the paths of Jerry Brown and Mike Curb crossed during Laurel Canyon's glory years, but as fate would have it, they were to cross in 1979 in Sacramento, California. Mike Curb, as it turns out, after being encouraged by Ronald Reagan to venture into politics, was elected to serve as Governor Jerry Brown's second-in-command. And so it was that these two men, both veterans of the 1960s Laurel Canyon scene, came to sit side-by-side in the governor's mansion, one sporting a "D" after his name and the other an "R."

Governor Brown, however, had little time to spend on actually governing the state of California. Tossing his hat into the presidential ring, he spent much of his time out of the state, working the campaign trail. That allowed Lieutenant Governor Curb, as acting governor of the state, to sign into law a withering array of reactionary legislation that was very far removed from what the people of California thought they were getting when they elected 'Governor Moonbeam.' This arrangement allowed the nominal liberal of the Laurel Canyon tag-team, Jerry Brown, to keep his hands clean even as his administration moved far away from its originally stated goals—and even as he made little effort to rein in his underling.

Brown and Curb weren't the only up-and-coming politicos who managed to find living space in Laurel Canyon back in the day. In July 2008, the venerable *Washington Post* revealed that a former reporter and novelist by the name of Alex Abella had "written a history of RAND, which was founded more than sixty years ago by the Air Force as a font of ideas on how that service might fight and win a nuclear war with the USSR... Abella focuses on Albert Wohlstetter, a mathematical logician turned nuclear strategist who was the dominant figure at RAND starting in the early 1950s and whose influence has extended beyond his death in 1997 into the current Bush administration... Wohlstetter epitomized what became known as the 'RAND approach'—a relentlessly reductive, determinedly quantitative analysis of whatever problem the independent, non-profit think tank was assigned, whether the design of a new bomber or improving public education in inner-city schools."

The RAND Corporation is a lot of things, but "independent" has never been one of them. Also in the *Post*'s book review, we find that "it was not so much Wohlstetter himself as his acolytes... who had a major impact in Washington." Most of those acolytes need little introduction: former Assistant Secretary of Defense Richard Perle (who once dated Wohlstetter's daughter); former US ambassador, President of the World Bank, and Deputy Secretary of Defense Paul Wolfowitz; former US ambassador to Iraq, Afghanistan, and the UN, Zalmay Khalilzad; and Andrew Marshall, who has served as the director of the United States Department of Defense's Office of Net Assessment for forty years and who served as a mentor to Dick Cheney, Donald Rumsfeld and Paul Wolfowitz.

In the latter half of the 1950s and into the early 1960s, while Wohlstetter was with the RAND Corporation and also serving as a professor at UCLA (and while his wife Roberta also worked as an analyst for RAND), Albert and his followers—the men who would serve as the architects of US foreign policy during the George W. Bush administration—regularly met in a heavily wooded neighborhood in Los Angeles known as Laurel Canyon. As Gregg Herken wrote in his review of Abella's book, "those bright, eager and ambitious young men... had sat cross-legged on the floor with their mentor at his stylish house in Laurel Canyon." Just as, not far away, Vito's eager young followers sat cross-legged with their mentor. And just as, also not far away, Charles Manson's eager young followers would sit cross-legged on the floor with their mentor.

Paul Young, writing in *LA Exposed*, revealed that, in the late 1960s and early 1970s, there was another curious group calling Laurel Canyon home: "The most infamous male madam [throughout LA's sordid history] would have to be Billy Bryars, the wealthy son of an oil magnate, and part-time producer of gay porn. Bryars was said to have a stellar group of customers using his 'brothel' at the summit of Laurel Canyon. In fact, some have claimed that none other than J. Edgar Hoover, the founder and chief executive officer of the FBI, was one of his best clients... when Bryars fell under police scrutiny in 1973, allegedly for trafficking in child pornography, officers obtained a number of confessions from some of his hustlers, and some of them identified Hoover and [Clyde] Tolson as 'Mother John' and 'Uncle Mike,' and claimed that they had serviced them on numerous occasions."

It appears then that the top law-enforcement officials in the nation were also a part of the Laurel Canyon scene, along with various other unnamed persons of prominence. And we also find, perhaps not too shockingly at this point, that Laurel Canyon was a portal of child pornography.

In January of 2011, the *San Francisco Chronicle* reported on the passing of "Ron Patterson, the flamboyant, free-spirited creator of the Renaissance and Dickens fairs," who had "died Jan. 15 at a friend's house in Sausalito after an illness. He was eighty." As staff writer Carolyn Jones noted in the article, Patterson's creation "was sort of a medieval precursor to Burning Man." And Burning Man is, of course, a rather explicitly occult ritual first performed on the summer solstice of 1986 and now performed every summer in Nevada's Black Rock Desert before an audience of over 50,000.

"In the beginning, the Renaissance Faire was an experiment in Mr. Patterson's backyard. In the early 1960s, Mr. Patterson and his wife, Phyllis, who were both interested in theater and art, began hosting children's improvisational theater workshops at their Laurel Canyon (Los Angeles County) home." One naturally wonders whether aspiring thespian and golden child Godo Paulekas (originally cast, it will be recalled, to play the lead in Kenneth Anger's *Lucifer Rising*) was involved in those workshops. In any event, there is something decidedly creepy about children's workshops being hosted in a small, tight-knit community that was home to a child pornography ring and more than its fair share of pedophiles.

Yet another curious character to take up residence in Laurel Canyon was producer Paul Rothchild, who played a key role in shaping the sound of both the Doors and Love. In June 1981, *Sports Illustrated* publisher Philip Howlett penned a short piece to introduce readers to new writer Bjarne Rostaing: "Born in Lincoln, N.Y., Rostaing grew up in various places in Connecticut, where he attended what he recalls as an even dozen schools. 'I got my B.A. and master's in English from the University of Connecticut,' he says. 'Then I did part of a Ph.D. at the University of Washington before going into the Army Intelligence Corps in 1959. We had Paul Rothchild, who later became producer for the Doors and Janis Joplin, to give you some idea of what the unit was like.'"

It was, in all likelihood, like countless other intelligence units designed to churn out shapers of public opinion, whether actors, novelists, newsmen, or, in this case, sportswriters and producers of popular music. It is quite shocking, of course, to learn that the handler of two of Laurel Canyon's most influential and groundbreaking bands had a background in intelligence work. Apparently the search is still on for *anyone* of any prominence in the Laurel Canyon scene who *didn't* have direct connections to the intelligence community.

Bjarne Rostaing would, perhaps not surprisingly, develop his own indirect connections to the Laurel Canyon music scene. His most notable contribution to the field of literature was penning the mass-market paperback version of *Phantom of the Paradise*, the campy tale of a Phil Spector-inspired music producer who had sold his soul to the devil for fame and fortune and who subsequently manipulated a disfigured young singer/songwriter into likewise selling his soul. The theatrical version, released on Halloween day 1974 and carrying the tagline "he sold his soul for rock'n'roll," starred Laurel Canyon's own Paul Williams as Swan, the demonic producer who surrounds himself with nubile young women eager to do his bidding. Williams, who lived on Lookout Mountain alongside numerous other singer/songwriters, also scored the film.

It is, I'm sure, entirely coincidental that two guys who emerged from the same intelligence unit in the early 1960s would follow such curious career paths—one, Paul Rothchild, becoming what many on the scene in those days would have described as a demonic rock music producer, and the other, Bjarne Rostaing, penning a novel about a demonic rock music producer.

There was one other person who, while he never took up residence in Laurel Canyon, had a profound influence on the scene. That guy was Augustus Owsley Stanley III, the premier LSD chemist of the hippie era. No one—not Ken Kesey, not Richard Alpert, not even Timothy Leary—did more to 'turn on' the youth of the 1960s than Owsley. Leary and his cohorts may have captured the national media spotlight and created public awareness, but it was Owsley who flooded the streets of San Francisco and Laurel Canyon with consistently high quality, inexpensive, readily available acid. By most accounts, he was never in it for the money and he routinely gave away more of his product than he sold. What then was his motive? According to Martin Lee and Bruce Shlain, writing in *Acid Dreams*, "Owsley cultivated an image as a wizard-alchemist whose intentions with LSD were priestly and magical."

Owsley is revered by many as something of an icon of the 1960s counterculture—a man motivated by nothing more than an altruistic desire to 'turn on' the world. But his rather provocative background and family history suggest that his intentions may not have necessarily been so altruistic.

Augustus Owsley Stanley III was the son, naturally enough, of Augustus Owsley Stanley II, who served as a military officer during WWII aboard the *USS Lexington* and thereafter found work in Washington, DC as a government attorney. He raised his son primarily in Arlington, Virginia. Young Owsley's grandfather was Augustus Owsley Stanley, who served as a member of the US House of Representatives from 1903 through 1915, as the Governor of Kentucky from 1915 through 1919, and as a US Senator from 1919 through 1925; Senator Stanley's father, a minister with the Disciples of Christ, served as a judge advocate with the Confederate Army. Owsley's mother was a niece of William Owsley, who also served as a Governor of Kentucky, from 1844 through 1848, and who lent his name to Owsley County, Kentucky.

During Owsley III's formative years, he attended the prestigious Charlotte Hall Military Academy in Maryland, but was reportedly tossed out in the ninth grade for being intoxicated. Not long after that, at the tender age of fifteen, Owsley voluntarily committed himself to St. Elizabeth's Hospital in the nation's capitol. St. Elizabeth's, it should be noted, had a far more sinister name upon its founding in 1855: the Government Hospital for the Insane. He remained confined there for treatment for the next fifteen months. During that time, his mother, in keeping with one of the recurrent themes of this saga, passed away.

Owsley apparently resumed his education following his curious confinement, but he had reportedly dropped out of school by the age of eighteen. Nevertheless, he apparently had no trouble at all gaining acceptance to the University of Virginia, which he attended for a time before enlisting in the US Air Force in 1956, at the age of twenty-one. During his military service, Owsley was an electronics specialist, working in radio intelligence and radar. After his stint in the Air Force, Owsley set up camp in the Los Angeles area, ostensibly to study ballet.

During that same time, he also worked at Pasadena's Jet Propulsion Laboratory, which was undoubtedly the primary reason for his move to LA In 1963, Owsley moved once again, this time to Berkeley, California, which just happened to be ground-zero of the budding anti-war movement. He may or may not have briefly attended UC Berkeley, which is where he allegedly cribbed the recipe for LSD from the university library. Owsley soon began cooking up both Methedrine and LSD in a makeshift bathroom lab near the campus of the university. On February 21, 1965, that lab was raided by state narcotics agents who seized all his lab equipment and charged Stanley with operating a meth lab. As Barry Miles recounted in *Hippie*, "Berkeley was awash with speed and Owsley was responsible for much of it."

Nevertheless, Owsley walked away from the raid unscathed, and, with the help of his attorney, who happened to be the vice-mayor of Berkeley, he even successfully sued to have all his lab equipment returned. He quickly put that equipment to work producing some four million tabs of nearly pure LSD in the mid-1960s.

Immediately after the raid of February 1965, Owsley and his frequent sidekicks, the Grateful Dead, moved down to the Watts area of Los Angeles, of all places, to ostensibly conduct 'acid tests.' The group rented a house that was conveniently located right next door to a brothel, curiously paralleling the *modus operandi* of various intelligence operatives who were (or had been) involved in conducting their own 'acid tests.' The band departed the communal dwelling in April 1965. It was a fortuitous departure as it turned out, since just a few months later, Watts exploded in violence that left thirty-four corpses littering the streets.

Owsley had been with the Dead from the band's earliest days, as both a financial backer and as their sound engineer. He is credited with numerous electronic innovations that changed the way live rock music was presented to the masses—and likely not in a good way, given that his work as a sound technician undoubtedly drew heavily upon his military training.

In 1967, Owsley unleashed on the Haight a particularly nasty hallucinogen known as STP. Developed by the friendly folks at Dow Chemical, STP had been tested extensively at Frank Zappa's former home, the Edgewood Arsenal, as a possible biowarfare agent before being distributed to hippies as a recreational drug. Owsley reportedly obtained the recipe from Alexander Shulgin, a former Harvard man who developed a keen interest in psychopharmacology while serving in the US Navy. Shulgin worked for many years as a senior research chemist at Dow and later worked very closely with the DEA.

In 1970, Owsley began serving time after a conviction on drug charges. That time was served, appropriately enough, at Terminal Island Federal Correctional Institution, the very same prison that had, just a few years earlier, housed both Charlie Manson and Flying Burrito Brothers' road manager Phil Kaufman. A few years later, it would also be home to both Timothy Leary and his alleged nemesis, G. Gordon Liddy. After his release, Owsley continued to work as a sound technician, eventually graduating to a new medium: television.

Owsley eventually moved to Australia in the 1980s, becoming a naturalized citizen in 1996. On March 12, 2012, the aging chemist was reportedly killed in an automobile accident near his Queensland home when his car veered off the road in a storm and plowed into some trees.

10

HELTER SKELTER IN A SUMMER SWELTER RETURN OF THE DEATH LIST

"Everybody was experimenting and taking it all the way. It opened up a negative force of energy that was almost demonic." Frank Mazolla, editor of the film Performance

IT IS NOW, SAD TO SAY, TIME TO ADD SOME MORE NAMES TO THE EVER-growing Laurel Canyon Death List. The first new name is Mr. Brian Jones of the Rolling Stones, who purportedly drowned without assistance in his home swimming pool on July 3, 1969, at the age of twenty-seven. (Jim Morrison would allegedly die precisely two years later, also at the age of twenty-seven.) Just three days after Jones' tragic death, the Stones, with the Hell's Angels providing security, played a previously scheduled concert in Hyde Park, footage of which appears in Kenneth Anger's *Invocation of My Demon Brother*. Despite being the founder of the Stones and being widely regarded as the main creative force within the band, Jones had been unceremoniously dumped by the group on June 9, less than a month before his death. He was replaced just four days later by Mick Taylor, who in turn was later replaced by Ron Wood. It would later be claimed that Jones was booted from the band due to his chronic substance abuse problems, although Keith Richards' legendary drug intake never seemed to pose a problem for the group.

The Rolling Stones were not, to be sure, a Laurel Canyon band, but they did spend a considerable amount of time there and they were very closely tied to the scene. As Barney Hoskyns writes in *Hotel California*, "In the summer of 1968 the English band was flirting heavily with Satanism and the occult... and spending a lot of time in Los Angeles." A lot of time, that is, in and around Laurel Canyon—and during that time, Mick Jagger was involved in two occult-drenched, Crowley-influenced film projects, Kenneth Anger's *Lucifer Rising* and Donald Cammell's *Performance*.

Jagger was the first musical superstar tapped by Anger to compose a soundtrack for his *Lucifer Rising* project, which at the time was to star Mansonite Bobby Beausoleil. Anger would later solicit a soundtrack for the long-delayed film project from Led Zeppelin's Jimmy Page, the proud owner of one of the world's largest collections of Aleister Crowley memorabilia, including Crowley's notorious Boleskine estate on the shores of Scotland's Loch Ness. When ultimately released, however, the film featured a soundtrack by neither Jagger nor Page, but rather one that was composed, recorded and arranged inside a prison cell by convicted murderer Bobby Beausoleil. The footage that Anger had shot of Beausoleil, meanwhile, ended up in a different film, the aforementioned *Invocation of My Demon Brother*. Costarring in *Lucifer Rising*, as Osiris, was *Performance* writer and co-director Donald Seaton Cammell, who happened to be a good friend of Roman Polanski.

Cammell, who some described as a master manipulator, was the son of Charles Richard Cammell, who happened to be a close friend and biographer of notorious occultist Aleister Crowley. Donald himself was, or at least claimed to be, Crowley's godson. Cammell's decidedly Crowleyian film was originally to star his good friend Marlon Brando, but the role ultimately went to actor James Fox. Brando and Cammell did, however, find time to write a novel together.

Speaking of Brando, he somehow found himself at the center of a curious string of deaths that began on May 16, 1990, when Marlon's son Christian gunned down Dag Drollet, the father of his sister Cheyenne's unborn child, in Marlon's Laurel Canyon-adjacent home. Though convicted, Christian got off with a rather light sentence, thanks primarily to Marlon having had his own daughter, the prosecution's potential star witness, locked away in a mental institution in Tahiti, safe from subpoena. A few years later, on April 14, 1995, twenty-five-year-old Cheyenne was found swinging from the end of a rope, her death unsurprisingly ruled a suicide. The next year, Christian Brando was released from prison and promptly became involved with a woman by the name of Bonnie Lee Bakley, who caught a bullet to the head on May 4, 2001, while in the company of new hubby Robert Blake (her tenth husband). Marlon dropped dead next, on July 1, 2004, though his death wasn't particularly shocking given that he was getting on in years. His home was promptly purchased by good friend and neighbor Jack Nicholson, who immediately announced plans to bulldoze it, declaring the structure to be decrepit. He never did though explain why a man wealthy enough to own his own Polynesian island was purportedly living in a derelict home. A few years later, on January 26 of 2008, Christian Brando dropped dead at the relatively young age of forty-nine.

Returning now, after that brief digression, to our discussion of Donald Cammell's *Performance*, we find that Mick Jagger was cast to play the role of 'Turner,' a debauched rock star (which, obviously, was a real stretch for Mick). James Fox played 'Chas,' a violent organized-crime figure. He was trained for the role by David Litvinoff, a real-life crime figure and associate of the notoriously sadistic Kray brothers. Litvinoff reportedly sent Fox to the south of London for a couple of months to hang out with his gangster buddies; when he returned, according to various accounts, Fox had literally *become* the violent character he portrayed in the film. After completing work on the project, Fox reportedly suffered a massive nervous breakdown, suspended his acting career and withdrew from public view for over a decade.

Recruited to create the film's soundtrack was Bernard Alfred "Jack" Nitzsche, an occultist and the son of a supposed 'medium.' Nitzsche, along with Sonny Bono, had begun his music career as a lieutenant for gun-brandishing producer Phil Spector (Nitzsche was one of the architects of Spector's famed "wall of sound"). Nitzsche was also a familiar presence on the Laurel Canyon scene, collaborating with such noted bands and artists as Buffalo Springfield, Neil Young, Randy Newman, Michelle Phillips, the Turtles, Captain Beefheart, Carole King, David Blue, Ricky Nelson and Tim Buckley.

Nitzsche's *Performance* soundtrack was composed, according to author Michael Walker, "in a witch's cottage in the canyon." (I'm not exactly sure what a "witch's cottage" is, but it's nice to know that Laurel Canyon had one.) One of the musicians hired by Nitzsche to play on that soundtrack was Lowell George, who we will also be adding to the Laurel Canyon Death List. For now, let's add Donald Cammell to the list, since on April 24, 1996, he became yet another of the characters in this story to catch a bullet to the head, and yet another to allegedly die by his own hand. David Litvinoff, *Performance*'s Director of Authenticity, reportedly also committed suicide. Nitzsche died of a heart attack on August 25, 2000. A few years earlier, he had made an appearance on primetime television—as a gun-brandishing drunkard arrested on the streets of Hollywood on *Cops*.

The next name on the Death List is Steve Brandt, who was a close friend of both John Phillips and one of the victims at 10050 Cielo Drive. Brandt allegedly overdosed on barbiturates in late November of 1969, some three-and-a-half months after the Manson murders. In the days and weeks following those murders, Brandt had placed numerous phone calls to the LAPD. Those calls became increasingly frantic in nature, and Brandt became increasingly fearful that his own life might be in jeopardy. He soon decided to put some distance between himself and LA, so he headed for New York City. On the night of his death, according to Phillips' autobiography, Brandt attended a Rolling Stones concert at Madison Square Garden, where he attempted to run on stage but was repelled and beaten by a security guard. He then went home and, according to official mythology, overdosed.

It seems obvious that if someone had information that desperately needed to be made public, and if it was the kind of information that authorities had, say, willfully failed to act upon, and if the information was of the type that could not be taken to the mainstream media, and if the year was 1969 and the mass communication technology that we now take for granted did not yet exist, then grabbing the mic at a Stones concert at Madison Square Garden might just be one of the most effective means of disseminating that information. Brandt failed in what may have been an attempt to do just that, and he turned up dead just hours later.

Next up is David Blue, another of the forgotten talents of Laurel Canyon. Blue was born Stuart David Cohen on February 18, 1941; shortly thereafter, his father was deployed overseas. According to David, his dad "came hobbling home on crutches and stayed depressed all his life" (not unlike, it seems fair to say, the family situation of our old friend Phil Ochs). David and his slightly older half-sister, Suzanne, endured a hellish existence consisting of alternating periods of rages and silences. Suzanne got out first, only to end up busted for prostitution in New York City in 1963. Suzanne's next stop, just a few months later, was at the county morgue.

David, meanwhile, had gotten out of the house as well, by dropping out of school and joining the US Navy at the age of seventeen—just as Lenny Bruce had done. And, like Jimi Hendrix, Blue was purportedly booted out of the service, after which he decided to become a folk singer. His first album was released in 1966. A later effort was produced by Graham Nash, who also, as previously noted, produced a record for the forgotten talent Judee Sill, with whom Blue had much in common. Like Sill, David Blue was one of the Laurel Canyon stars who never quite shone as brightly as they should have. And also like Sill, Blue was one of the first few acts signed by David Geffen's fledgling Asylum label. Finally, as with Judee, David was long forgotten by the time of his death, on December 2, 1982, when the forty-one-year-old Blue dropped dead while jogging in New York's Washington Square Park. The former rising star (and occasional actor) lay in the morgue for three days before anyone noticed that he was missing.

Next on the list is Ricky Nelson, who—like Brandon DeWilde, Kenneth Anger, Mickey Dolenz and Van Dyke Parks—began his Hollywood career as a child actor. He was the son, as everyone surely knows, of America's favorite 1950s TV mom and dad, Ozzie and Harriet Nelson. Ricky began his rock'n'roll career in 1957, when he was just seventeen. By 1962, he had scored no fewer than thirty top forty hits, trailing only superstars Elvis Presley and Pat Boone.

Speaking of Elvis, he arrived in LA in 1956 to begin what would prove to be a prolific film career that would continue throughout the 1960s and would result in the inexcusable creation of nearly three dozen motion pictures. In the early years of his film career, Elvis reportedly spent his off-hours hanging out with his two best Hollywood pals—a couple of young roommates and Canyonites named Dennis Hopper and Nick Adams. In later years, Presley's backing musicians—considered to be among the best session musicians in the business—were in high demand among the Laurel Canyon crowd. Elvis' bass player, for example, can be heard on some of the Doors' tracks. The entire band was recruited by "Papa" John Phillips to play on his less-than-memorable solo project. Mike Nesmith's critically acclaimed post-Monkees project, the First National Band, featured Presley's band as well. Gram Parsons also hired Elvis' band to back him up on the two solo albums he recorded at what proved to be the twilight of his life and career.

Those two solo efforts by Parsons, by the way, prominently featured the voice of a young singer/guitarist named Emmylou Harris, a relatively late arrival to the canyon scene. Harris was the daughter—brace yourselves here for a real shocker, folks—of a career US Marine Corps officer. As with so many other characters in this story, she grew up in the outlying suburbs of Washington, DC, primarily in Woodbridge, Virginia—which happens to be the home of an imposingly large Army research and development installation known as the Harry Diamond Laboratories Woodbridge Research Facility.

In 1972, during the time that Parsons and Harris were recording and performing together, columnist Jack Anderson revealed that, "Experiments to control human behavior with science fiction devices are being conducted secretly at the Army's high-fenced Harry Diamond Laboratories in Washington... Ultimately, human guinea pigs will be used to test the devices. Although a classified memorandum in our hands specifies the tests are for riot and civil disturbance control, the memo admits the general purpose is 'short-time-span control of human behavior.'" It sounds as though Emmylou Harris probably fit right in with the rest of the Laurel Canyon crowd.

But here I seem to have digressed from our discussion of Elvis, which was, if I remember correctly, itself a digression from our discussion of Ricky Nelson. Given though that he had only peripheral connections to Laurel Canyon, I guess I don't really have much more to say about Elvis other than that he reportedly died on August 16, 1977, the victim of a drug overdose at the young age of forty-two. As with Morrison, however, there have been persistent rumors that Elvis didn't actually die at all, but rather reinvented himself to escape from the fishbowl. Also as with Morrison, Elvis apparently had a keen interest in the occult, particularly the writings of Madame Blavatsky.

As for Nelson, in the mid-1960s he successfully shed his 'teen idol' image and emerged as a respected pioneer of the country-rock wave that Canyonites Jackson Browne, Linda Ronstadt and the Eagles would soon ride to dizzying heights of commercial success. One future member of the Eagles, Randy Meisner, played in Nelson's Stone Canyon Band. As the name of the band would seem to imply, Nelson had moved to one of the many neighboring canyons, but he had previously lived on Mt. Olympus in Laurel Canyon and he and his band were very much a part of the early country-rock scene that included bands like the Byrds, Poco, the Flying Burrito Brothers and the First National Band.

Nelson was killed on New Year's Eve, 1985, in a rather unusual plane crash. According to Nelson's Wikipedia entry, "the original NTSB investigation long ago stated that the crash was probably due to mechanical problems. The pilots attempted to land in a field after smoke filled the cabin. An examination indicated that a fire originated in the right hand side of the aft cabin area at or near the floor line. The passengers were killed when the aircraft struck obstacles during the forced landing; the pilots were able to escape through the cockpit windows and survived." Nothing unusual about that, I suppose. Shit happens.

For the final eight years of his life, Nelson lived in a rather unique home. In 1941, swashbuckling actor Errol Flynn had purchased an eleven-and-a-half-acre chunk of the Hollywood Hills just off Mulholland Drive and had a sprawling home built to his specifications. According to Laurie Jacobson and Marc Wanamaker, writing in *Haunted Hollywood*, the mansion featured "several mysterious secret passageways, and more than a few peepholes." The home appeared to have been designed to allow for surreptitious observation of guests in the home's numerous bedrooms. It is claimed that Flynn incorporated the unusual design features so that he could satisfy his own voyeuristic impulses. Researcher/writer Charles Higham, however, has cast Flynn as a Western intelligence asset, and if true, then it is far more likely that the home was built not so much for Flynn's personal pleasure but rather as a means of compromising prominent public figures.

After Nelson's death, the palatial home stood vacant until a curious incident took place; referring once again to Jacobson and Wanamaker, we find that "A gang broke in and murdered a girl in the living room. Then a mysterious fire burned half the house. The ruins were torn down." Like I said, shit happens.

Moving on to the next name on the list, we find that on December 31, 1943—precisely forty-two years before the plane crash that would claim the life of Ricky Nelson—Henry John Deutschendorf, Jr., better known as John Denver, was born in Roswell, New Mexico. A few years later, the town of Roswell would make a name for itself and become something of a tourist destination. But that is not really the focus here, though it should be noted that Henry John Deutschendorf, Sr. might well have known a little something about that incident, given that he was a career US Air Force officer assigned to the Roswell Army Air Field (later renamed the Walker Air Force Base), which was likely the origin of the object that famously crashed in Roswell.

After spending his childhood being frequently uprooted, as did many of our cast of characters, Denver attended Texas Tech University in the early 1960s. In 1964, he apparently heard the call of the Pied Piper and promptly dropped out of school and headed for LA. Once there, he joined up with the Chad Mitchell Trio, the group from which Jim McGuinn had recently departed to co-found the Byrds. By November 1966, Denver was front-and-center at the so-called 'Riot on the Sunset Strip,' alongside folks like Peter Fonda, Sal Mineo and a popular husband-and-wife duo known as Sonny and Cher.

A decade later, in the latter half of the 1970s, Denver could be found working alongside a spooky chap by the name of Werner Erhard, creator of so-called 'EST' training. After graduating from the training program, Denver penned a little ditty that became the organization's theme song. In 1985, Denver testified alongside our old friend Frank Zappa at the PMRC hearings. Twelve years later, in autumn of 1997, Denver died when his self-piloted plane crashed soon after taking off from Monterey Airport, very near where the Monterey Pop Festival had been held thirty years earlier. The date of the crash, curiously enough, was one that we have stumbled across before: October 12.

The next name we need to add to the list is one that has already worked its way into this narrative a time or two, Sonny Bono. As previously noted, Bono began his Hollywood career as a lieutenant for reclusive murderer Phil Spector. In the early 1960s, Bono hooked up with an underage Cherilyn Sarkisian LaPierre to form a duo known first as Caesar and Cleo, and then as Sonny and Cher. The pair were phenomenally successful, first on the Sunset Strip and later on television. Bono, of course, ultimately gave up the Hollywood life and found work in a different branch of the federal government: the US House of Representatives.

On January 5, 1998, Sonny Bono died after purportedly skiing into a tree. At the time, he occupied a seat on the House Judiciary Committee, which was about to come to sudden prominence with the investigation and impeachment of President Clinton. The ball was already rolling by the time of Bono's death, and on January 26, 1998, just three weeks after the alleged skiing incident, Clinton held his now-notorious press conference. By that time, Bono's seat on the panel had been set aside for his robowife.

Let's turn our attention now to Phil Hartman, the *Saturday Night Live* alumnus who was murdered in his Encino home on May 28, 1998. That much is not in dispute. Decidedly less clear is the answer to the question of who it was that actually shot and killed Hartman. The official story holds that it was his wife Brynn, who shortly thereafter shot herself—with a different gun, naturally, and reportedly after she had left the house and then returned with a friend, and *after* the LAPD had arrived at the home. There is a very strong possibility, however, that both Phil and his wife were murdered, with the true motive for the crime covered up by trotting out the tired but ever-popular murder/suicide scenario.

In most people's minds, of course, Phil Hartman is not associated with the Laurel Canyon scene of the late 1960s and early 1970s. But as it turns out, Hartman did indeed have substantial ties to that scene. To begin with, during the time that Jimi Hendrix lived in LA (in the spacious mansion just north of the Log Cabin on Laurel Canyon Boulevard), Hartman worked for him as a roadie. Soon after that, Phil found work as a graphic artist and he quickly found himself much in demand by the Laurel Canyon rock royalty. In addition to designing album covers for both Poco and America, Hartman also designed a readily recognizable rock symbol that has endured for over forty years: the distinctive CSN logo for Crosby, Stills & Nash.

Hartman was also the brother of record executive/club proprietor John Hartmann, who was an associate of David Geffen. Hartmann had begun his career as a protégé of Elvis handler Colonel Tom Parker, who, in the 1940s, had worked with cowboy actor/Log Cabin owner Tom Mix. And Tom Mix, in turn, had frequently used the Spahn Movie Ranch as a filming location. That same ranch later became the home of Charles Manson and his girls, including Lynette "Squeaky" Fromme, who happened to have been a high school chum of Phil Hartman. Curiously enough, the Log Cabin's guesthouse, also known as the Bird House, was designed and built by architect Robert Byrd, who also, according to one report, designed the house at 10050 Cielo Drive where Sharon Tate and friends were murdered, *and* the house at 5065 Encino Avenue where Phil Hartman was murdered.

Phil Hartman was not the only Laurel Canyon luminary who had past school ties to Squeaky Fromme; Mark Volman, co-lead vocalist for the Turtles, knew Ms. Fromme from their days together in Westchester where they attended Orville Wright Junior High School.

During the days of the Manson clan's stay at the now infamous Spahn Ranch, there was a similarly dilapidated movie set that was located right across the road. Its name, being the small world that it is, was the Wonderland Movie Ranch. Speaking of Wonderland, let's turn our attention next to four individuals whose names will probably not be familiar to most readers: Ronald Launius, Billy Deverell, Barbara Richardson and Joy Miller. All died on July 1, 1981, all by bludgeoning, and all at the same location: 8763 Wonderland Avenue in Laurel Canyon. All were members of a gang that trafficked heavily in cocaine and occasionally in heroin.

The leader of the group was Ron Launius, who reportedly embarked on his criminal career, and established his drug connections, while serving for Uncle Sam over in Vietnam, which is also where he began to build his carefully crafted reputation as a merciless, cold-blooded killer. At the time that he became a murder victim himself, Launius was a suspect in no fewer than twenty-seven open homicide investigations. He was also a drug supplier to various members of the Laurel Canyon aristocracy, including Chuck Negron of Three Dog Night.

Victim Billy Deverell was Launius' second-in-command, and victim Joy Miller was Billy's girlfriend as well as the renter of the Laurel Canyon drug den. Victim Barbara Richardson was the girlfriend of another member of the gang, David Lind, who conveniently was not at the home at the time of the mass murder. That could well have been due to the fact that Lind was, according to various rival drug dealers, a police informant for both the Sacramento and Los Angeles Police Departments. He was also a member of the ultra-violent prison gang known as the Aryan Brotherhood (as is, by several accounts, Bobby Beausoleil). Lind, who met Launius when the two had served time together, is alleged to have overdosed in 1995, though it is widely believed that he actually went into the federal witness protection program.

A year-and-a-half earlier, another drug dealer with close connections to the music scene was brutally murdered in his Laurel Canyon home, though his death was dismissed by the LAPD as a suicide. Lawrence Eugene "Larry" Williams was a singer, songwriter, musician, producer and actor born on May 10, 1935, in New Orleans, Louisiana. He achieved some success in the late 1950s as a solo artist before being convicted and sent to prison on drug dealing charges in 1960. Following a three-year prison stint, he returned to the music business, working frequently with longtime friend Little Richard. He also continued to spend a good deal of time in the violent world of drug trafficking and prostitution.

Williams had no shortage of fans among the Laurel Canyon and British Invasion bands. The Beatles scored a hit with his Dizzy Miss Lizzy and the Rolling Stones covered his She Said Yeah. In the late 1960s and the early 1970s, Williams also tried his hand at acting, including a co-starring role alongside O.J. Simpson in 1974's *The Klansman*. He failed to achieve significant success in the entertainment business; his lavish lifestyle, however, indicated that he did very well for himself as a pimp and drug trafficker.

On January 7, 1980, Williams was found dead in his Laurel Canyon home with a gunshot wound to his head and his blood splattered all over his garage walls. Though ruled a suicide, no one who was familiar with Larry's violent lifestyle was much convinced of that. In a bizarre turn of events, another blues singer named Martin Allbritton appropriated his name before Williams' body was even cold. He continues to this day to claim that he is the real Larry Williams and even tours and performs under the name "Big" Larry Williams.

The next name on the list is Brian Cole, bass player for the Association, a Laurel Canyon folk-rock band known for the hit songs Along Comes Mary and Never My Love. The Association was formed by Terry Kirkman and Jules Alexander; Kirkman had formerly played in a band with Frank Zappa, while Alexander was fresh from a stint in the US Navy. Jerry Yester, a guitarist and keyboardist with the band, was formerly with the Modern Folk Quartet, a band managed by Zappa manager Herb Cohen and produced by Byrds manager Jim Dickson. Guitarist Larry Ramos had formerly been with the New Christy Minstrels, which also produced Gene Clark of the Byrds.

On June 16, 1967, Cole and his band were the first to take the stage at the Monterey Pop Festival, followed by such Laurel Canyon stalwarts as the Byrds, Buffalo Springfield, and the Mamas and the Papas. Five years later, on August 2, 1972, Cole was found dead in his Los Angeles home. The cause of death was reportedly a heroin overdose. Cole was one month shy of his thirtieth birthday at the time of his death.

Another new name on the Laurel Canyon Death List is Lowell George, the founder and creative force behind the critically acclaimed but largely obscure band known as Little Feat. George was the son of Willard H. George, a famous furrier to the Hollywood movie studios. Lowell's first foray into the music world was with a band known as the Factory, which cut some demos with a guy by the name of Frank Zappa. The Factory evolved into the Fraternity of Man, though without George, who had left to serve as lead vocalist for the Standells. George returned, however, to join the band in the studio for the recording of their second album. By that time, as we have already learned, the Fraternity of Man had taken up residence in the Log Cabin, alongside Carl Franzoni and his fellow freaks.

George next joined up with Frank Zappa's Mothers of Invention, though his tenure there was destined to be a short one; like so many others, Lowell left embittered by Zappa's dictatorial approach to making music and his condescending treatment of his bandmates. After parting company with Zappa, George formed Little Feat, a band composed mostly of musicians from the Fraternity of Man sessions. Lowell, who is credited with being a pioneer of the use of slide guitar in rock music, served as singer, songwriter and lead guitarist for the band, which released its debut album in 1970. Though well regarded within the industry and by critics, the band's albums failed to sell and George ultimately announced the demise of the band and recorded a solo album. After playing a show on June 29, 1979, at George Washington University in support of that album, George was found dead in an Arlington, Virginia, hotel room, very near the Pentagon. Cause of death was said to be a massive heart attack, though George was just thirty-four years old at the time.

According to Barney Hoskyns, writing in *Hotel California*, "A regular social stop-off for George was a Laurel Canyon house on Wonderland Avenue belonging to Three Dog Night singer Danny Hutton. A drop-in den of debauchery, the Hutton house featured a bedroom with black walls and a giant fireplace. Lowell would often swing by and entertain the likes of Brian Wilson or Harry Nilsson." Nilsson and his regular drinking buddy, John Lennon, were frequent guests at this "den of debauchery."

Former Beatle John Lennon is, to be sure, one of the most famous names to be found on the Laurel Canyon Death List. Lennon also has the distinction of being one of the few Laurel Canyon alumni whose cause of death is acknowledged to have been homicide. The ex-Beatle, of course, never lived in the canyon, but he was a fixture on the Sunset Strip and at various Laurel Canyon hangouts, frequently in the company of Harry Nilsson.

Lennon was, as is fairly well known, murdered on December 8, 1980, in front of New York's Dakota Apartments, which had been portrayed by filmmaker Roman Polanski in his film *Rosemary's Baby* as a den of Satanic cult activity. Not long before Lennon's murder, assassin Mark David Chapman had approached occult filmmaker Kenneth Anger and offered him a gift of live bullets. Just days after Lennon was felled, Anger's long-delayed final cut of *Lucifer Rising* made its New York debut, very near the bloodstained grounds of the Dakota Apartments.

Precisely three weeks after Lennon's death, Tim Hardin—Canyonite, folk musician, close associate of Frank Zappa, onetime tenant in Lenny Bruce's Laurel Canyon-adjacent home, and former United States Marine—died of a reported heroin and morphine overdose in Los Angeles. At the time of his death, on December 29, 1980, Hardin was just thirty-nine years old, one year younger than Lennon.

Eight years later, on July 18, 1988, singer/songwriter/keyboardist Christa Paffgen, better known as Nico, died of a reported cerebral hemorrhage in Ibiza, Spain, under unusual circumstances. After achieving some level of fame as a vocalist with the Velvet Underground, Nico had left the Warhol stable and migrated west to Laurel Canyon, where she formed a bond with a then-unknown singer-songwriter named Jackson Browne, who contributed a few songs to Nico's 1967 debut album, *Chelsea Girl*. The title was derived from New York's Chelsea Hotel, where Devon Wilson took a dive and where the persona of John Train murdered the persona of Phil Ochs.

11

DETOURS RUSTIC CANYON & GREYSTONE PARK

"By the time Manson shifted base from Rustic Canyon to an old ranch in Chatsworth, he'd begun formulating the notion that he and his followers had to prepare themselves for a race war with Black America." Barney Hoskyns, writing in Hotel California

WE MUST NOW TEMPORARILY RELOCATE TO RUSTIC CANYON, WHICH LIES about nine miles west of Laurel Canyon in the Hollywood Hills. It was there, in Lower Rustic Canyon, that Beach Boy Dennis Wilson lived in the late 1960s in what Steven Gaines described in *Heroes and Villains* as "a palatial log-cabin-style house at 14400 Sunset Boulevard that had once belonged to humorist Will Rogers." The expansive home sat on three lushly landscaped acres.

In the summer of 1968, as is fairly well known, Charlie Manson and various members of his entourage moved in with Wilson. Considerably less well known is that Charles "Tex" Watson, for reasons that have never really been explained, was already living there. As many as two-dozen members of Manson's clan spent the entire summer there, with Wilson picking up the tab for all expenses. The Mansonites, mostly nubile young women, regularly drove Wilson's expensive cars and demolished at least one of them. Dennis didn't seem to mind; he was busy recording Manson in brother Brian's home studio and inviting fellow musicians, like Neil Young, over to the house to hear Charlie perform. (Young was so impressed that he urged Mo Ostin to sign him.)

Dennis would later claim that he had destroyed all the Manson demo tapes, that he remembered almost nothing of his time with Charlie and the Family, and that he certainly knew nothing about the Tate and LaBianca murders, which were committed in the summer of 1969, about a year after the Family had vacated the Rustic Canyon residence. At some point in time though, Wilson had a change of heart and decided that maybe he did indeed know a little something about the murders. "I know why Charles Manson did what he did," said Dennis. "Someday, I'll tell the world. I'll write a book and explain why he did it." That book, however, was never written and Wilson's story, if indeed he had one, was never told. Instead, Dennis Wilson drowned under questionable circumstances on December 28, 1983, in the marina where his beloved yacht had previously been docked.

But this story isn't really about Dennis Wilson; it's about Charlie Manson and his alleged motive for allegedly ordering the Tate and LaBianca murders. According to the 'Helter Skelter' scenario popularized by lead prosecutor Vincent Bugliosi, who later penned a wildly disinformational book on the JFK assassination, Manson was hoping to spark an apocalyptic race war. It is said that Charlie believed that America's black population would prevail over whitey, but that, having won the war, the victors would be incapable of governing themselves. And that, alas, is when Charlie and his retinue would emerge from the shadows to take command.

According to Barney Hoskyns, Manson began formulating his race war theory during his stay in Rustic Canyon. If true, then Charlie appears to have been following in the footsteps of a long-forgotten former Rustic Canyon guru—one who preceded him by a few decades, and who, like Manson, had a certain fondness for swastikas.

Just to the north of Dennis Wilson's former home is a vast wilderness of undeveloped canyon lands. Lower Rustic Canyon soon gives way to Upper Rustic Canyon, and all signs of human civilization abruptly vanish. The land remains wild and undeveloped save for an old, unpaved fire road that winds along the summit between Rustic Canyon and a neighboring canyon. That road is closed to the public and vehicle traffic is nonexistent. Aside from an occasional hiker wandering in from nearby Will Rogers State Park, there is nary a human to be seen.

The farther in one hikes, the more wild and untamed it becomes. Along with the sights of the city, the sounds and the scents quickly disappear as well. Within a very short time, it is surprisingly easy to forget that one is still within the confines of the city of Los Angeles. And in its fall splendor, the canyon looks nothing like the Los Angeles that most Angelenos know and don't quite love. It is beautiful... serene... pastoral. And yet, filled with mist and heavily overgrown, it is also vaguely ominous.

If one knows where to look, there is a narrow concrete stairway that is accessible from the fire road. That stairway descends down to the floor of the canyon, and it is a very, very long descent. Five hundred and twelve steps long, to be exact. As one makes the descent, this stairway, which seems to go on forever, seems wildly out of place. With time to kill on the way down, one may find oneself pondering how many man-hours it took to set forms for 512 poured concrete steps, and how truckloads of concrete were poured out here in the middle of nowhere.

Reaching the canyon floor, one finds that, though the native flora has struggled mightily to reclaim the land, remnants of a past civilization can be seen everywhere. Some structures remain largely intact—a nearly 400,000 gallon, spring-fed reservoir serving a sophisticated potable water system; a concrete-walled structure that once housed twin electrical generators capable of lighting a small town; more concrete stairways, hundreds of steps long, each snaking its way up the canyon walls; weathered livestock stables; professionally graded and paved roads; countless stone retaining walls; an incinerator; concrete foundations and skeletal remains of former dwellings; the rusting carcass of a Mansonesque VW bus; and, at the former entrance, an imposing set of electronically controlled, wrought iron security gates.

It is the kind of place that seems tailor-made for Charlie and his Family—remote and secluded, yet accessible by the Family's custom-built dune buggies; with just enough crumbling infrastructure to provide rudimentary shelter for the clan; and with elaborate security provisions, including sentry positions and a formerly electrified fence completely encircling the fifty-acre compound (as well as, by some reports, an underground tunnel complex). And it was located just a short hike up the canyon from the place that Charlie Manson called home in the summer of 1968.

While exploring this place, obvious questions begin to come to mind: Who developed this remote portion of the canyon, in what feels like the middle of nowhere? The goal appears to have been to create a hidden and completely self-sustaining community, and an extraordinary amount of money was invested in infrastructure development... but why?

Very few Angelenos know of the curious ruins in Rustic Canyon, and fewer still know the history of those ruins. Every now and then though, a local reporter will pay a visit and the story will make a one-time appearance in a local publication, briefly casting some light on a bit of the hidden history of Los Angeles. In May 1992, Marc Norman of the *Los Angeles Business Journal* was one such reporter. According to Norman, "County records show 'Jessie Murphy, a widow,' purchasing fifty-plus acres north of [Will] Rogers' property in 1933, but the owners were actually named Stephens—Norman, an engineer with silver-mining interests, and Winona, the daughter of an industrialist and a woman given to things supernatural. Local lore has it that Winona fell under the spell of a certain unnamed gentleman."

This trio, along with unnamed others, began "a ten-year construction program costing $4 million... starting with a water tank holding 375,000 gallons and a concrete diesel-powered generator station with foot-thick walls—both of which are still visible. The hillsides were terraced for orchards, an electrified fence circled the boundaries and a huge refrigerated locker was built into a hillside... The one thing Murphy/Stephens couldn't seem to get right was their main house. The first architect hired was Welton Becket, but there are also sketches by Lloyd Wright, and in 1941, Paul Williams drafted blueprints for a sprawling mansion with twenty-two bedrooms, a children's dining room, a gymnasium, pool and a workshop in the basement."

Thirteen years later, in September 2005, Cecelia Rasmussen of the *Los Angeles Times* added a few details to the story: "Southern California has been the cradle to many odd cults, credos, utopias and dystopias. Among the most mysterious are the ruins of a Rustic Canyon enclave once known as Murphy Ranch... on [Rustic Canyon's] secluded and woodsy floor stand the eerily burned-out and graffiti-scarred remains of concrete and steel structures, underground tunnels and stairways leading from the top of the canyon to the bottom... Behind the locked and rusted wrought iron entrance gates and flagstone wall stand the traces of a small community that had the capacity to grow its own food, generate its own electricity and dam its own water... The hillsides were terraced with 3,000 nut, citrus, fruit and olive trees, and fitted with water pipes, sprinklers and an elaborate greenhouse. A high barbed-wire fence discouraged intruders... research indicates that it could have been home to up to forty local Nazis from about 1933 to 1945... armed guards patrolled the canyon dressed in the uniform worn by Silver Shirts, a paramilitary group modeled after Hitler's brownshirts... A man known through oral histories only as 'Herr Schmidt' supposedly ruled the place and claimed to possess metaphysical powers."

Herr Schmidt, needless to say, was the gentleman whose spell Winona Stephens fell under. According to Marc Norman, Schmidt "convinced her that the coming world war would be won by Germany, that the United States would collapse into years of violent anarchy and that the chosen few (read: the Stephenses, the certain gentleman and other true believers) would need a tight spot in which to hole up, self-sufficient, until the fire storm had passed. Then they could emerge not only intact but, thanks to the superiority of their politics, rulers of the anthill and, not incidentally, the origin of its new population."

Sound familiar?

Murphy Ranch also reportedly featured a 20,000 gallon diesel fuel tank, livestock stables, and dairy and butchering facilities. Along both sides of the compound "rise eight crumbling, narrow stairways of at least 500 steps each," as the *LA Times* noted. Those stairways apparently led to sentry positions high on the canyon walls (for the record, they are not actually crumbling, though most are overgrown with impenetrable vegetation). During Murphy Ranch's years of operation, nearby residents reportedly complained of late-night military exercises and the sounds of live gunfire echoing through the canyons.

To summarize then, it appears that the city of Los Angeles was home to a very secret, militarized Nazi compound that was in operation both before and during WWII. Remnants of that blacked-out chapter of LA history can be seen to this day, though few make the trek. The purpose of the decaying compound was to ride out an anarchic, apocalyptic war, so that the chosen few could emerge as the rulers of the new world. It was all so very Mansonesque, and, ironically enough, Manson and his crew spent an entire summer camped out at a home that was within a two-mile hike of this curious place.

In the late 1940s, after the close of the war, Murphy Ranch was reportedly converted into an artists' colony. Architect Welton Becket, who designed several of the structures at the ranch, would go on to design two of LA's landmark structures: the Capitol Records building and the Music Center. In 1973, the property once known as Murphy Ranch was purchased by the city of Los Angeles. As far as is known, the city has no plans to reopen the facility.

"Van Cortlandt and Untermyer functioned as outdoor meeting sites for the cult." Maury Terry, writing in The Ultimate Evil, in reference to the cult behind the 'Son of Sam' murders

NESTLED IN BETWEEN THE MOUTHS OF LAUREL AND COLDWATER Canyons lies a large estate known as Greystone Park, home of the long-vacant Greystone Mansion. The home, and the grounds it sits on, is said to be, to this day, the most expensive private residence ever built in the city of Los Angeles. Constructed in the 1920s, the home and grounds carried the then-unfathomable price tag of $4 million. (By way of comparison, the Lookout Inn, built a decade-and-a-half earlier, was projected to cost from $86,000–$100,000; in other words, the single-family residence cost at least forty times what the lavish seventy-room inn cost—and the inn required bringing infrastructure and building materials to a remote mountaintop.)

The massive, 46,000 square-foot edifice sits amid twenty-two lavishly landscaped acres of prime Hollywood Hills real estate. This rather ostentatious home was built by uberwealthy oil tycoon Edward L. Doheny as a wedding present for his son, Edward "Ned" Doheny, Jr. If that plotline sounds vaguely familiar, it is probably because Edward Doheny was the inspiration for Upton Sinclair's *Oil*, and thus for the homicidal

Daniel Plainview character in *There Will Be Blood* (some of the interior shots near the end of that film, of expansive, marble-floored rooms, appear to have been shot in the real Greystone).

Upon the home's completion, in September 1928, young Ned Doheny and his new bride moved into the humble abode. Within months, the home would be bloodstained; soon after, it would be permanently abandoned.

Poor Ned, you see, was found dead in the cavernous home on February 16, 1929. Near him lay the lifeless body of his assistant/personal secretary, Hugh Plunkett. Both men had been shot. Despite an inordinately long delay in reporting the deaths, and an admission that the bodies had been moved prior to the arrival of police, who were called only after the family doctor and numerous relatives, all of whom arrived at the home before the LAPD, no formal inquest was ever conducted and the case was written off in less than forty-eight hours as a murder/suicide arising from a gay lovers' quarrel. Despite an unlikely lack of fingerprints on the gun, Plunkett was said to be the triggerman and the media quickly went into a frenzy playing up the scandalous homosexuality angle and portraying young Plunkett as positively demented.

It is anyone's guess whether or not the two really were gay lovers, but it matters little; the rest of the story was almost certainly a work of fiction. In reality, both men were likely murdered as part of the massive cover-up/damage-control operation that followed the disclosure of the Harding-era Teapot Dome scandal, which the Doheny family, as it turns out, was very deeply immersed in. Both Ned Doheny and Plunkett had been scheduled to testify before a Senate investigating committee, as was Doheny's father, one of the wealthiest men in the world at the time. Due to manufactured public sympathy for the grieving father, however, the congressional investigation was shelved.

News reports of the tragedy contained no mention of the victims' deep involvement in the scandal and the tired murder/suicide scenario was trotted out because, as is seen so often in more modern times, if the alleged perpetrator is already dead, it pretty much eliminates the need for things like an investigation and trial.

Some forty years after those gunshots rang out in the opulent Greystone Mansion, a new Ned Doheny, scion of the very same Doheny oil clan, joined the ranks of the Laurel Canyon singer-songwriters club. Like fellow Canyonites Terry Melcher and Gram Parsons, Doheny was viewed by many as a pampered 'trust-fund kid.' His closest circle of friends included country-rockers Jackson Browne, J.D. Souther and Glen Frey. In addition to recording his own solo albums (his self-titled debut was released in 1973), Doheny contributed to albums by such Laurel Canyon superstars as Frey, Browne, Don Henley, Linda Ronstadt and Graham Nash.

Strangely enough, New York City once had a large estate known as Greystone as well. That Greystone was donated to the city as parkland, and it thereafter became known as Untermyer Park—the same Untermyer Park identified by Maury Terry as one of the two principal ritual sites used by the Process faction behind the 'Son of Sam' murders. The other site used by the cult was Van Cortlandt Park, named for Jacobus Van Cortlandt, a former Mayor of New York and one of David Van Cortlandt Crosby's forefathers. Another of Crosby's forefathers lent his name to Schuyler Road, which happens to run along the western boundary of the Greystone estate in the Hollywood Hills.

I have no idea what, if anything, any of that means, but I thought it best that I toss it into the mix.

12

RIDERS ON THE STORM
THE DOORS

"By that, I mean, 'Get me a lead singer. He's got sort of an androgynous blonde hair, very pretty. We need a guitar player, sort of hatchet-faced, wears a hat, plays very fast, very dramatic. He must be very dramatic. Get me a pound of bass player, pound of drummer'... they're making little cardboard cutouts. They hire a producer, they hire writers... And in the current stuff now, they don't even bother getting people to play. Don't bother with that guitar player, bass player, drummer—nonsense... The people in those bands can't write, play, or sing." David Crosby, describing the synthetic, manufactured nature of today's rock bands

AT THE VERY BEGINNING OF THIS JOURNEY, IT WAS NOTED THAT JIM Morrison's story was not "in any way unique." That, however, is not exactly true. It is certainly true that Morrison's family background did not differ significantly from that of his musical peers, but in many other significant ways, Jim Morrison was indeed a most unique individual, and quite possibly the unlikeliest rock star to ever stumble across a stage.

Morrison essentially arrived on the scene as a fully developed rock star, complete with a backing band, a stage persona and an impressive collection of songs—enough, in fact, to fill the Doors' first few albums.

How exactly he reinvented himself in such a radical manner remains something of a mystery, since before his sudden incarnation as singer/songwriter, James Douglas Morrison had never shown the slightest interest in music. None whatsoever. He certainly never studied music and could neither read nor write it. By his own account, he never had much of an interest in even listening to music. He told one interviewer that he "never went to concerts—one or two at most." And before joining the Doors, he "never did any singing. I never even conceived of it." Asked near the end of his life if he had ever had any desire to learn to play a musical instrument, Jim responded, "Not really."

So here we had a guy who had never sang, who had "never even conceived" of the notion that he could open his mouth and make sounds come out, who couldn't play an instrument and had no interest in learning such a skill, and who had never much listened to music or been anywhere near a band, even just to watch one perform, and yet he somehow emerged, virtually overnight, as a fully formed rock star who would quickly become an icon of his generation. Even more bizarrely, legend holds that he brought with him enough original songs to fill the first few Doors' albums. Morrison did not, you see, do as other singer/songwriters do and pen the songs over the course of the band's career; instead, he allegedly wrote them all at once, before the band was even formed. As Jim once acknowledged in an interview, he was "not a very prolific songwriter. Most of the songs I've written I wrote in the very beginning, about three years ago. I just had a period when I wrote a lot of songs."

In fact, all of the good songs that Morrison is credited with writing were written during that period—the period during which, according to rock legend, Jim spent most of his time hanging out on the rooftop of a Venice apartment building consuming copious amounts of LSD. This was just before he hooked up with fellow student Ray Manzarek to form the Doors. Legend also holds, strangely enough, that that chance meeting occurred on the beach, though it seems far more likely that the pair would have actually met at UCLA, where both attended the university's rather small and close-knit film school.

In any event, the question that naturally arises (though it does not appear to have ever been asked of him) is: How exactly did Jim "The Lizard King" Morrison write that impressive batch of songs? I'm certainly no musician myself, but it is my understanding that just about every singer/songwriter across the land composes his or her songs in essentially the same manner: on an instrument—usually either a piano or a guitar. Some songwriters, I hear, can compose on paper, but that requires a skill set that Jim did not possess. The problem, of course, is that he also could not play a musical instrument of any kind. How then did he write the songs?

He would have had to have composed them, I'm guessing, in his head. So we are to believe then that a few dozen complete songs, never heard by anyone and never played by any musician, existed only in Jim Morrison's acid-addled brain. Anything is possible, I suppose, but even if we accept that premise, we are still left with some nagging questions, including the question of how those songs got *out of* Jim Morrison's head. As a general rule of thumb, if a songwriter doesn't know how to read and write music, he can play the song for someone who does and thereby create the sheet music (which was the case, for example, with all of the songs that Brian Wilson penned for the Beach Boys). But Jim quite obviously could not play his own songs. So did he, I don't know, maybe hum them?

And these are, it should be clarified, *songs* that we are talking about here, as opposed to just lyrics, which would more accurately be categorized as *poems*. Because Jim, as is fairly well known, was quite a prolific poet, whereas he was a songwriter only for one brief period of his life. But why was that? Why did Morrison, with no previous interest in music, suddenly and inexplicably become a prolific songwriter, only to just as suddenly lose interest after mentally penning an impressive catalog of what would be regarded as rock staples? And how and why did Jim achieve the accompanying physical transformation that changed him from a clean-cut, collegiate, and rather conservative-looking young man into the brooding sex symbol who would take the country by storm? And why, after a few years of adopting that persona, did Jim transform once again, in the last year or so of his life, into an overweight, heavily bearded, reclusive poet who seemed to have lost his interest in music just as suddenly and inexplicably as he had obtained it?

It wasn't just Morrison who was, in retrospect, a bit of an oddity; the entire band differed from other Laurel Canyon bands in a number of significant ways. As *Vanity Fair* once noted, "The Doors were always different." All four members of the group, for example, lacked previous band experience. Morrison and Manzarek, as noted, were film students, and drummer John Densmore and guitarist Robby Kreiger were recruited by Manzarek from his Transcendental Meditation class—which is, I guess, where one goes to find musicians to fill out one's band. That class, however, apparently lacked a bass player, so they did without—except for those times when they used session musicians and then claimed that they did without.

Anyway, the point is that none of the four members of the Doors had any real band credentials. Even a band as contrived as the Byrds, as we shall soon see, had members with band credentials. So too did Buffalo Springfield, with Neil Young and Bruce Palmer, for example, having played in the Mynah Birds, backing a young vocalist who would reinvent himself as Rick "Superfreak" James (Goldy McJohn of Steppenwolf, oddly enough, was a Mynah Bird as well). The Mamas and the Papas were put together from elements of the Journeymen and the Mugwumps. And so on with the rest of the Laurel Canyon bands.

The Doors could cite no such band lineage. They were just four guys who happened to come together to play the songs written by the singer who had never sung but who had a sudden calling and a magical gift for songwriting. And as you would expect with four guys who had never actually played in a band before, they didn't really play very well. And that is kind of an understatement. Don't take my word for it though; let's let the band's producer, Paul Rothchild, weigh in: "The Doors were not great live performers musically. They were exciting theatrically and kinetically, but as musicians they didn't make it; there was too much inconsistency, there was too much bad music. Robby would be horrendously out of tune with Ray, John would be missing cues, there was bad mic usage too, where you couldn't hear Jim at all."

As fate would have it, I have heard some audio of a young and quite inebriated Jim Morrison at the microphone, and I would have to say that not being able to "hear Jim at all" might have, in many cases, actually improved the performance. But performing poorly as a live band, of course, did not really set the Doors apart from its contemporaries. Another thing that *was* unusual about the band, however, is that, from the moment the band was conceived, the lineup never changed. No one was added, no one was replaced, no one dropped out of the band over 'artistic differences,' or to pursue a solo career, or to join another band, or for any of the other reasons that bands routinely change shape.

It would be difficult to identify another Laurel Canyon band of any longevity that could make the same claim. After their first two albums, the Byrds changed lineups with virtually every album release. Frank Zappa's Mothers of Invention were in a near-constant state of flux. Love and Steppenwolf changed lineups on a regular basis, with leaders John Kay and Arthur Lee routinely firing band members. Laurel Canyon's country-rock bands were also constantly changing shape, usually by incestuously swapping members amongst themselves.

But not the Doors. Jim Morrison's band arrived on the scene as a fully formed entity, with a name (taken from Aldous Huxley's *The Doors of Perception*), a stable lineup, a backlog of soon-to-be hit songs... and no previous experience writing, arranging, playing or performing music. Other than that though, they were just your run-of-the-mill, organic, grass roots, 1960s rock'n'roll band, albeit one with a curious aversion to political advocacy. Jim Morrison was, by virtually all accounts, a voracious reader. Former teachers and college professors expressed amazement at the breadth and depth of his knowledge on various topics, and at the staggering array of literary sources that he could accurately cite. And yet he was known to tell interviewers that he "[had]n't studied politics that much, really." But that was okay, according to drummer John Densmore, since "a lot of people at our concerts at least, they're sort of—it seems like they don't really come to hear us speak politics."

That's the way it was in the 1960s, you see; the young folks of that era just didn't concern themselves much with politics, and certainly didn't want their anti-war icons engaging in anything resembling political discourse.

During the Doors' glory days on the Sunset Strip, Morrison "struck up an intimate friendship" with Whisky-a-Go-Go owner Elmer Valentine, according to a *Vanity Fair* article published in September 2006. At the time, Valentine was also, coincidentally of course, very close to his own secretary/booking agent, Gail Sloatman, whom Jim had known since kindergarten through Naval officers' circles. Valentine was also—by pretty much all accounts, including his own—a 'made man.'

Valentine arrived in LA by way of Chicago, where he had worked as a vice cop—a decidedly corrupt vice cop. By his own account, he worked as a police captain's bagman, "collecting the filthy lucre on behalf of the captain." He also boasted that, even while working as a vice cop, his night job was "running nightclubs for the outfit—for gangsters." One "very close friend" from his days in Chicago was "Felix Alderisio, also known as Milwaukee Phil, who was arguably the most feared hit man in the country in the 1950s and sixties, carrying out at least fourteen murders for Sam Giancana and other Chicago bosses."

Valentine was ultimately indicted for extortion, though he naturally managed to avoid prosecution and conviction. Venturing out to LA circa 1960, he soon found himself running PJ's nightclub at the corner of Crescent Heights and Santa Monica Boulevards (which, as you may recall, was co-owned by Eddie Nash and was the favored hangout of early rocker/murder victim Bobby Fuller). It wasn't long though before Valentine had his very own club to run—the legendary Whisky-a-Go-Go, where numerous Laurel Canyon bands, including the Doors in the summer of 1966, served their residency.

Valentine obviously had considerable financial backing to launch his business empire and it wasn't much of a secret on the Strip where that backing came from. Frank Zappa once cryptically referred to Valentine's backers as an "ethnic organization," while Chris Hillman of the Byrds simply noted that, "whoever financed Elmer, I don't want to know."

Valentine received far more than just financial backing to launch the Whisky; he got a generous assist from the media as well. As *Vanity Fair* noted, "Within months of the Whisky's debut, *Life* magazine had written it up, Jack Paar had broadcast an episode of his post-*Tonight* weekly program from the club, and Steve McQueen and Jayne Mansfield had installed themselves as regulars." Legendary actor McQueen, it should be noted, was a former US Marine who had served in an elite unit tasked with protecting President Harry Truman's private yacht.

Turning now to the Byrds, the band that started the folk-rock revolution, we find that they were, by any reasonable assessment, an entirely manufactured phenomenon. As a fledgling band, they had any number of problems. The first and most obvious was that the band's members did not own any musical instruments. That problem was solved though when Naomi Hirschorn, better known for funding quasi-governmental projects such as the Hirschorn Museum in Washington, DC, stepped up to the plate to provide the band with instruments, amplifiers and the like. But that didn't solve a bigger problem, which was that the band's members, with the notable exception of Jim (later Roger) McGuinn, didn't have a clue as to how to actually play those instruments.

Cast to play the bass player was Chris Hillman, who had never picked up a bass guitar in his life. As he candidly admitted years later, he "was a mandolin player and didn't know how to play bass. But [the other band members] didn't know how to play their instruments either, so I didn't feel too bad about it." On drums was Michael Clarke, who had never before held a set of drumsticks in his hands but who bore a resemblance to Rolling Stone Brian Jones, which was deemed to be of more significance than actual musical ability. As Crosby co-author Carl Gottlieb recalled, "Clarke had played beatnik bongos and conga drum, but had no experience with conventional drumming."

Richie Unterberger noted in *Turn! Turn! Turn!* that the guys in the Byrds "had barely known each other before getting thrown into the studio, were still learning electric instruments, and in a couple cases had never really even played their assigned instruments at all. Actually, Michael Clarke didn't even have an instrument to start with; on his first rehearsals, and even some recording sessions, he kept time on cardboard boxes."

Gene Clark, though by far the most gifted songwriter in the band and a talented vocalist as well, could barely play his guitar and so was relegated to banging the tambourine, which was Jim Morrison's (and various non-musically inclined members of the Partridge Family's) instrument of choice as well. David Crosby, tasked with rhythm guitar duties, wasn't much better. Crosby himself admitted, in his first autobiography (does anyone really need to write more than one autobiography, by the way?), that, "Roger was the only one who could really play."

The band had another problem. With the clear exception of Gene Clark, the group was a bit lacking in songwriting ability. To compensate, they initially played mostly covers. Fully a third of the band's first album consisted of covers of Dylan songs, and nearly another third was made up of covers of songs by other folk singer/songwriters. Clark contributed the five original songs, two of them co-written with McGuinn. As for Crosby, who emerged as the band's biggest star, his only contribution to the Byrds' first album was backing vocals.

Carl Franzoni perhaps summed it up best when he declared rather bluntly that, "the Byrds' records were manufactured." The first album in particular was an entirely engineered affair created by taking a collection of songs by outside songwriters and having them performed by a group of nameless studio musicians (for the record, the actual musicians were Glen Campbell on guitar, Hal Blaine on drums, Larry Knechtel on bass, Leon Russell on electric piano, and Jerry Cole on rhythm guitar), after which the band's trademark vocal harmonies, entirely a studio creation, were added to the mix.

As would be expected, the Byrds' live performances, according to Barney Hoskyns' *Waiting for the Sun*, "weren't terribly good." But that didn't matter much; the band got a lot of assistance from the media, with *Time* being among the first to champion the new band. And they also got a tremendous assist from Vito and the Freaks and from the Young Turks, as previously discussed.

We shall return to the Byrds, and to the ubiquitous Vito Paulekas, in the next chapter. For now, I leave you with this curious little story about Byrd Chris Hillman's initial arrival in Laurel Canyon, as told by Michael Walker in *Laurel Canyon*: "In the autumn of 1964, a nineteen-year-old bluegrass adept and virtuoso mandolin player named Chris Hillman stood at the corner of Laurel Canyon Boulevard and Kirkwood Drive contemplating a FOR RENT sign on a telephone pole across from the Canyon Country Store... It didn't take him long to find [a place to stay], and, in the canyon's emerging mythos of enchanted serendipity, one presented itself as if by magic. 'This guy drives up and he says you looking for a place to rent?' Hillman recalls. 'I said yeah, and he said, Well, follow me up. It was this young guy who was a dentist. It was his parents' house, a beautiful old wood house down a dirt road—and he lived on the top, and he was renting out the bottom part. I just went, Wow, perfect. The guy ended up being my dentist for a while... It was the top of the world, a beautiful, beautiful place. I had the best place in the canyon.'"

In the Los Angeles of the 1960s, you see, it was quite common for a very wealthy person to offer exquisite living accommodations to a random, scruffy vagrant. We know this to be true because it happened to Charles Manson on more than one occasion. In any event, Chris Hillman's former mountaintop home no longer exists because, as tends to happen in Laurel Canyon, it burned to the ground on what Walker described as a "hot, witchy day in the sixties." According to Hillman, "Crosby was at my house an hour before the blaze. I can't connect it yet—where the Satan factor came into play with David—but I'm working on it."

13

EIGHT MILES HIGH AND FALLING FAST THE BYRDS

"I'd have to say that, personally speaking, Crosby was worse for the good feelings of [the local] rock'n'roll [scene] than Manson was." Terry Melcher

One of the most influential people lurking about the periphery of the Laurel Canyon scene was the Byrds' first producer, Terry Melcher. It is fairly well known that Melcher was the son of 'virginal' actress Doris Day, who was just sixteen when impregnated and seventeen when Terry was born. Melcher's father was trombonist Al Jorden, who reportedly regularly beat Day, and likely Terry as well. Jorden wasn't around for long though; his death, when Melcher was just two or three years old, was yet another Hollywood suicide.

After an equally short-lived second marriage, Doris Day married her agent and producer, Marty Melcher, who was universally regarded as one of the biggest assholes in Hollywood—and that's not an easy title to attain, given the fierce competition. Like Jorden, Melcher was well known for being a tyrannically violent and abusive man. He also reportedly embezzled some $20 million from his wife/client. On the bright side though, he did adopt and help raise Terry, who took his name.

Terry Melcher, perhaps more so than anyone else, had deep ties to virtually all aspects of the canyon scene, including the Laurel Canyon musicians, the Manson Family, the group of young Hollywood actors generally referred to as 'The Young Turks,' and the Vito Paulekas dance troupe. As it turns out, Melcher first met Vito Paulekas when Terry was still in high school in the late 1950s. As Melcher later recalled, "Vito was an art instructor. When I was in high school, we'd go to his art studio because he had naked models." A half-decade or so later, Melcher and Paulekas would, each in his own way, become key players in launching not just the career of the Byrds but the entire Laurel Canyon music scene, as well as the accompanying youth countercultural movement.

Also while still in high school, Melcher befriended Bruce Johnston, the adopted son of a top executive with the Rexall drugstore chain. While growing up on the not-so-mean streets of Beverly Hills and Bel Air, the two recorded together as singing duo Bruce and Terry. Johnston also played in a high school band with Phil Spector, who, it will be recalled, shared with Melcher (and various others in this story) the distinction of having lost a parent to an alleged act of suicide.

As has been pointed out already, it was Spector's crack team of studio musicians, dubbed the Wrecking Crew, who provided the instrumental tracks for countless albums by Laurel Canyon bands. Bruce Johnston, meanwhile, went on to become a Beach Boy, replacing Wrecking Crew member Glen Campbell, who had briefly replaced Brian Wilson after Brian abruptly decided that he no longer wanted to perform live. Brian's brother Dennis forged a close bond with Terry Melcher, as well as with Gregg Jakobson, a would-be actor and talent scout who was married to famed comedian Lou Costello's daughter.

The trio of Wilson, Melcher and Jakobson, who dubbed themselves the "Golden Penetrators" (with Wilson referring to himself rather subtly as "The Wood"), infamously forged a close bond with a musician/prophet/penetrator by the name of Charles Manson. In 1966, Melcher, along with Mark Lindsay of the band Paul Revere and the Raiders, leased and moved into the soon-to-be infamous home at 10050 Cielo Drive in Benedict Canyon. (Lindsay would later have the dubious distinction of also living for a time in that other infamous canyon death house, on Wonderland Avenue; Lindsay was also a regular visitor to the Log Cabin.) The two were soon joined by Melcher's girlfriend, actress Candice Bergen. Melcher and Bergen remained in the home until early 1969, frequently entertaining high-profile guests from both the music and film industries.

During the summer of 1968, when Charlie Manson and numerous members of his entourage, including Charles "Tex" Watson and Dean Moorehouse, were shacking up with Melcher's sidekick, Dennis Wilson, Watson and Moorehouse were known to regularly visit the Melcher/ Bergen home on Cielo Drive. Charlie Manson is known to have visited the Melcher home on several occasions as well, and to have occasionally borrowed Melcher's Jaguar. Just after Melcher and Bergen vacated the home, Jakobson reportedly arranged for Moorehouse to live there briefly, before Tate and Polanski took possession in February of 1969. During Moorehouse's stay, Tex, who would later be portrayed as the leader of the Tate and LaBianca hit squads, came calling regularly. His address book would later be found to contain a phone number for a former Polanski residence.

Watson had moved out to LA from Texas in 1966 after opting to drop out of college, which those who knew him viewed as being wildly out of character. By the spring of 1968, when Charles Watson met Charles Manson at Dennis Wilson's home, Tex was the modish co-owner of Crown Wig Creations on the corner of Santa Monica Boulevard and Rodeo Drive in Beverly Hills. Through that business enterprise, he had developed extensive Hollywood contacts—contacts that came in handy when he began handling large drug transactions and large piles of cash for Charlie Manson. Tex Watson soon grew so close to Manson that, according to Ed Sanders, he was known to complain at times "that he actually thought he was Charlie."

According to *Vanity Fair*, Tex Watson was also "a regular patron of the Whisky," which isn't too surprising given that Elmer Valentine's club was well known to be a major drug trafficking site during the late 1960s. Watson's frequent sidekick Dean Moorehouse, by the way, hailed from Minot, North Dakota, identified by Maury Terry as the longtime home of a Process faction with deep ties to Offutt Air Force Base. Though it is purely speculation, it seems entirely possible that Moorehouse served as a handler for both Charlies—Manson and Watson. Perhaps tellingly, Vincent Bugliosi mentioned Moorehouse only once in his nearly 700-page treatment of the Manson case (in much the same way that David Crosby ignored Vito Paulekas in his wordy autobiography).

In the spring of 1969, the trio of Wilson, Melcher and Jakobson got close to Bobby Beausoleil as well. Jakobson made at least two trips to the Gerard Theatrical Agency to hear demo tapes that Bobby had recorded. The agency, headed by Jack Gerard, specialized in supplying topless dancers to seedy clubs, and actors and actresses for porno film shoots. Beausoleil's primary job with the agency was to deliver carloads of girls to the clubs; more than a few of those girls were members of Charlie's Family. In March of 1969, just months before he was arrested for the torture-murder of Gary Hinman, Bobby signed a songwriting contract with the agency and began recording demos.

Beausoleil also accompanied Melcher and Jakobson on at least two trips out to the Spahn Movie Ranch, once in May of 1969 and then again the next month. Jakobson was a frequent visitor to Spahn and was known to boast of having held over 100 hours of conversations with the all-knowing prophet known as Charles Manson. Gregg also lobbied NBC to shoot a documentary film about the Manson Family's 'hippie commune' and the network was for a time quite interested in the project. Along with Dennis Wilson, Jakobson also arranged for Charlie to record at an unnamed studio in Santa Monica; that session was also attended by Terry Melcher, Bobby Beausoleil and several of the Manson girls.

Lest anyone think otherwise, by the way, the Manson Family certainly had no shortage of talented musicians. Convicted murderer Charles Manson, of course, was widely viewed by his contemporaries in the canyon as a talented singer/songwriter/guitarist. So too was Bobby Beausoleil, who had jammed with Dennis Wilson, played rhythm guitar for the pre-Love lineup known as the Grass Roots, knew Frank Zappa and had visited the Log Cabin, and later composed and recorded the film score for Kenneth Anger's *Lucifer Rising*. Convicted murderer Patricia Krenwinkle was an accomplished guitarist and songwriter. Convicted murderer Steve "Clem" Grogan was a talented musician as well; he later played in the prison band assembled by Beausoleil to record the *Lucifer Rising* soundtrack. In addition, Family members Brooks Poston and Paul Watkins were accomplished musicians, and Catherine "Gypsy" Share was a virtuoso violin player as well as being a singer and occasional actress (see, for example, *Ramrodder*, costarring Bobby Beausoleil and filmed partially at—where else?—Spahn Movie Ranch).

Catherine Share is notable in other ways as well, including her unparalleled feat of raising the bar so high on parental suicides that no one else, even in Laurel Canyon, is likely to be able to clear it. Orphaned as a child when *both* biological parents purportedly committed suicide, Gypsy was adopted by a psychologist and his wife. Her adoptive mother then allegedly committed suicide as well, leaving her to be raised by her adoptive father. Share is also notable for being the oldest of Charlie's girls, nearly twenty-seven at the time of the murders (most of the others were under twenty-one, and many, including Dean Moorehouse's daughter, Ruth Ann "Ouisch" Moorehouse, were minors). Gypsy lived with Bobby Beausoleil before meeting and living with Manson, and she seemed to serve as a recruiter for both of them.

According to Ed Sanders, Gypsy Share also "arranged for Paul Rothchild, the producer of the Doors, to hear the family music." It seems as though just about everyone had an opportunity to hear the Family's music. Some of it was recorded in Beach Boy Brian Wilson's state-of-the-art home recording studio. Some was recorded by Terry Melcher and Gregg Jakobson at Spahn Ranch using a mobile recording studio. Some was recorded in Santa Monica. By some reports, some was recorded by a major Hollywood studio. Other recordings were likely made as well, though nobody really likes to talk about such things. Gregg Jakobson recorded many of his marathon conversations with Charlie, but as with the demo recordings made by Dennis Wilson, everyone likes to pretend that such recordings were lost or destroyed or never existed.

The Family was filmed at Spahn Ranch by Melcher as well. Family members also shot an extensive amount of film making 'home movies,' which some witnesses have claimed included Family orgies and ritualized snuff films. A vast amount of NBC camera equipment and film was found to be in the possession of Charlie's motley crew, all of which was claimed to be stolen. It seems likely, however, given the network's known involvement with the Family, that the equipment was provided to them so that they could film their exploits.

When not hanging out with Charlie and Tex and Bobby, Terry Melcher also found time to produce the records that first catapulted the Byrds to fame: Mr. Tambourine Man and Turn! Turn! Turn! The first, recorded in January 1965 and released a few months later, was the record that announced to the world the arrival of a new breed of music. Those early hits were created, simply enough, by borrowing from the songbooks of folk legends Bob Dylan and Pete Seeger and then playing those songs on amplified equipment. Dylan himself followed suit not long after, at the Newport Folk Festival in July 1965, much to the consternation of the gathered crowd of folkies.

In *Hotel California*, Barney Hoskyns writes that the Byrds were, from the very outset, "conceived as an electric rock'n'roll group." What Hoskyns doesn't really clarify though is who exactly it was that initially conceived of this hugely influential band in those terms. Surely it wasn't the band members themselves who decided that they were going to pioneer a new musical genre, since they probably had their hands full with just learning to play their instruments. It would probably be slightly more accurate to say that the Byrds appear to have been initially conceived as an electric *folk-rock* group. By July of 1966, however, when the band released its third album, featuring the Gene Clark-penned Eight Miles High, it had morphed into something different and by doing so helped pioneer another genre of music: psychedelic rock. With the later addition of Gram Parsons and the growing influence of Chris Hillman, the Byrds would next morph into a country-rock band, thus helping to spawn that genre of music as well.

According to rock'n'roll legend, the first two Byrds to get together were James Joseph McGuinn III and Harold Eugene Clark. McGuinn hailed from Chicago, the son of best-selling authors James and Dorothy McGuinn. Considered a very talented guitarist, Jim had played with Bobby Darin, the Limeliters, and the Chad Mitchell Trio. In 1962, he left the Chad Mitchell Trio and worked for a time in New York City as a studio musician—before hearing the call that so many others seemed to hear and making his way to Los Angeles. Once there, he wasted no time hooking up with Gene Clark.

Clark had been born in Tipton, Missouri, the second-oldest in a family of thirteen siblings. An undeniably talented songwriter and vocalist, Clark cut his first record with a local rock'n'roll combo when he was just thirteen years old. He later joined the New Christy Minstrels, a vocal ensemble known during his tenure primarily for the hit song Green, Green. Like so many others, however, Gene soon found himself packing his bags for—where else?—Los Angeles, where he met up with the recently-arrived Jim McGuinn. The newly formed folk duo soon added a third voice to the mix—our old friend David Crosby, who had formerly been a vocalist with Les Baxter's Balladeers.

Crosby brought in manager Jim Dickson, with whom he had done some solo sessions in 1963. The year before that, Dickson had produced a self-titled album for a band known as the Hillmen, featuring a young mandolin player out of San Diego named Chris Hillman. Hillman had cut his first album, with a band known as the Scottsville Squirrel Barkers, while still in high school. He was a highly regarded young bluegrass musician and was generally considered to be a virtuoso mandolin player, which I guess is why Jim Dickson cast him to play the part of the bass player in the world's first folk-rock band. And as we already know, Hillman lucked out in securing luxurious living accommodations right in the heart of what was to become the music community's epicenter, so he was all set to become a rock star.

Raised on a ranch in San Diego, Hillman had traveled alone to Berkeley when he was just fifteen, ostensibly to take private mandolin lessons. At about that same time, his father had—wait for it—reportedly committed suicide. Those two closely aligned events would, I guess, have had a profound impact on the young musician.

Hillman would ultimately become a skilled bass player and a major figure in the Laurel Canyon-spawned country-rock movement. Like many others of that bent, Hillman had been a huge fan of Spade Cooley during his formative years and he later cited Cooley as a major influence on his own musical direction. Most readers are probably not familiar with the story of the "King of Western Swing," which is kind of a shame because as stories go, it's a pretty good one, so let's digress here briefly and meet the man who was frequently cited as one of the forefathers of country-rock, and whom Brian Wilson has cited as a major influence as well.

Throughout the 1940s and 1950s, Donnell Clyde "Spade" Cooley was a popular local musician and bandleader. His weekly shows at the Redondo Beach Pier could draw as many as 10,000 appreciative fans, few of whom knew of his alcoholism, violent temper, or prior arrest for attempted rape. His popularity ultimately landed him his own local television show, *The Spade Cooley Hour*. His career, however, came to an abrupt end on April 3, 1961, when he tortured and murdered his young wife, Ella Mae Cooley, while forcing his fourteen-year-old daughter to watch in horror.

According to court transcripts, Ella Mae had been spending a considerable amount of time in the company of two men, identified as Luther

Jackson and Bud Davenport, both of whom worked in the sprawling, CIA-infested medical research facility at UCLA. On the day of her death, Ella Mae had made the rather bold decision to inform Spade that the two men had initiated her into a 'free love' cult and that she had decided to give up her family and all her possessions to join the group, which was in the process of buying land near the ocean to build and operate a private compound.

Spade Cooley's response to his wife's declaration was to brutally beat, stomp and strangle her to death, but only after repeatedly burning her with a lit cigarette. All of this was witnessed by daughter Melody, who had been told by her father that "now you're going to watch me kill this whore." After doing just that, Spade then asked his daughter if she thought that Ella Mae was really dead, adding, "Well, let's see if she is." He then proceeded to burn her lifeless body repeatedly with another lit cigarette, until he apparently was satisfied that she was indeed dead.

Unlike so many other celebrity homicide suspects, Cooley was convicted of first-degree murder and sentenced to serve a life sentence. He was sent to the rather notorious Vacaville facility where he served eight years before being offered early parole. Just before his scheduled release, he arranged a November 23, 1969, comeback concert in Oakland for which his captors had agreed to release him on a three-day pass. The concert was reportedly a huge success and it looked as though Cooley's star was about to shine once again upon his pending release from prison. But that's not quite how this story ends; instead, Cooley walked back to his dressing room right after the show and promptly dropped dead, thus ending the saga of Spade Cooley and allowing us to return to where we left off... after, that is, taking one more quick detour here to note that not long after Spade Cooley was scheduled for release, another peripheral character in this story decided that it might be a good idea to kill his wife as well. "Humble" Harve Miller was a popular DJ on LA's number one pop music station during that era, KHJ on the AM dial. During the latter half of the 1960s, Miller was yet another of the players who helped launch the careers of the Laurel Canyon bands, by being the first to get their new singles on the radio. But then he, like Cooley, killed his wife and was sent to prison. Also like Cooley, he was granted early release. But unlike Spade, Miller successfully resumed his career. And now, at long last, we can return to the Byrds.

By mid-1964, the nucleus of what would become the band had formed with the bonding of McGuinn and Clark. Between the two of them, they would provide the band with its signature twelve-string guitar sound, its two lead vocalists, and (in the early years, at least) its best songwriters. Then along came David Crosby, who added little more than harmony vocals, at least on the first two albums, but who seems to have largely hijacked the band with the help of manager Jim Dickson, who added fake bass player (but real musician) Chris Hillman. Crosby then rounded out the band by adding fake drummer Michael Clarke.

Clarke had been born Michael Dick in Spokane, Washington. At seventeen, Dick ran away from home and hitchhiked to the land of enchantment known as California, apparently becoming Michael Clarke along the way. The year was 1963. According to rock history as told by David Crosby, Clarke and Crosby met in Big Sur, which coincidentally happens to be the location of the notorious Esalen Institute (where CSNY would play some years later). A year later, the vagrant teenager with no drumming experience would find himself cast to play the role of the drummer in the band designed to be America's answer to the Beatles. According to Crosby, Clarke's first LA address was the home of Terry Melcher.

The band, now complete, first dubbed themselves the Jet Set and then the Beefeaters, even recording a less-than-memorable single under the latter moniker, before finally settling on the Byrds. Before the end of 1964, Jim Dickson had signed the band to a deal with Columbia Records. As Barney Hoskyns recounts in *Waiting for the Sun*, "The obvious ineptitude of Michael Clarke and shakiness of most of the others was still a problem when Jim Dickson got the band signed to Columbia in November." Columbia assigned the new band to staff producer Terry Melcher.

That assignment, it would seem, was a rather fortuitous one given that the fledgling band's rehearsal space just happened to be in the very same basement studio that Melcher snuck off to while in high school. Just two months after signing with Columbia, the band, or rather its surrogates, were already in the studio recording Mr. Tambourine Man, at the insistence of Jim Dickson. Despite the objections of various band members, Dickson reportedly pushed hard for the song to be the band's first single. On March 26, 1965, just two months after pretending to lay down the instrumental tracks for *Mr. Tambourine Man*, the Byrds played their first real live show, as the first act at the refurbished and reopened Ciro's nightclub.

I wasn't there so I can't say for sure, but I'm going to go out on a limb here and guess that a band whose entire rhythm section was just learning to play their instruments probably did not put on a very compelling performance. The Byrds apparently played one other live show before the Ciro's opening, though the nature of that show appears to be in dispute (or perhaps there were two previous shows). According to Jim Dickson, "The Byrds first public gig was booked by Lenny Bruce's mother, Sally Marr. She got them a job at Los Angeles City College, noon assembly, for a half hour." According to Carl Franzoni and various others, however, it was Vito Paulekas who booked the Byrds' first live show, at a rented hall on Melrose Avenue just a day or two before the show at Ciro's.

In any event, *Mr. Tambourine Man* was released about a month after the band had its big public debut at Ciro's, and the LA music scene would never be the same again. Before long, clubs big and small were popping up all along the fabled Sunset Strip and bands were spilling out of Laurel Canyon to play them. As Terry Melcher recalled, "kids came from everywhere. It just happened. One day you couldn't drive anymore. It was, like, overnight—you couldn't drive on the Strip."

That would soon change. By the summer of 1967, the mythical Summer of Love, the club scene on the Strip was quickly dying. It had been killed, deliberately or not, by some of the key players who had created it: Terry Melcher, producer of the scene's first band; Lou Adler, business partner of club owner Elmer Valentine; and John Phillips, leader of the Mamas and the Papas. It was the show they produced, you see, the fabled Monterey Pop Festival held on June 16–18, 1967, that killed the Sunset Strip scene. The bands that had filled the clubs became, literally overnight, too big to play such intimate venues. Over the course of the next decade, Laurel Canyon bands quickly moved from clubs to concert halls to massive sports arenas. But here we are, I suppose, getting ahead of ourselves.

As for the Byrds, they carried on for a good many years, albeit with numerous personnel changes. First out was the man who many feel was the most talented member of the group, Gene Clark, who dropped out in March of 1966, just one year after the band had first taken the stage at Ciro's. Clark was also the first original Byrd to pass away, on May 24, 1991, at just forty-six years of age, reportedly due to a bleeding ulcer. Two-and-a-half-years later, on December 19, 1993, Michael Clarke died as well when his liver failed. Both deaths were attributed to chronic alcoholism.

Jim McGuinn, who remained a Byrd through numerous band line-ups, joined the Subud religious sect in 1965. Two years later, upon the advice of the cult's founder, he changed his name to Roger. A decade later, he became a born-again Christian. In a similar vein, Chris Hillman became an Evangelical Christian in the 1980s, but then later switched to the Greek Orthodox faith. Hillman played in various Byrds lineups, with Gram Parsons' Flying Burrito Brothers, and in David Geffen's failed attempt at creating a second supergroup, one known as Souther, Hillman, Furay. David Crosby, of course, left the Byrds and became one-third of David Geffen's first supergroup, Crosby, Stills & Nash. These days he primarily spends his time inseminating lesbians and occasionally reuniting with former bandmates.

Jim Dickson and Terry Melcher continued to work with some of the Byrds, particularly Gram Parsons and Chris Hillman. Melcher formed a particularly close bond with fellow 'trust-fund kid' Parsons, as did Melcher's sometime sidekick, John Phillips. Both Melcher and Phillips, of course, had ties to Charles Manson (Melcher raved about him to Ned Doheny), whose former prison buddy, Phil Kaufman, was, as already noted, Parsons' road manager. In unrelated news, Bill Siddons, the Doors' road manager, was once a paramour of Mansonite Lynette "Squeaky" Fromme.

The Family's fingerprints, it appears, can be found in nearly every nook and cranny of the Laurel Canyon scene.

14

THE GREAT SERENDIPITY
BUFFALO SPRINGFIELD

"This is going to break your heart, but much of the music you heard in the sixties and early seventies wasn't recorded by the people you saw on the album covers. It was done by me and the musicians you see on these walls... Many of these kids didn't have the chops and were little more than garage bands... At concerts, people hear with their eyes. Teens cut groups slack in concert, but not when they bought their records." Hal Blaine, longtime drummer for the Wrecking Crew, quoted in the Wall Street Journal on March 23, 2011

THE BYRDS WERE THE VERY FIRST FOLK-ROCK BAND TO TAKE FLIGHT OUT OF Laurel Canyon, and they were also the one that achieved the greatest fame, but to many discerning ears, the Sunset Strip's other folk-rock powerhouse, Buffalo Springfield, was the more talented band.

In the literature chronicling the 1960s music scene, few stories have been repeated more frequently than the legend surrounding the formation of what would later be regarded as perhaps the first 'supergroup.' All such accounts unquestioningly retell the story as though it were the gospel truth, seemingly oblivious to the improbability of virtually every aspect of the legend. And curiously, virtually every version of the story contains some form of the word "serendipity," as though everyone has been copying off the same kid's homework.

As the story goes, Stephen Stills and Richie Furay, both formerly of the Au Go-Go Singers, had recently transplanted themselves to Los Angeles after the breakup of the manufactured folkie group. Stills had been the first to relocate, in August of 1965. Furay flew out to join him in February 1966, after spending a little time working at defense contractor Pratt & Whitney, and the two set their sights on putting together a folk-rock band.

Meanwhile, up in Toronto, Neil Young and Bruce Palmer were playing in a band known as the Mynah Birds—a band fronted by an AWOL Navy man known as Ricky James Matthews, who would later morph into funkmeister/torturer/rapist Rick James, but whose real name was James Ambrose Johnson, Jr. The Mynah Birds broke up in March of 1965, just after authorities came calling on Matthews and tossed him in the Brooklyn Brig. In search of a new band, Young made the curious decision to head out to LA, for no better reason than that he had what Palmer described as "a hunch, a feeling that... Stephen Stills was in LA."

Of course, Young had no clue if Stills was in fact there, nor did he know anyone else in LA And you would think that he would have realized that, even if Stills was there, there was virtually no chance of finding some random person in a city of millions, especially when the person doing the searching had no idea how to get around the city. But no matter. Neil had a calling, so he jumped into an old hearse, of all things, recruited Palmer to ride shotgun, and the two set off on the lengthy trek to Los Angeles.

They arrived, the legend tells us, on April 1, 1966—April Fool's Day, appropriately enough—and began the search for Stills. Several days of searching yielded no results, however, and on the afternoon of April 6, the frustrated pair decided to head off to San Francisco in the hopes that maybe they would have better luck finding Stephen there. Perhaps they were going to go on a tour of all the big cities in America, in the hopes that somewhere along the way they might find Stephen Stills.

But as fate would have it, just as they were about to head out of town, Stephen Stills *found them*. As Barney Hoskyns tells the story in *Hotel California*, "Early in April 1966, Stills and Richie Furay were stuck in a Sunset Strip traffic jam in Barry Friedman's Bentley. As they sat in the car, Stephen spotted a 1953 Pontiac hearse with Ontario plates on the other side of the street. 'I'll be damned if that ain't Neil Young,' Stills said. Friedman executed an illegal U-turn and pulled up behind the hearse. One of rock's great serendipities had just occurred. Young, a lanky Canadian, had just driven all the way from Detroit in the company of bassist Bruce Palmer. They'd caught the bug that was drawing hundreds of other pop wannabes to the West Coast."

The pair had actually driven out from Toronto, not Detroit, and the hearse was a 1959 model by most accounts, and Stills and Furay were in a van rather than a Bentley, but such inconsistencies are typical of all Hollywood legends. In any event, John Einarson, in *For What It's Worth*, supplies a somewhat longer and more hyperbole-filled version of the legend: "What transpired next is no longer considered simply a chance encounter. Transcending mere fact, the events of the next few minutes have taken on mythic proportions to become, in the annals of popular culture, legendary. More than pure luck, coincidence or serendipity, at that very moment the planets aligned, stars crossed, everyone's karma turned positive, divine intervention interceded, the hand of fate revealed itself—whatever you subscribe to in order to explain the unexplained. Though each of the five participants in that moment in time tell it slightly differently, the fact remains that the occupants of the white van, individually or collectively, depending on who's retelling it, noticed the black hearse with the foreign plate heading the other direction. Once the light of recognition came on, the van hastily pulled an illegal, and likely difficult in rush hour, U-turn, maneuvering its way through the line of northbound cars, horn honking frantically all the while, to pull up behind the hearse. One of the passengers leapt out, ran up and pounded on the driver's side window of the strange vehicle, yelling to the startled travelers inside who had taken no notice of the blaring car horn directly behind them. 'Hey Neil, it's me, Steve Stills! Pull over, man!' The drivers of the two vehicles managed to find curb space or a vacant store parking lot, again depending on whose version is being related, and the five piled out to embrace and introduce one another… On April 6, 1966, in that late afternoon line of traffic, the course of popular music was altered forever."

Anyone who actually lives and drives in LA likely knows that "difficult" is not really the word to describe the feasibility of making an impromptu U-turn in rush hour traffic on the Sunset Strip; the correct word would be "impossible," which is the same word that accurately describes the likelihood of that van "maneuvering its way through the line of northbound cars," or of it finding "curb space" on Sunset Boulevard. But let's just play along and assume that Neil Young and Stephen Stills, each of whom, for some reason, had been dreaming about forming a band with the other, had a random, chance encounter on Sunset Boulevard. In that brief moment in time, a band was formed—or at least four-fifths of a band.

Retiring to the home of Barry Friedman, who would later legally change his name to Frazier Mohawk, the quartet of musicians quickly decided that their newly formed band would only perform original material, though they didn't yet actually have any original material. They did though have three singer/songwriter/guitarists on board (Furay, Young and Stills), along with a bass player (Bruce Palmer), so all that was needed was a drummer. Three days later, on April 9, 1966, they acquired one, in the form of Dewey Martin, formerly with the Dillards.

The Dillards, in another awesome bit of serendipity, had just decided to go back to their acoustic bluegrass roots, so they no longer needed a drummer. They also decided that they had no further need for a whole bunch of new electric instruments and stacks of amplifiers, so Dewey, according to legend, brought all of that with him. Because the Dillards, you know, were just going to throw it all away anyway. So now, with the stars all properly aligned, the band was not only complete but they each had shiny new electric instruments to play—and it all had magically come together in just seventy-two hours!

There was still much work to be done, of course. For one thing, they all had to familiarize themselves with those shiny new electric instruments. And they all had to learn to play together as a band. And they had to build up a repertoire of original songs. And they had to rehearse and polish those songs. But not to worry; they had, as we'll see, at least a couple of hours to work on each of those things.

Unlike the Byrds, the members of the Buffalo Springfield were, by all accounts, talented musicians from the outset. Stills and Young were both skilled lead guitarists and songwriters, though Young's vocals were, to be sure, an acquired taste. Furay was an accomplished rhythm guitarist and songwriter, as well as being the group's best lead vocalist. Bruce Palmer was a respected bass player who, shockingly, actually had experience playing the instrument. And Dewey Martin, several years older than the rest of the crew, had drummed for such legendary artists as the Everly Brothers, Charlie Rich, Roy Orbison, Patsy Cline, and Carl Perkins.

None of that, however, explains the absurdly meteoric rise of Buffalo Springfield. On April 11, 1966, just five days after the quartet had purportedly first met and *just two days* after they had added a drummer and acquired instruments, the band played its first club date at one of Hollywood's most prestigious venues, the Troubadour. Four days later, on April 15, they played the first of six dates around the southland opening for the Byrds, the hottest band on the Strip. That mini-tour was followed almost immediately by a six-week stand at the hottest club in town, the Whisky-a-Go-Go. That gig wrapped up on June 20, 1966.

A month later, on July 25, the band landed the opening slot on the most anticipated concert of the year—the Rolling Stones show at the Hollywood Bowl, sponsored by local radio station KHJ. The station, by the way, had just been launched the previous year, in May of 1965, just a few weeks after the Byrds had taken the world by storm with the release of *Mr. Tambourine Man* and sparked a folk-rock revolution. Just as new clubs magically appeared along the Sunset Strip in anticipation of the about-to-explode music scene, so too did a radio station magically appear to promote those new clubs and the artists filling them. Such things tend to happen, as we know, rather, uhmm, serendipitously.

Three days after the Stones concert at the Bowl, Buffalo Springfield released its first single, the Neil Young-penned Nowadays Clancy Can't Even Sing, which failed to connect with the record-buying public. Several months later though, the band would release what was to be its only hit single and what would become the most recognizable 'protest' song of the 1960s.

Buffalo Springfield had signed with Atlantic Records, which had been founded in 1947 by Ahmet Ertegun and dentist/investor Herb Abramson. Born in Istanbul, Turkey in 1923, the year the Turk Republic was established, Ahmet was both the son and the grandson of career diplomats/civil servants. His father had been named the first Turkish representative to the League of Nations in 1925 and thereafter served as the Turk Republic's ambassador to Switzerland, France and England. In 1935, he was named the first Turkish ambassador to the United States and he promptly relocated the family to Washington, DC.

From about the age of twelve, Ahmet grew up along DC's Embassy Row, attending elite private schools with the sons and daughters of senators, congressmen, and intelligence operatives. In 1947, three years after his father died, Ertegun founded Atlantic Records. At first the label was home to jazz and R&B artists, including Ray Charles, the company's first big star. In the late 1950s, Ertegun took on his first assistant—a guy by the name of Phil Spector. Atlantic soon shifted focus and rock luminaries like Eric Clapton, Led Zeppelin and the Rolling Stones would later join the label's stable of talent.

Curiously enough, Columbia Records, the corporate entity that signed the Byrds, was also born in the nation's capitol. The name is derived from the District of Columbia, where the label was founded and first headquartered some 125 years ago. It would appear then that the two record labels that signed and launched Laurel Canyon's first two folk-rock bands were not only major record labels but also happened to be corporate entities that had deep ties to the nation's center of power. With Laurel Canyon's other bands as well, it was the major record labels, not upstart independents, that signed the new artists. It was the major labels that provided them with instruments and amplifiers. It was the major labels that provided them with studio time and session musicians. It was the major labels that recorded, mixed and arranged their albums. And it was the major labels that released and then heavily promoted those albums.

As Unterberger duly notes in his expansive, two-volume review of the folk-rock movement, "much folk-rock was recorded and issued by huge corporations, and broadcast over radio and television stations owned for the most part by the same or similar pillars of the establishment." The corporate titans of all three branches of the mainstream media—print, radio and television—did their part to help out the titans of the record industry. Unterberger notes that, "AM radio (and sometimes primetime network television) would act as a primary conduit for this countercultural expression." Conservative, corporate-controlled AM stations across the country almost immediately began giving serious airplay to the new sounds coming out of Southern California, and network television gave the rising stars unprecedented coverage and exposure: "primetime variety hours were much more likely to showcase rock acts than they would be in subsequent decades. New releases by the Byrds were often accompanied by large ads in trade magazines that simultaneously plugged the records and upcoming TV appearances."

The boys in Buffalo Springfield, for example, managed to find themselves appearing as guests on an impressive array of network television shows, including *American Bandstand, The Smothers Brothers Show, Shebang!, The Della Reese Show, The Go Show, The Andy Williams Show, Hollywood Palace, Where the Action Is,* Joey Bishop's late night show, and a local program known as *Boss City*. They also made guest appearances, curiously enough, on primetime hits like *Mannix* and *The Girl From U.N.C.L.E.*

The print media did its part as well to raise awareness of the new music/countercultural scene. In September 1965, the nation's premier newsweeklies, *Time* and *Newsweek*, "ran virtually simultaneous stories on the folk-rock craze," just months after the first folk-rock release had climbed to the top of the charts. The country's biggest daily newspapers chimed in as well, providing an inordinate amount of coverage of the emerging scene. By the end of 1967, the movement had its very own publication, *Rolling Stone*. Initially designed to look as though it were a product of the underground press, it was, without question, very much a corporate mouthpiece. Another avenue of the print media provided the scene with considerable exposure as well; as Einarson notes, many of the Laurel Canyon stars, particularly members of Buffalo Springfield and the Monkees, were "the darlings of the California teen magazines," including *Teenset*, *Teen Screen*, and *Tiger Beat*.

In 1964, just months before the birth of folk-rock, the *LA Free Press*, widely believed to be the first underground newspaper of the 1960s, was launched from offices at the corner of Sunset and Crescent Heights, at the very mouth of Laurel Canyon. The publication, which quickly became the voice of the canyon, was initially financed by comedian Steve Allen. In the late 1970s, it was purchased and killed off by pornographer Larry Flynt.

As the story is usually told, the 1960s countercultural movement posed a rather serious threat to the status quo. But if that were truly the case, then why was it the "pillars of the establishment," to use

Unterberger's words, that initially launched the movement? Why was it 'the man' that signed and recorded these artists? And that heavily promoted them on the radio, on television, and in print? And that set them up with their very own radio station and their very own monthly magazine?

It could be argued, I suppose, that this was simply a case of corporate America doing what it does best: making a profit off of anything and everything. Blinded by greed, a devil's advocate might say, the corporate titans inadvertently created a monster. The question that is begged by that explanation, however, is why, after it had become abundantly clear that a monster had allegedly been created, was nothing done to stop the growth of that monster? Why, for example, did the state not utilize its law enforcement and criminal justice powers to silence some of the most prominent countercultural voices?

It's not as if it would have required resorting to heavy-handed measures. Since many of the Laurel Canyon stars were openly using, dealing, or at least advocating the use of illegal substances, they were practically begging for the powers-that-be to take action. And yet that never happened. As just one example, three members of Buffalo Springfield (Neil Young, Richie Furay and Jim Messina, along with a dozen others, including Eric Clapton) were arrested in a drug bust at a Topanga Canyon home only to then walk away as if nothing had happened. Why wasn't this case, and so many others like it, aggressively prosecuted?

David Crosby has candidly acknowledged that "the DEA could have popped me for interstate transport of dope or dealing lots of times and never did." John Phillips, busted for wholesale trafficking of pharmaceuticals, was, by his own account, "looking at forty-five years and got thirty days." He began serving his sentence on April 20, appropriately enough, and served just twenty-four days in a minimum security prison that offered "residents" such activities as "basketball, aerobics, softball, tennis, archery, and golf," and that featured a "delicious kosher kitchen, an elaborate salad bar, and a tasty brunch on Sundays."

Time and time again, 'the man' was handed golden opportunities to crack down on Laurel Canyon's most prominent voices, and time and time again those 'dangerous dissidents' were handled with kid gloves. Indeed, the LAPD appears to have adopted a hands-off policy towards the Laurel Canyon crowd. As musician-turned-photographer Henry Diltz acknowledged to writer Harvey Kubernik, "There was not a presence of the heat in Laurel Canyon." Radio personality Elliot Mintz agreed, noting that he couldn't "recall a law enforcement presence in Laurel Canyon." Given the unique geography of the canyon community, it would have been very easy for the police to cut off access and conduct regular sweeps, but nothing like that ever happened. Instead, police seem to have stayed out of the canyon entirely.

The state had another powerful tool at its disposal to silence young critics—involuntary military service. There was, after all, a war going on and hundreds of thousands of draft-age young men across the country were being fed into the war machine. As Richie Unterberger noted in *Turn! Turn! Turn!*, "Most folk rockers (if they were male), like their audience, were of draft age." But curiously enough, "Very, very few had their careers interrupted by the draft." Actually, Unterberger appears to have been playing it safe with the "very, very few" wording since the reality is that *none* of the folks living the rock'n'roll life in the canyons, whether folk rockers, country rockers or psychedelic rockers, had their careers interrupted by the Vietnam War.

The literature is littered with mentions of various rock stars receiving their draft notices, but those mentions are invariably followed by amusing anecdotes about how said people fooled the draft board by pretending to be gay, or pretending to be crazy, or pretending to be otherwise unfit for service. Of course, if it had really been that easy to pull the wool over the draft board's eyes, then Uncle Sam probably wouldn't have been able to come up with all those bodies to send over to Vietnam. The reality is that thousands of young men across the country tried those very same tricks, but they only ever seemed to work for the Laurel Canyon crowd.

How is it possible that not one of the musical icons of the Woodstock generation, almost all of them draft age males, was shipped off to slog through the rice paddies of Vietnam? Should we just consider that to be another one of those great serendipities? Was it mere luck that kept all the Laurel Canyon stars out of jail and out of the military during the turbulent decade that was the 1960s? Not likely. The reality is that 'The Establishment,' as it was known in those days, had the power to prevent the musical icons of the 1960s from ever becoming the megastars that they became. The state, working hand-in-hand with corporate America, could quite easily have prevented the entire countercultural movement from ever getting off the ground—because then, as now, the state controlled the channels of communication.

A real grass-roots cultural revolution would probably have involved a bunch of starving musicians barely scratching out a living playing tiny coffee shops in the hopes of maybe someday landing a record deal with some tiny, independent label, and then, just maybe, if they got really lucky, getting a little airplay on some obscure college radio stations. But that's not how the sixties folk-rock 'revolution' played out. Not by any stretch of the imagination.

And now, without further adieu, let's circle back around and take a look at the Buffalo Springfield story from the beginning, starting from January 3, 1945, when Stephen Arthur Stills was born to William and Talitha Stills. As John Einarson recounts in *For What It's Worth*, Stephen's roots were "firmly planted in Southern soil. His family traces its history back to the plantations of the rural antebellum South. After the Union armies laid waste to much of the Southern farm economy, the family relocated to Illinois."

Einarson describes William Stills as "somewhat of a soldier of fortune, an engineer, builder, and dreamer who frequently uprooted the family to follow his dreams and schemes." That is, I suppose, as good a definition as any for what he actually appears to have been: a military intelligence operative who was frequently on assignment in various hotspots in Central America. Stephen's childhood was spent in Illinois, Texas, Louisiana, Florida, and various parts of Central America, including Costa Rica, El Salvador and the Panama Canal Zone.

At a fairly young age, Stills attended the Admiral Farragut Military Academy in St. Petersburg, Florida. In later years, his authoritarian manner and military bearing would earn him the nickname "the Sarge." He joined his first band, the Radars, as a drummer. In his next band, the Continentals, he played guitar alongside another young guitarist named Don Felder, who would later turn up in Laurel Canyon as a member of the Eagles—because, as we have seen repeatedly, all roads seemed to lead to Laurel Canyon.

According to Einarson, "An unfortunate incident with the administration at his Tampa Bay high school resulted in Stephen's dismissal in 1961, after which he joined his wayward family then settled in Costa

Rica." What that "unfortunate incident" may have been, and why he had been separated from his family at a fairly young age, remains a mystery. In any event, Stephen's next few years are rather murky. Some reports have him graduating from a high school in the Panama Canal Zone. Others have him shuffling back and forth between Florida and Central America. Stills himself has, as previously noted, at times claimed that he served a stint in Vietnam. Whatever the case, circa March of 1964, he surfaced in New Orleans with his sights set on a career in music.

By the summer of 1964, he had drifted to New York's Greenwich Village, where he became fast friends with a young folk singer/songwriter by the name of Peter Torkelson, who, like so many others in this story, hailed from Washington, DC. The two played together briefly as a duo before Torkelson "migrated to Connecticut then Venezuela," which was, I suppose, a typical migratory route for folkies in those days. Torkelson would soon enough make his way to Laurel Canyon, where he would become Monkee Peter Tork. Stills would also audition for the show, but his bad teeth and thinning hair would render him unfit for a leading role on primetime TV.

In July 1964, Stills found work as one of the nine members of the Au Go-Go Singers, the newly formed house band for New York's famed Café Au Go-Go. Singing alongside of Stills was a young folkie named Richie Furay, the son of a pharmacist who had run a family drugstore in Yellow Springs, Ohio. By November 1964, the Au Go-Go Singers already had an album out. But trouble soon arose, due primarily to the fact that the band was under contract to Morris Levy, a known organized crime figure who would soon be indicted on an array of criminal charges. The band soon broke up and Furay headed off to Connecticut where a cousin got him a job at Pratt & Whitney. While working there, he took a little time off to audition for a slot in the Chad Mitchell Trio, but he was beat out by a military brat from Roswell named John Deutschendorf.

Stephen Stills, meanwhile, hung out in New York for a while longer before heeding the call of the Pied Piper and heading out to LA in August of 1965. That was the summer, according to Einarson, that "the epicenter of American rock'n'roll shifted coasts, Los Angeles replacing New York as the power base of the music industry." Richie Furay apparently soon found himself missing Stills but didn't know how to reach his former sidekick, so he sent a letter to Stills' dad in El Salvador, according to legend, and William Stills forwarded the message to Stephen.

What exactly the elder Stills was doing in El Salvador circa 1965/66 is unknown, but former State Department official William Blum provided some possible clues in his authoritative *Killing Hope*: "Throughout the 1960s, multifarious American experts occupied themselves in El Salvador by enlarging and refining the state's security and counter-insurgency apparatus: the police, the National Guard, the military, the communications and intelligence networks, the coordination with their counterparts in other Central American countries... as matters turned out, these were the forces and resources which were brought into action to impose widespread repression and wage war."

Meanwhile, up in Canada, Neil Young and Bruce Palmer were handling guitar and bass duties for the Mynah Birds. Neil Percival Kenneth Ragland Young was born on November 12, 1945, in Toronto to Scott Young, a sportswriter and novelist, and Edna "Rassy" Ragland, a Canadian television personality. Scott Young had spent a considerable amount of time abroad during WWII, first as a journalist and then as a member of the Royal Canadian Navy. Scott's father (Neil's grandfather), like Richie Furay's, had been a pharmacist/drug store owner.

As Einarson recounts, "Neil Young and Stephen Stills had more in common than music. Both had grown up in transient families, Neil's journalist father Scott uprooting his mother Edna 'Rassy,' Neil, and older brother Bob several times during Neil's first fifteen years." Novelists, it would appear, need to move around a lot. Just after his seventeenth birthday, Neil formed his first band, the Squires, and began playing local gigs. According to legend, it was during those early years that Young and Stills first briefly crossed paths up in Canada. That meeting would, a couple years later, allegedly send Young and Palmer—also born in Toronto, to a violinist father and artist mother—off on a cross-country quest to find Stephen Stills.

The Mynah Birds also at one time featured Nick St. Nicholas and Goldie McJohn, both of whom would become members of Steppenwolf. And all the intertwined characters in the preceding narrative—Stephen Stills, Richie Furay, Neil Young, Bruce Palmer, John Denver, Don Felder, Nick St. Nicholas, Goldy McJohn, and Peter Tork—would soon find themselves transplanted to Laurel Canyon.

15

BEYOND BUFFALO SPRINGFIELD AND THE MONKEES, TOO

"He was great, he was unreal—
really, really good."

"He had this kind of music that nobody else was doing. I thought he really had something crazy, something great. He was like a living poet." Neil Young, sharing his thoughts on Charles Manson

AT THE TIME OF THE LEGENDARY 'SERENDIPITOUS' ENCOUNTER ON SUNSET Boulevard, Stills was living at the home of Barry Friedman, a former circus clown, fire-eater, TV producer and freelance publicist. To say that his home was a bit odd would probably be an understatement. According to folkie Nurit Wilde, "It had a bathtub in the middle of the living room and a secret room behind the bathroom where people carried on liaisons." The massive bathtub sat right in front of the equally massive fireplace. As Friedman himself would later acknowledge, "This was a very strange house."

Not strange by canyon standards, perhaps, but strange nonetheless. Stranger homes can certainly be found, such as in the Holly Mont neighborhood near the base of nearby Beachwood Canyon. One such home is described in the book *Haunted Hollywood*. The house isn't actually haunted, of course, but it does contain some rather unusual features, as a past owner discovered: "the house's most startling feature—a secret passageway behind a built-in bookshelf he'd discovered during remodeling. It connected to a series of subterranean tunnels linking several houses on the hillside... While exploring the tunnel beneath his house, Grey found a makeshift grave. The headstone read 'Regina 1922.'"

In Friedman's not-quite-as-strange home, he had taken both Stills and Furay under his wing, providing them with a place to live and rehearse, doling out spending money, and introducing them to various music industry contacts. Friedman had been present when the fabled meeting took place, and it was to his home that the group adjourned after stopping on the Strip. It was also Friedman who found them their drummer, Walter Milton Dwayne Midkiff, otherwise known as Dewey Martin. Though Martin was, like Young and Palmer, Canadian, he had served a stint in the US Army.

Friedman was working for Byrds' manager Jim Dickson, who also managed the Dillards. It was Dickson who hooked Friedman up with Martin, and with a full slate of electric instruments, just as he had set the Byrds up with instruments and a bass player. Dickson and Friedman would soon become neighbors when Friedman moved from his odd house on Fountain Avenue to a home in, naturally enough, Laurel Canyon. That home, on 8524 Ridpath, would become a rather notorious party house. As Jackson Browne, who Friedman later took under his wing, recalled, "It was always open house at Paul Rothchild's and Barry Friedman's."

Barney Hoskyns writes in *Hotel California* that, "Friedman... orchestrated scenes of sexual and narcotic depravity that soon spun out of control." Among the regular visitors was "a gaggle of girls who mainly lived at Monkee Peter Tork's house"—which was also in Laurel Canyon, where gaggles of young girls were known to cluster around rock stars, sculptors, and mass murderers. Just a few doors down from Friedman, at 8504 Ridpath, lived Billy James, who also played a behind-the-scenes role in the success of the Byrds. A very young Jackson Browne, fresh from the "imposing Browne family home in the tony, old-money neighborhood of Highland Park," lived with James for a year, during which time Friedman worked to build a band around Browne. Toward that end, he recruited someone else who came from "old-money," a kid by the name of Ned Doheny.

Curiously, publicist/talent scout James had moved into his Laurel Canyon home in January 1964, a full year before the Byrds recorded the single that started a cultural revolution. Within no time at all, that home would be surrounded by the homes of numerous rock stars. Just another one of those amazing serendipities, I suppose.

Most members of Buffalo Springfield also took up residence in everyone's favorite secluded canyon. Richie Furay initially moved in with Mark Volman of the Turtles, who already had a place up on Lookout Mountain. After marrying in March of 1967, Furay got his own place on the main thoroughfare, Laurel Canyon Boulevard. Neil Young, ever the recluse, found himself what has been described as a "shack" at 8451 Utica Drive, which was far from actually being a shack. And Stills eventually moved into Peter Tork's home, which was also on Laurel Canyon Boulevard and which once belonged to actor/comedian Wally Cox, a onetime roommate and close friend of fellow canyonite Marlon Brando. It is unclear whether Palmer and Martin took up residence in the canyon.

The band would prove to have a difficult time keeping their lineup intact. Bruce Palmer had a habit of getting himself arrested on a regular basis, usually on drug charges. Some of those arrests led to deportations, since both he and Young were in the country illegally. He never seems to have had much trouble getting back into the country, however, and not too surprisingly, none of his crimes seem to have actually been prosecuted in any meaningful way. He did though go missing on a fairly regular basis. During the band's two-year run, Ken Koblun, Jim Fielder (formerly of Zappa's Mothers of Invention), and Jim Messina all filled in on bass for varying lengths of time. And Doug Hastings filled in for an occasionally absent Neil Young, who had a habit of quitting the band due to ego clashes with the Sarge.

The Springfield's second single, recorded and mixed on December 5, 1966, and written just a couple weeks earlier, was released locally in December 1966 and nationally in early January 1967. It was the group's only hit single and it is remembered today as the quintessential protest song of the 1960s. That song, of course, is For What It's Worth, the opening lines of which kicked off this book. As a protest song, however, it doesn't quite measure up. Despite what is commonly believed today, the song was not a commentary on anti-war demonstrations. Far from it. The event under consideration was the so-called Riot on the Sunset Strip, which involved about 1,000 kids who were demonstrating against the imposition of a curfew and the announcement that a popular club (Pandora's Box, at 8118 Sunset Boulevard) was slated to be closed.

Pandora's was a small coffee shop that featured poetry readings, folk music, and, with the birth of folk-rock, Laurel Canyon bands like Love and Buffalo Springfield. The crowds drawn to the club caused a bit of a problem though, as Pandora's sat on a traffic island at the intersection of Sunset and Crescent Heights (the gateway to Laurel Canyon) and overflow crowds would frequently spill out onto the boulevard, blocking traffic and endangering pedestrians. Even before the problems began, the building had been scheduled to be demolished as part of a planned road-widening project. Nevertheless, the announcement of its closing sparked a demonstration and on the night of November 12, 1966, 200 cops squared off against an estimated 1,000 kids. The LAPD, being the LAPD, began cracking heads and arresting everyone in sight. Protestors responded by throwing rocks, setting a car ablaze, and attempting to ignite a bus. Just one month later, a song commemorating the event was blaring from car radios across the city. Eight months after that, Pandora's was bulldozed.

Even if the song had been about anti-war protests, it still would be an odd choice for a protest song. Lyrics such as "Singing songs and carrying signs, mostly say hooray for our side," seem to largely dismiss the concerns of protestors. And the line "nobody's right if everybody's wrong" seems to suggest that protestors are no better than that which they are protesting against. Another curious irony about the song is that it was authored by Stephen Stills, an authoritarian, law-and-order kind of guy if ever there was one. Stills himself later heaped derision on the very notion of writing protest songs: "We didn't want to do another song like For What It's Worth. We didn't want to be a protest group. That's really a cop-out and I hate that. To sit there and say, 'I don't like this and I don't like that' is just stupid."

While For What It's Worth is now the best-remembered 'protest' song of the 1960s, the most successful one at the time was Barry McGuire's recording of P.F. Sloan's The Eve Of Destruction, which was also a curious choice for a protest song, for reasons best explained by Paul Jones of the band Manfred Mann: "I think that Barry McGuire must have been paid by the State Department. The Eve Of Destruction protests about nothing. It is simply a 'Thy Doom at Hand' song with no point."

It is probably safe to say that, to most music fans, there is a world of difference between a band like Buffalo Springfield and a band like the Monkees. That perception, however, is not necessarily accurate. As Unterberger has written, "there was not nearly as much gauche commercialism separating the Monkees and the bold Sunset Strip vanguard as is commonly believed. The Byrds, Buffalo Springfield, and Barry McGuire might have been landing hit records with social protest both gentle and incendiary, but they were tethered to a corporate media establishment in order to deliver those messages. On television's *Where the Action Is* you could see the Byrds lip-synching The Bells Of Rhymney in front of vacuous, grinning beach bunnies and muscle men cavorting on diving boards and plastic inner tubes. When Buffalo Springfield mimed to For What It's Worth on *The Smothers Brothers Show*, they suffered the insertion of a shot of Tom Smothers pointing a gun at the camera during the line 'there's a man with a gun over there,' to a burst of uproarious canned laughter."

The parallels between the bands actually ran far deeper than their mutual fondness for cheesy television appearances. Stephen Stills, it will be recalled, auditioned to be a Monkee (as did singer/songwriters Harry Nilsson and Paul Williams). Stills and Tork remained close friends and frequently jammed together at various Laurel Canyon gathering spots. Both Tork and fellow Monkee Mickey Dolenz at times joined the Springfield on stage at various local shows. And Stills, Young and Dewey Martin all sat in on Monkees recording sessions.

On July 2, 1967, guitarist extraordinaire Jimi Hendrix played the Whisky and reportedly blew the roof off the place (figuratively speaking, of course). Shortly thereafter, he moved into Peter Tork's house in Laurel Canyon. By the middle of July, Hendrix had joined the Monkees on tour as their opening act. He was dropped after just a few dates, however, due to the fact that Monkees fans couldn't quite wrap their heads around Jimi's brand of music. Throughout the remainder of the summer of 1967, Stephen and Dewey's Malibu home became the site of informal jam sessions involving Stephen Stills, Jimi Hendrix, Buddy Miles, David Crosby, and Peter Tork. All of them ultimately ended up living at Tork's Laurel Canyon spread, which, as previously mentioned, came complete with a gaggle of young groupies who spent an inordinate amount of time lounging around the pool in various states of undress.

Those jam sessions, both in Malibu and Laurel Canyon, were fueled by massive amounts of LSD. According to an anonymous insider interviewed by John Einarson, LSD guru Augustus Owsley Stanley, "used to give Bruce [Palmer] baggies full of acid, a thousand tabs of purple. Somehow he befriended Bruce so we [the band and various hangers-on] never lacked for LSD."

There was yet one more curious tie between the Monkees and the Springfield: while together in Chicago, unnamed members of both bands were allegedly immortalized by the notorious Cynthia Plaster Caster. Our old friend Frank Zappa soon took Cynthia under his wing and relocated her to LA to continue with her important work, just as he had taken the nubile young women who would become the GTOs under his wing. It could reasonably be argued that Zappa did more than anyone to create one of the more peculiar artifacts of the 1960s: the rock'n'roll supergroupie.

The aforementioned Ahmet Ertegun, by the way, played a key role in launching the career of Mr. Zappa, so much so that Frank named one of his sons after him. Meanwhile, Zappa's shady manager, Herb Cohen, "was involved with the [Buffalo Springfield] financially... Stephen knew Herbie from New York," according to Einarson. The Laurel Canyon crowd, to be sure, was a close-knit group—all the more so because so many of them seem to have known one another before arriving there.

Just a couple of weeks before Jimi's Whisky debut, he had dazzled the crowd at the Monterey Pop Festival, where the band currently under review, Buffalo Springfield, had also played—though by most accounts, not very well. Neil Young was taking one of his leaves-of-absence from the band and Doug Hastings filled in on second lead guitar. In addition, Stills brought his buddy David Crosby out on stage to join the band, which by many accounts was a rather poor decision on Stephen's part. According to bassist Bruce Palmer, "Crosby stunk to high heaven. He didn't know what he was doing... he was all ego. He came on for forty minutes and embarrassed us." Guitarist Hastings agreed, explaining that Crosby's "problem was that he couldn't play rhythm guitar very well, though he thought he could... that was one of the reasons why we sounded so bad at Monterey."

After spending the Summer of Love jamming with members of both Jimi Hendrix's Band of Gypsys and the Monkees, Buffalo Springfield hit the road in November 1967 as the opening act for the Beach Boys, a pairing nearly as odd as the Monkees and Jimi Hendrix. Bruce Palmer, whom we have already learned was not one to mince words, had this to say about the Beach Boys as a performing band: "They were real lousy musicians but they had terrific harmony and a name. They were a studio group. On stage it was like the Monkees. They would spend weeks and months in the studio with Brian Wilson perfecting harmonies and overdubs, but you put them on stage and they stunk."

That Beach Boys/Buffalo Springfield tour included a stop, curiously enough, at West Point Military Academy, which isn't really a regular stop on most rock tours. While on the road, the members of the Springfield formed a close bond with Dennis Wilson, a bond that would be built upon in April of 1968 when the Springfield again went out on tour with the Beach Boys. That tour was launched on April 5, almost two years to the day from the fabled meeting that allegedly forged the band. It was the last major tour the group would undertake. Just after returning from that 1968 tour, Dennis Wilson bonded with another local musician, a guy by the name of Charles Manson. When Dennis introduced his new friend Charlie to his buddies in Buffalo Springfield, Neil Young in particular was quite smitten.

On April 28, the band began playing its last series of local shows. On May 5, at the Long Beach Arena, Buffalo Springfield played together as a band for the last time. They had been scheduled to play two shows that day, the first at a venue in Torrance, but that earlier show never materialized. The band released its third and final album, *Last Time Around*, some three months later. As with albums released nearly simultaneously by the Byrds (*Sweetheart of the Rodeo*) and the International Submarine Band (*Safe at Home*), the Springfield's final album is often cited as being a pioneering effort in the creation of the country-rock genre.

That was just one curious shift that occurred in the local music scene. The folk-rock movement, as it turns out, didn't really last very long in its original incarnation. To the contrary, it quickly splintered into three distinct new genres: country-rock, psychedelic rock, and the 'introspective singer-songwriter' school of folk-rock most closely associated with former mental patient James Taylor. None of those musical genres, notably, posed much of a threat to the 'establishment.' The navel-gazers eschewed social concerns in favor of focusing on tales of personal anguish, the acid rockers largely preached the mantra of 'turn on, tune in, drop out,' and the country-rockers largely stuck to traditional—which is to say, quite conservative—country music themes.

Following the breakup of Buffalo Springfield, Richie Furay and sometime bassist Jim Messina went on to form the band Poco. Through various formations, the band was critically acclaimed but never had a great deal of commercial success. Jim Messina ultimately left to become half of Loggins and Messina; his replacement, Randy Meisner, went on to become an Eagle. A guy by the name of Gregg Allman, who played briefly with Poco during its formative days, went on to front the Allman Brothers.

Poco debuted at the Troubadour, which served as the breeding ground for the country-rock movement, in November 1968. The band's first album, *Pickin' Up the Pieces*, hit the shelves six months later, not long after the release of the debut album by country-rock rivals the Flying Burrito Brothers, formed by former Byrds Gram Parsons and Chris Hillman. Byrd David Crosby, meanwhile, teamed up with Springfield's Stephen Stills and ex-Hollie Graham Nash (who had arrived in Laurel Canyon in December 1968 and quickly found lodging in Joni Mitchell's canyon home) to form a band first known as the Frozen Noses, a name inspired by the trio's fondness for cocaine.

By the late 1960s, the drug that would eventually become the drug of choice of the disco crowd had already begun pouring into Laurel Canyon. As glam-rocker Michael Des Barres recalled, "Every drug dealer was in Laurel Canyon." Along with the drugs came lots of guns and huge piles of cash. Before long, according to Laurel Canyon chronicler Michael Walker, "cocaine became a pseudo-currency, like cigarettes in prison." A decade later, the world would catch a glimpse of that dark canyon undercurrent when four battered bodies were bagged and removed from a house on Wonderland Avenue… but we've already covered that.

The newest Laurel Canyon band was quickly renamed Crosby, Stills & Nash, and by the summer of 1969 they had the top-selling album in the country. That disc would remain on the charts for an unprecedented two years. When the band got ready to hit the road though, there was a little problem; given that Stills was the only serious musician in the band, and it was he who had played virtually all the instruments on that debut album, it was going to be difficult, as Barney Hoskyns noted, "to translate their layered studio sound to the stage." The solution was, as Einarson has written, to bring Neil Young on board, "to provide more umph to their live sets." And so it was that by the end of the year, CSN had become CSNY.

Now the band just needed a rhythm section. Dallas Taylor, who had played on sessions for the first album, was recruited as a drummer. Stills and Young summoned Bruce Palmer to come down from Canada to handle bass duties. According to Palmer, however, that didn't work out, primarily because once he got to LA and "started rehearsing at Stephen's house with Crosby and Nash, it became real evident that they were nothing but backup singers. They didn't like it and decided to change it. They couldn't take that; they thought they were too big, too famous, too talented. They weren't talented, they were backup singers... It looked to them as if it was Crosby and Nash backing up Buffalo Springfield, being nothing more than harmony singers for Stephen, Neil, myself, and Dallas Taylor."

According to Palmer, the first CSN album was "ninety-five percent Stephen doing everything and he's got his backup singer boys with him." Considering that Stills composed the majority of the material, played most of the instruments, and produced and arranged the album, Palmer's assessment seems a reasonable one. In any event, CSNY didn't last too long, dissolving after their 1970 tour. Stills next recruited the ubiquitous Chris Hillman to form Manassas, which also proved to be short-lived. Not long after, David Geffen teamed Hillman with Richie Furay and J.D. Souther to create a failed clone of Crosby, Stills & Nash.

The real CSN was not the only new Laurel Canyon band to release a debut album in 1969. Three Dog Night, mentored and first recorded by Beach Boy Brian Wilson, released their self-titled debut in January, and in June, a psychedelic rock band from the LC issued its first LP. Throughout 1968, the band, then known as Nazz, had been a regular presence on the Sunset Strip, where they gained a reputation for being heavy on the theatrics but light on the musicianship. The band was fronted by Vincent Furnier, the boyfriend of Miss Christine of the GTOs. Miss Pamela, aka Pamela Des Barres, described Furnier as "a rich kid from Phoenix." A staunch supporter of the war in Vietnam, Vince would later become a golf partner of notoriously conservative Senator Barry Goldwater.

Furnier would soon change his own name and the name of his band to Alice Cooper, after deciding that he was the reincarnation of a witch who purportedly lived in the seventeenth century. Frank Zappa signed the band, whose debut album, *Pretties For You*, was the first release on Zappa's Straight label. After transforming into a shock-rock band, the group would hit it big a few years later with the release of *School's Out*.

Cooper had a curious connection to another rather eccentric canyon character, Mr. Brian Wilson. In later years, both Cooper and Wilson would receive wildly controversial psychiatric treatment from a certain Eugene Landy, who took complete control of Wilson's life for an entire decade. Another star client of Landy's was Academy Award winning actor Gig Young. On October 19, 1978, Young and his fifth wife, Kim Schmidt, were found shot through the head in their New York City apartment. The sixty-four-year-old Young—raised, as would be expected, in Washington, DC—had just married the young art gallery worker three weeks earlier. There was no note found and no one close to the pair could come up with a motive for either to commit suicide, so the incident naturally was written off as a murder/suicide. Young had just taped an episode of the Joe Franklin television show that day and he presumably had given no indication that anything was amiss. The show never aired.

As for the original members of Buffalo Springfield, Stephen Stills and Neil Young are still known to perform at times. Richie Furay founded the Cavalry Chapel near Boulder, Colorado, and for quite some time served there as senior pastor. Bruce Palmer died of a heart attack on October 1, 2004. And Dewey Martin was found dead by his roommate on February 1, 2009. He had been living in a nondescript apartment in Van Nuys, California.

16

ALTAMONT PIE
GRAM PARSONS

"No one could recall ever seeing or hearing about Gram being involved in a protest of any sort." Author Ben Fong Torres, who interviewed scores of people close to Gram Parsons while researching Hickory Wind

LET'S BEGIN WITH THE OBVIOUS: GRAM PARSONS WAS FAR FROM BEING THE biggest star to emerge from the Laurel Canyon scene. In his short lifetime, he failed to achieve any significant level of commercial success. None of his albums, whether recorded solo or with the International Submarine Band, the Byrds, or the Flying Burrito Brothers, climbed very high on the sales charts. But to many fans and musicians alike, he is considered a hugely influential and tragically overlooked figure.

It is safe to say that Parsons does not have nearly the number of fans that David Crosby or Frank Zappa have, and compared to contemporaries who died during the same era and at roughly the same age—legendary artists like Jim Morrison, Janis Joplin and Jimi Hendrix—Parsons is all but unknown. His life story, nevertheless, is a fascinating one, primarily because it contains all the classic Laurel Canyon elements: the royal bloodlines, the not-so-well-hidden intelligence connections, the occult overtones, the extravagantly wealthy family background, an incinerated house or two, and, of course, a whole lot of curious deaths.

We begin back about 1,000 years ago, with Ferdinand the Great, the first King of Castille on the Iberian Peninsula. It is to him that the wealthy Connor family claims their family lineage can be traced. Also in the family tree was King Edward II of England, son of Edward I and Eleanor of Castille. According to some sources, Eddie II was murdered by having a red-hot iron rod shoved up his rectum, though most of his loyal subjects probably didn't shed many tears for the hated ruler. Bringing the royal bloodline to America was one Colonel George Reade, born in the UK in 1608 and married in Yorktown, Pennsylvania, sometime thereafter.

Reade's offspring would ultimately spawn Ingram Cecil Connor, Jr., a well-to-do gent who settled in Columbia, Tennessee. Like his father before him, Cecil attended Columbia Military Academy. In May 1940, at the outset of WWII, he enlisted in the US Army Air Force as a Second Lieutenant. In March of 1941, Cecil, who during the war would become known as "Coon Dog" (though no one seems to remember why), was shipped off to Hawaii. Nine months later, Pearl Harbor came under attack by Japanese bombers.

Not to worry though—Cecil was never in harm's way, having opted to forgo living in officer's quarters on the military base in favor of staying at a luxurious, massive estate near Diamond Head owned by wealthy heiress Barbara Hutton. Hutton, for the record, was the granddaughter of Frank Woolworth, the founder of the Woolworth's five-and-dime store chain. She was also the daughter of Franklyn Laws Hutton, co-founder of E.F. Hutton, one of the nation's most prestigious brokerage firms until it ran afoul of the law for such crimes as check kiting, money laundering and mail fraud. Barbara was also the niece of Marjory Post Hutton, the daughter of C.W. Post, founder of what would become General Foods.

Like so many of the other characters who have populated this story, Barbara was traumatized in childhood by the alleged suicide of a parent. According to news reports, it was five-year-old Barbara who discovered her mother Edna's lifeless body in May of 1917. An empty bottle of strychnine was reportedly recovered by police from a nearby bathroom. There was no autopsy performed and no official inquest was ever conducted, as would be expected when an extremely wealthy person dies under questionable circumstances (see, for example, the Ned Doheny story).

In 1930, just after the onset of the Great Depression, Barbara was thrown a lavish debutante ball attended by those at the very top of the food chain, including members of the Astor and Rockefeller families. The next year, she inherited a fortune estimated to be worth the equivalent of $1 billion today. She was just nineteen at the time. Two years later, she received further inheritance that raised her net worth to an estimated $2–2.5 billion in today's money. Much of the rest of the country was busily wallowing in abject poverty.

Ms. Hutton lived a very troubled life, with numerous failed marriages and relationships. One of her many paramours was a gentleman by the name of Phillip van Rensselaer, who later penned a book about her life which he entitled *Million Dollar Baby*. Van Rensselaer, it will be recalled, was an ancestor of Laurel Canyon's own David Crosby—the man whom Gram Parsons would briefly replace in the Byrds. And that, conveniently enough, brings us back to the subject of this chapter.

As WWII dragged on, Ingram Cecil Connor, Jr. worked his way up the chain of command to the rank of Major. Deployed in the Pacific theater of operations, he was a decorated hero and a squadron commander who flew numerous combat missions. After the war, he continued to serve in the Air Force at a base in Bartow, Florida, very near the Snively family home in Winter Haven. The Snively clan had first come to America circa 1700, about a century after the arrival of the guy who spawned the Connor clan. According to historical records and genealogical charts, Johann Jacob Schnebele, a Swiss Mennonite, was born in 1659. When in his late fifties, around 1715 or shortly thereafter, he ventured across the Atlantic and settled near Cornwall, Pennsylvania. Johann died and was buried in 1743 near Lancaster, Pennsylvania.

Brought over with him to America was his son Jacob, born on the winter solstice of 1694, and his daughter Maria, born in 1702. In 1724, in Mannheim, Pennsylvania, Maria Schnebele married the son of immigrants Hans Hersche and Anna Geunder. That son had Americanized his name and become known as Andrew Hershey. The Schnebele name was likewise Americanized to Snavely (or Snively). The Hershey and Snavely clans would continue to happily intermarry, ultimately producing, in 1857, Milton Snavely Hershey, the son of Henry Hershey and Fanny Snavely.

Milton S. Hershey, of course, would go on to found the world's largest producer of chocolate confections. Less well known is that Hershey failed miserably in his first several attempts to launch a candy company, first in Philadelphia, then in Chicago, and finally in New York City. All of those ventures were financed with Snively/Snavely family money. Hershey ultimately succeeded in launching the successful Lancaster Caramel Company in 1883. In 1900, he sold the caramel company to focus exclusively on chocolate confections. With proceeds from that sale, he purchased 40,000 acres of undeveloped land and built not only the world's largest chocolate facility, but an entire company town as well.

As for Maria's brother, Jacob Schnebele, he died in August of 1766 in Cumberland County, Pennsylvania, but not before fathering an astounding nineteen children. One of those was son Andrew, who himself fathered fourteen kids. From that branch of the family tree would emerge John Andrew "Papa John" Snively, who headed off to Florida in the early 1900s to seek his fortune. By the 1950s, Snively Groves was the largest shipper of fresh fruit in the state of Florida.

Avis Snively, who exchanged vows with Ingram Cecil Connor, Jr. on March 22, 1945, was the daughter of Papa John. On November 5, 1946, Coon Dog and Avis gave birth to their first child and only son, Ingram Cecil Connor III, later known as Gram Parsons. Soon after, the family relocated to Waycross, Georgia, where, as with Winter Haven, the Snively family owned a massive amount of land devoted to citrus fruit production. It was there that young Ingram "Gram" Connor was raised.

The Connor family home in Waycross, as would be expected, was large and luxurious and there were numerous servants in attendance, all of whom had considerably more skin pigmentation than did the Connors. Coon Dog and Avis entertained frequently and both were well known to be heavy drinkers; there were hushed rumors that they were 'swingers' as well. As Gram's younger sister, known as Little Avis, would later recall, "Things were mighty strange around the house."

In September of 1957, when Gram was not yet eleven, he was sent off to attend the Bowles School, a combination prep school and military academy in Jacksonville, Florida. While attending Bowles, he became a member of the Centurions, the school's version of an elite fraternity. The following year, just before Christmas 1958, Ingram Cecil "Coon Dog" Connor, Jr. was found sprawled across his bed in the family home, a bullet hole in his right temple. A .38-caliber handgun was found nearby. There was no note to be found. Cecil's brother Tom had visited just the month before, around Thanksgiving, and Coon Dog had told him that he'd never been happier and that life with Avis was wonderful. Curiously, his death was initially ruled to be accidental but the cause of death was later changed to suicide.

Just ten months before Cecil's death, Papa John Snively, Avis' dad, had also died, so she suddenly found herself with both of the men in her life gone. And yet, according to a family member, she never appeared to grieve and she displayed a "total lack of remorse" over anything she may have done to drive Coon Dog to allegedly commit suicide (by some reports, she had been having an affair). Some six months after Cecil's death, Avis, Gram and Little Avis boarded a train for a cross-country trip. They were gone the entire summer. Not long after returning, the family moved from the house that Cecil had died in and Avis soon met Robert Ellis Parsons, who owned a business that ostensibly specialized in leasing heavy construction equipment. Parsons' clients, curiously enough, happened to be in Cuba, then under the brutal hand of Batista, and in various South American countries that were also under the thumb of US-installed dictators

The Snively clan took an immediate dislike to Parsons, who was described by one family member as a "greedy son of a bitch." Nevertheless, Avis quickly married him and Bob Parsons quickly took control of her life. One of his first moves was to adopt Gram and Avis, even going so far as to have new birth certificates drawn up listing him as their biological father (though it remains unclear exactly how he could have done that). He also promptly impregnated Avis and convinced her to file a $1.5 million lawsuit against her brother, John, Jr., and her sister, Evalyn. The suit was settled out of court with Avis receiving an unspecified number of citrus groves, but the real repercussions would be felt some fifteen years later with the bankruptcy of much of the family business in 1974.

In 1960, just a year after marrying, Bob and Avis added daughter Diane to the family. Also added was eighteen-year-old babysitter Bonnie, whom Bob immediately began an affair with, which apparently was not a very well-kept secret. What was a somewhat better kept secret is that, in the early 1960s, following the Cuban revolution, Robert Ellis Parsons became involved in what was referred to as the 'Cuban cause,' which is to say that he had very close ties to the leaders of an exile group that was being trained in Polk County, Florida, to overthrow the Cuban government. On at least one occasion, he brought young Gram along to visit the group's training camp. As luck would have it, a team from *Life* magazine happened to also be there that day and Gram was photographed at the camp. When Avis was informed of that development, she worked quickly to insure that those photos were never published. To this day, they have never surfaced.

During that same era, Bob Parsons converted a downtown warehouse that he owned into a teen nightclub to showcase the talents of his 'son,' Ingram "Gram" Parsons, who sang and played keyboards and the guitar. Circa 1963, Gram got a folk combo together that was known as the Shilos. During the summer of 1964, the summer before Gram's senior year of high school, the band spent a month in New York. During that brief time, Parsons, as fate would have it, met and bonded with Brandon DeWilde, Richie Furay, and John Phillips. He would meet up with all three again a couple years later in Laurel Canyon.

Despite having expressed an early preference for Annapolis or West Point, Gram applied to Harvard and Johns Hopkins. And despite decidedly unimpressive grades and test scores, he was accepted by Harvard, purportedly due to an essay he submitted that he likely didn't actually write. During his last year of high school, Gram and the Shilos booked an hour-long gig at the campus radio station at, of all places, Bob Jones University. At his high school graduation in June of 1965, Gram was in his cap and gown and all set to proceed with the ceremonies when he was pulled aside and informed that his mother Avis had suddenly and unexpectedly passed away. Seemingly unaffected by the news, he chose to participate in the ceremonies. A classmate and friend has said that there was no sign that anything was troubling Gram that day as he went through the graduation rituals.

Avis had died in the hospital, reportedly of alcohol poisoning, right after Bob Parsons had smuggled her in a bottle of scotch. Gram's mother was just forty-two at the time of her death. His father, Coon Dog, had only made it to the age of forty-one. Neither of their kids, Gram or Little Avis, would make it even that far.

Soon after his mother's death, Gram received a draft notice from the Selective Service. Not to worry though—Bob quickly got him a 4-F deferment and Gram happily went off to Harvard, enrolling in September of 1965. By February of 1966, just five months later, Gram had had enough of Harvard and he withdrew. According to some sources, he never really attended school at all, but rather spent all his time taking in the folk music scene in Cambridge and putting his own band together. Gram arrived at Harvard a few years too late to catch that scene at its peak. In the early 1960s, the college town had been one of the cradles of the resurgent folk movement, hosting such luminaries as Joan Baez, Bob Dylan, Bob Neuwirth, Tom Rush, Pete Seeger, Richard and Mimi Fariña, Geoff and Maria Muldaur, Eric Andersen and Joni Mitchell.

The epicenter of the Cambridge folk scene was the legendary Club 47, opened in 1958 as a jazz and blues venue. A very young Joan Baez, whose reputedly CIA-connected father worked at nearby MIT, was the first folkie to take the stage, not long after the club opened. Dylan reportedly first performed there in 1961, taking the stage between the billed acts. The scene hit its peak in the summer of 1962, which was the Cambridge equivalent of the Haight's Summer of Love. The Cambridge scene, and others in Greenwich Village and elsewhere, were necessary precursors to the Laurel Canyon scene, which was essentially created by taking the music of that earlier scene, particularly the work of Dylan and Seeger, and mixing it with the instrumentation being utilized across the pond by a band known as the Beatles. It is entirely fitting then that, as with Laurel Canyon, the Cambridge scene came complete with its own resident psycho killer.

In addition to the folk scene hitting its peak in the summer of 1962, something else newsworthy happened in Cambridge that summer: a lot of women started turning up dead—six of them in that first summer alone, and seven more over the next couple of years. And as Susan Kelly noted in *The Boston Stranglers*, one of those victims was killed right across the street from Club 47: "Just across the street from [victim Beverly Samans'] apartment, a very young and not yet famous Joan Baez and an equally youthful and unknown Bob Dylan were playing to reverently hushed audiences at the Club 47."

As the title of Kelly's book implies, there actually was no such person as the Boston Strangler, but that didn't stop authorities and the media from pinning all the murders on one Albert DeSalvo, far better known as the Boston Strangler. Just as Laurel Canyon would have Charles Manson as its unofficial mascot, the earlier scene in Cambridge had Albert DeSalvo. Cambridge had something else that Laurel Canyon would later have—Paul Rothchild, who worked at Club 47 and went on to produce the Doors.

Folkie Richard Fariña, by the way, was the husband of Mimi Baez, Joan's younger sister. Fariña had attended Cornell University as an engineering major. Cornell also happened to be where Joan and Mimi's dad, Albert Baez, conducted classified research. Albert Baez tended to move around a lot, popping up for varying periods of time at Stanford, UC Berkeley, Cornell, and MIT, all of which have been revealed through declassified documents as hotbeds of MK-ULTRA research. Albert Baez also traveled abroad, to France, Switzerland, and, in 1951, to Baghdad, Iraq, where he spent a year purportedly teaching physics and building a physics laboratory at the University of Baghdad. Nineteen-fifty-one also happened to be the year that Mossadegh was duly elected in neighboring Iran and the CIA immediately began planning a coup to oust him, but I'm sure that that is just a coincidence.

Anyway, Fariña married Mimi when he was twenty-six and she was just seventeen. The two of them, along with Joan, became stars of the Cambridge folk music scene, which they were introduced to when Albert Baez moved the family to Boston in 1958 when he went to work at MIT. Richard and Mimi's marriage was a short one, alas, as Richard Fariña was killed in a motorcycle accident in Carmel, California, on, of all days, April 30, 1966. On that very same day, in nearby San Francisco, Anton Szandor LaVey declared it to be the dawn of the Age of Satan.

But perhaps I've gotten sidetracked here...

During Gram's brief time at Harvard, he began gathering together what would become the International Submarine Band. When he dropped out in early 1966, he and his new bandmates moved to the Bronx in New York, where Gram rented an eleven-room party house where marijuana and LSD flowed freely. One unofficial member of his band was child-actor-turned-aspiring-musician Brandon DeWilde, known in the 1950s as "the king of child actors." Parsons and DeWilde worked together on demo tapes during their time in New York.

In November/December 1966, nine months after leaving Harvard for New York, Gram ventured out to California. While there he met a certain Nancy Ross, who at the time was living with David Crosby. In Ben

Fong-Torres' *Hickory Wind*, Ross provides some interesting biographical details: "I grew up with David Crosby here in town... I was thirteen when we met. David and I were part of the debutante set... My father was a captain in the Royal Air Force of England... I married Eleanor Roosevelt's grandson, Rex, at sixteen, seventeen. I was still married to Rex when I was with David... The marriage lasted a couple of years. I got an apartment and started designing restaurants for Elmer Valentine of Whisky-a-Go-Go."

At age nineteen, Ross went with Crosby "up to his little bachelor apartment, where I drew pentagrams on the wall." Soon after, Crosby bought a house on Beverly Glen and Ross moved in with him. That is where Gram Parsons found Nancy Ross and stole her away from David Crosby: "Brandon DeWilde, who was a good friend of David's and Peter Fonda's, brought Gram up to our Beverly Glen house one Christmas time." According to Nancy, Gram quickly stole her heart. Shortly after, in early 1967, Parsons permanently relocated to Los Angeles with his band in tow. According to Fong-Torres, Gram—who received up to $100,000 a year from his trust fund, a considerable amount of money in the mid-1960s—"found a house for the rest of the band on Willow Glen Avenue, off Laurel Canyon Boulevard and just north of Sunset." He and Nancy found an apartment together nearby.

Meanwhile, back home, Bob Parsons had married Bonnie shortly after the death of Avis, and the newlywed couple had then moved with Little Avis and Diane to New Orleans. Back in Waycross, the Connor family home that had been abandoned after Coon Dog's alleged suicide had been occupied since 1960 by the family of Sheriff Robert E. Lee (and no, I'm not making that up). In late 1968, on the eve of the election that put Richard Nixon in the White House, the stately home exploded from within and caught fire. The cause of the explosion was never determined.

Once ensconced in the hills above Los Angeles, Gram Parsons and his band began recording what would prove to be their only album, *Safe at Home*, which some pop music historians regard as the first country-rock album, but others regard as a straight country album performed by guys who look like they should be playing in a rock band. Whatever the case, by the time the album was released, in 1968, Gram had disbanded the International Submarine Band and unofficially joined the Byrds, replacing the recently departed David Crosby, who had determined that there just wasn't quite room in the band for both he and his ego.

Parsons' time with the Byrds was rather brief, just four to five months, after which he was replaced by virtuoso guitarist Clarence White, who had been part of the Cambridge folk scene. Despite his brief tenure, Parsons is credited with having a major influence on the album that the band produced during that period, *Sweetheart of the Rodeo*. Soon after leaving the Byrds, Parsons ran into Richie Furay, who was casting about for a new band after the breakup of Buffalo Springfield. Gram and Furay considered working together but quickly realized that they wanted to go in different musical directions, so Furay went to work putting Poco together while Parsons assembled the Flying Burrito Brothers. By 1969, Gram's new band had taken shape, with Gram supplying lead vocals and guitar, Chris Hillman also on guitar, Chris Etheridge on bass, and "Sneaky Pete" Kleinow on pedal steel guitar. With various other local musicians sitting in, the band recorded and released *The Gilded Palace of Sin*. Byrd Michael Clarke would later join the band, as would soon-to-be-Eagle Bernie Leadon.

Also in 1969, late in the year, twenty-three-year-old Gram hooked up with sixteen-year-old Gretchen Burrell. His new love interest was the daughter of high-profile news anchor Larry Burrell, who was very well-connected in Hollywood. Before long, Gretchen had moved into Parsons' place at the notorious Chateau Marmont Hotel, with her parents' blessings—because most wealthy parents, I would think, want their teenage daughter living in a debauched rock star's drug den. Another guest at the hotel at that same time, incidentally, was Rod Stewart, at whose home one of the victims of the so-called Sunset Strip Killers would later be last seen.

At the tail end of 1969, Parsons and his fellow Burrito Brothers had the dubious distinction of playing as one of the opening acts at the Rolling Stones' infamous free show at Altamont Speedway. Gram had become a very close confidant of the Stones, particularly Keith Richards, and he would later be credited with being the inspiration for the country flavor evident on the Stones' *Let it Bleed* album.

Parsons had first met up with the Stones when they were in Los Angeles in the summer of 1968 to mix their *Beggar's Banquet* album. Also hooking up with the Stones around that same time was Phil Kaufman, who once boasted that he had slept with every one of the convicted murderesses in the Manson Family. Kaufman initially lived with Charlie and his girls after being released from prison in March of 1968, and he thereafter remained what Kaufman himself described as a "sympathetic cousin" to Manson. He also went to work as the Rolling Stones' road manager for their 1969 American tour, which is the type of job apparently best filled by ex-convict friends of Charles Manson.

In late summer of 1969, following the curious death of Brian Jones in July, the Stones were back in LA to complete their *Let It Bleed* album and prepare for yet another tour. According to Ben Fong-Torres, writing in *Hickory Wind*, "Mick and Keith stayed at Stephen Stills' house near Laurel Canyon... Before Stills, the house had been occupied by Peter Tork of the Monkees." For the record, other reports hold that that house was in, not near, Laurel Canyon.

On December 6, 1969, temporary Laurel Canyon residents Mick and Keith, along with permanent Laurel Canyon residents Crosby, Stills, Nash & Young and the Flying Burrito Brothers, all gathered at a desolate speedway known as Altamont to stage a free concert. By the time it was over, four people were dead and another 850 concertgoers were injured to varying degrees, mostly by members of the Hell's Angels swinging leaded pool cues. The Angels had, of course, been hired by the Stones to ostensibly provide security. That decision is almost universally cast as an innocent mistake on the part of the band, though such a claim is difficult to believe. It was certainly no secret that the reactionary motorcycle clubs, formed by former military men, were openly hostile to hippies and anti-war activists; as early as 1965, they had brutally attacked peaceful anti-war demonstrators while police, who had courteously allowed the Angels to pass through their line, looked on. It was also known that the Angels were heavily involved in trafficking meth, a drug that was widely blamed for the ugliness that had descended over the Haight.

Perhaps less well known was that more than a few of the biker gangs of the 1960s had uncomfortably close ties to Charlie Manson, particularly a club known as the Straight Satans, one of whose members, Danny DeCarlo, served as the Family's sergeant-at-arms, watching over Charlie's arsenal of weapons. DeCarlo also, by some reports, had close ties to the Process. At least one of the performers taking the stage at

Altamont, curiously enough, also had close ties to some of the outlaw biker gangs; as was revealed in his autobiography, Crosby "had friends in every Bay Area chapter of the Hell's Angels."

The death that the concert at Altamont will always be remembered for is that of Meredith Hunter, the young man who was stabbed to death by members of the Hell's Angels right in front of the stage while the band (in this case, the Rolling Stones) played on. The song they were playing, contrary to most accounts of the incident, was the Process-inspired Sympathy For The Devil, as was initially reported in *Rolling Stone* based on the accounts of several reporters on the scene and a review of the unedited film stock.

Most accounts claim that Hunter was killed while the band performed Under My Thumb, but all such claims appear to be based on the mainstream snuff film *Gimme Shelter*, in which the killing was deliberately presented out of sequence. In the absence of any alternative filmic versions of Hunter's death, the Maysles brothers' film became the default official orthodoxy. Not well known is that someone went to great lengths to insure that there would be only one available version of events; as *Rolling Stone* reported, shortly after the concert, "One weird Altamont story has to do with a young Berkeley filmmaker who claims to have gotten 8MM footage of the killing. He got home from the affair Saturday and began telling his friends about his amazing film. His house was knocked over the next night, completely rifled. The thief took only his film, nothing else."

Contrary to the impression created by *Gimme Shelter*, Hunter was killed not long into the Stones' set. But as the film's editor, Charlotte Zwerin, explained to Salon.com some thirty years later, the climax of the movie always has to come at the end: "We're talking about the structure of a film. And what kind of concert film are you going to be able to have after somebody has been murdered in front of the stage? Hanging around for another hour would have been really wrong in terms of the film." What wasn't wrong, apparently, was deliberately altering the sequence of events in what was ostensibly a documentary film.

One of the young cameramen working for the Maysles brothers that day, as it turns out, was a guy by the name of George Lucas. (It is unclear whether it was Lucas who captured the conveniently unobstructed footage of the murder.) Not long after, Lucas would begin a meteoric rise to the very top of the Hollywood food chain. He would be joined there by another film director by the name of Steven Spielberg; the two of them would emerge as arguably the most critically acclaimed and influential filmmakers of their generation. Just as the second wave of Laurel Canyon bands, with names like the Eagles and CSN, would transform the music industry from a community of artists into a vast money-making machine—ushering in the era of stadium concerts, multi-million selling albums and unprecedented profits—Spielberg and Lucas would perform a similar trick with the film business, producing blockbusters like *ET*, *Raiders of the Lost Arc*, *Jaws* and *Star Wars*. It seems perfectly natural then that in the mid- to late-1960s, USC film student Spielberg was living on Lookout Mountain in Laurel Canyon.

Many of the accounts of the tragedy at Altamont include the dubious claim that Hunter can unmistakably be seen drawing a gun just before being jumped and killed by the Angels. Some accounts even have Hunter firing the alleged gun. What can certainly be fairly clearly seen is the large knife being brought down into Hunter's back, but the footage is ambiguous at best as far as Hunter allegedly brandishing a gun. The Angel who was charged with the murder and then ultimately acquitted, Alan David Passaro, was found floating facedown in a reservoir in March of 1985 with $10,000 in his pocket. Despite a widespread belief to the contrary, Passaro's acquittal was not based on the jury having been convinced that Hunter had drawn a gun, but rather on the fact that the knife wounds that killed Hunter were apparently upstrokes, which meant that they were not the wounds inflicted on-camera by Passaro; someone else continued to stab Hunter after he was down, and it was those wounds, which the cameras didn't clearly record, that killed him.

About one year after Altamont, otherwise obscure singer/songwriter Don McLean penned the lyrics to what was destined to become one of the most iconic songs in the annals of popular music: American Pie. Those lyrics are essentially a chronological recitation of various tragedies that shaped the world of popular music. Not long after a reference to the August 1969 Manson murders and their connection to the Laurel Canyon music scene, and just before a reference to the October 1970 death of Janis Joplin, can be found the following verse in which McLean characterized the death of Hunter as a ritualized murder, with Mick Jagger in the role of Satan:

"And there we were, all in one place, a generation Lost in Space / With no time left to start again / So, come on, Jack be nimble, Jack be quick, Jack Flash sat on a Candlestick, 'cause... / Fire is the Devil's only friend / Oh, and as I watched him on the stage, my hands were clenched in fists of rage / No angel born in hell, could break that Satan's spell / And as the flames climbed high into the night, to light the sacrificial rite / I saw Satan laughing with delight, the day the music died."

As was the custom with big events in the mid- to late-1960s, particularly in the northern California area, Altamont was drenched in acid. And as was also the custom at that time, that acid was provided free-of-charge by Mr. Augustus Owsley Stanley III, also known as The Bear. At the so-called "Human Be-In" staged in January of 1967, for example, Owsley had kindly distributed 10,000 tabs of potent LSD. For the Monterey Pop Festival just five months later, he had cooked up and distributed 14,000 tabs. For Altamont, he did likewise. Also present that day, and featured in the Maysles brothers' film gyrating atop a raised platform near the stage, was the King of the Freaks himself, Vito Paulekas.

Along with Mick and the boys, Gram Parsons made a hasty exit from the chaos at Altamont via the Stones' private helicopter. The next year, his Flying Burrito Brothers released their second album, *Burrito Deluxe*, which was produced by Jim Dickson, the man who had played such a pivotal role in shaping Laurel Canyon's first band, the Byrds. By June, Parsons had been booted out of the band, reportedly due to chronic alcohol and drug abuse. He quickly signed with A&M Records and was partnered with Terry Melcher. Gram soon became a regular visitor to Melcher's Benedict Canyon home, where the self-destructive pair worked on songs together, with Gram on guitar and Melcher on piano. John Phillips became a close associate of Parsons at that time as well.

Meanwhile, sister Avis had been institutionalized back in New Orleans. She had gotten pregnant, after which Bob Parsons had moved quickly to have her committed and to have her marriage annulled. Little Avis reached out repeatedly to big brother Gram for help, but got none.

In late October of 1970, Gram went to A&M and signed out the master tapes of ten songs that he had recorded with Melcher; those tapes were never seen or heard again, as seems to happen from time-to-time with recordings made with Melcher. During roughly that same period of time, Parsons was busted with a briefcase full of prescription drugs. As would be expected, however, the charges were quietly dropped and Gram walked away unscathed.

In 1971, Gram married Gretchen Burrell. The lavish affair was held, curiously enough, at the New Orleans home of step-dad Bob Parsons, a fact that has left Gram's chroniclers somewhat puzzled. Bob Parsons was, after all, the man who had—at least in the eyes of many family members—terrorized and institutionalized Gram's younger sister, carried on a scandalous affair with the family's babysitter, murdered Gram's mother and subsequently married that babysitter, and repeatedly looted the family coffers. And yet it was Bob Parsons, of all people, who Gram trusted to host his wedding, suggesting a bond between the two that would seem to defy conventional explanations.

That same year, Gram spent some time in France, hanging out once again with the Rolling Stones. The following year he was signed to Reprise Records by Mo Ostin and he and Gretchen moved back into the Chateau Marmont, where Gram and Emmylou Harris, who had been raised on various military bases in Virginia, began working on the songs that would make up his first solo album. In 1973, with that first solo album, entitled simply *GP*, due for release, "Gram and Gretchen finally moved out of the Chateau Marmont and found a cozy brown wood-shingled house on Laurel Canyon Boulevard, which wound its way north from Hollywood through the stars' favorite canyon," as recounted by Fong-Torres.

Together again with Emmylou, Gram began working on tracks for what would be his posthumously released second solo album, *Grievous Angel*. But as July of 1973 rolled around, a series of tragedies befell Parsons and the people around him. In July of the previous year, Gram's friend Brandon DeWilde—who had introduced Gram to Peter Fonda, Dennis Hopper, Bruce Dern and Jack Nicholson, resulting in Gram's involvement in *The Trip*—had been killed in a traffic accident. A year later, on July 15, 1973, Gram's friend and fellow musician, Clarence White, was hit by a car and killed. According to Fong-Torres, "Around the same time that Clarence White was killed, Sid Kaiser, a familiar face in the Los Angeles rock scene, a close friend of Gram's and, not so incidentally, a source of high-quality drugs, died of a heart attack." Just after those two deaths, "In late July 1973... [Gram's] house in Laurel Canyon burned down."

Other sources, for the record, have placed that house in Topanga Canyon rather than Laurel Canyon. Whatever the case, Gram was home when the house caught fire and he was briefly hospitalized for smoke inhalation. Having lost their home and all their possessions, Gram and Gretchen "moved into Gretchen's father's spacious home on Mulholland Drive in Laurel Canyon." Gram wouldn't live in the Burrell estate long though; on September 19, 1973, Ingram Cecil Connor III died in a nondescript room at the Joshua Tree Inn. His death is usually attributed to a drug overdose, but toxicology reports suggest otherwise. Parsons' death received minimal press coverage, partly because, as fate would have it, singer/songwriter Jim Croce went down in a blaze of glory the very next day, on September 20, 1973. But though the media had moved on, the Gram Parsons story wasn't quite over yet.

Parsons had been a regular visitor to Joshua Tree National Park, where one of his favorite pastimes was said to be ingesting hallucinogenic drugs and then searching for UFOs. Sometimes he would take friends like Keith Richards along with him to help with the search. In September of 1973, Gram was accompanied to Joshua Tree by his personal assistant, Michael Martin, Martin's girlfriend, Dale McElroy, and Parsons' former high school sweetheart, Margaret Fisher. As the story goes, the group soon ran out of pot and quickly dispatched Martin back to LA to pick up a fresh supply. He was, therefore, officially not there at the time of Gram's death, though why he hadn't returned has never been explained, especially given that his job was, specifically, to keep an eye on Gram and monitor his drug intake.

How Gram Parsons died is anyone's guess. There are as many versions of the event as there were witnesses to it. Actually, that's not quite true—there are *more* versions than there were witnesses, because some of those witnesses have told more than one story. Officially, Parsons died of an overdose, but forensic testing revealed no morphine or barbiturates in his blood. Morphine showed up in his liver and urine, but as experts have noted, those toxicology results indicate chronic, but not recent, use. Police seem to have had little interest in getting at the truth and made no apparent effort to reconcile the various conflicting accounts. Details of the incident—such as how long Gram had been left alone, whether he was still alive when discovered, who made that discovery, etc.—were wildly inconsistent in the accounts of Fisher, McElroy, and Frank and Alan Barbary (the Inn's owner and his son). The Barbarys' accounts conflicted both with each other and with the girls' accounts.

At the hospital, police spoke briefly with the two girls and then released them. Within two hours, Phil Kaufman was on the scene to pick up Fisher and McElroy. Bypassing the police and the hospital, Kaufman went directly to the Inn, which the girls had returned to, and quickly hustled them straight back to LA. Police never spoke to either of the women again, despite the conflicting accounts and the open question of what exactly it was that killed Gram.

On the autumnal equinox of 1973, Kaufman and Martin, driving a dilapidated hearse provided by McElroy, arrived at LAX to claim the body of Gram Parsons. If this story is to be believed, then nobody, including the police officer who was nearby, found it at all unusual that two drunken, disheveled men in an obviously out-of-service hearse (it had no license plates and several broken windows) had arrived without any paperwork to claim the body of a deceased celebrity. In fact, according to Kaufman's dubious account, the cop even helped the pair load the casket into the hearse—and then looked the other way when Martin slammed the hearse into a wall on the way out of the hangar.

Kaufman and Martin then drove the body back out to Joshua Tree, doused it with gasoline and set it ablaze. Local police initially speculated that the cremation was "ritualistic," which indeed it was, but such reports were, and continue to be, scoffed at.

On September 26, LAPD detectives, led by anchorman Larry Burrell, came knocking on Kaufman's door with warrants to serve. Bizarrely enough, director Arthur Penn was there with a full crew shooting scenes for the film *Night Moves* with star Gene Hackman. When you are a friend of Charlie Manson's, it would appear, everyone in Hollywood wants to hang out with you. While the crew continued working, Kaufman was taken in by police but he was back just a few hours later. In the end, he and Martin were fined $300 each plus reimbursement for the cost of the coffin.

In January 1974, four months after Parsons' death, *Grievous Angel* was released to critical acclaim and public indifference. Later that year,

Gram's adoptive father, Bob Parsons, died from complications of an alcohol-related illness. He had apparently been making moves aimed at gaining control of the deceased musician's estate. By sheer coincidence, no doubt, the deaths of Gram and Bob Parsons were followed by the 1974 bankruptcy of much of the Snively family business. Around that same time, Little Avis gave birth to daughter Flora. Sixteen years later, both were killed in a boating accident in Virginia. Avis had made it all the way to age forty.

17

THE LOST EXPEDITION OF GENE CLARK

"In later years, toward the end, he would have really bad nightmares. He would wake up in the middle of the night screaming..." Kai Clark, Gene Clark's son

In many ways, the Gene Clark story reads a lot like the Gram Parsons story. Both were considered by their peers to be among Laurel Canyon's brightest stars, yet both are now largely forgotten. Both of their lives were cut tragically short (though Clark lived considerably longer than Parsons). Both of their deaths were overshadowed to some extent by unusual events that occurred just after their passing. Both were considered pioneers of the country-rock genre. Both played for a time with the Byrds. Both recorded duets with Emmylou Harris, and both employed many of the same musicians on their various solo projects. Both had legions of female admirers. Both had a keen interest in UFOs and believed in alien visitations. And both were notorious drug and alcohol abusers.

Harold Eugene Clark was born on November 17, 1944, in Tipton, Missouri, though the year of his birth was frequently reported as 1941. It seems quite likely that Gene Clark himself was the source of that erroneous biographical detail, to avoid questions about the fact that his alleged father was actually overseas for all of 1944.

Tipton is a small town—the kind of town where everyone knows one another by name. In fact, Tipton is kind of like a big park where the same oversized family reunion is held every day of the year. As Bonnie Clark Laible told author John Einarson, "When I was in Tipton, Missouri, the year my grandfather died, in 1954, I found out I was related to almost everyone in the community. Everyone had married people they knew through the various families like Faherty and Sommerhauser. I couldn't throw a stone without hitting a family member!"

Tipton was founded by Mr. William Tipton Seely, a rather wealthy and influential gent who opened a general store circa 1830. A community soon sprang up around his store, as tended to happen in those days, and Seely named his new little fiefdom Round Hill. A decade or so later, in the 1840s, a group of German immigrant families arrived in the area—the Nieuffers, the Lutzs, the Kammerichs, the Schmidts, the Hoens, the Shrecks and the Sommerhausers. Those families proceeded to intermarry to a rather extreme degree.

In the 1850s, Seely lobbied hard to have both the Pacific Railroad and the Butterfield Overland Mail route pass through his little kingdom. Those efforts proved successful, though the railroad was routed a few miles north of Round Hill. Around that new railroad station was born Seely's second town, tiny Tipton, where Gene Clark would spend the early years of his life.

Meanwhile, just before 1800, a group of Irish families led by a Mr. Edmund Faherty settled in southwestern Illinois. In addition to the Fahertys, the group included the Whelans, the O'Haras and the O'Neills. These families also proceeded to intermarry. Some factions of the family eventually crossed over the border into Perryville, Missouri, where they became slave owners. James and Helena Faherty split from the rest of the Missouri herd and moved to Cole Camp, not too far southwest of Tipton. According to chronicler Einarson, the move was recommended by a "priest who feared too much inbreeding among the families."

Oscar Faherty, Gene Clark's maternal grandfather, was born and raised near Tipton, as was the woman who was to be his wife and Gene's grandmother, Rosemary Sommerhauser. Before long, the Fahertys and the Sommerhausers were intermarrying at a furious pace. According to Bonnie Clark, "The Faherty and Sommerhauser families had double cousins going on." On the summer solstice of 1920, Rosemary Sommerhauser Faherty gave birth to Mary Jeanne Faherty, Gene Clark's mother. After completing elementary school, Mary Jeanne was sent away to work as a "domestic servant" for an unnamed wealthy family living near Kansas City, Kansas. The Depression years were pretty rough, from what I hear, but selling off your barely teenage daughter seems a bit harsh.

The other half of Gene Clark's family tree is, curiously enough, shrouded in mystery and secrecy. As chronicler Einarson notes, "Unlike Jeanne Faherty Clark's well-documented family history, the lineage of Gene's father, Kelly George Clark, is far more murky and mysterious." Indeed, Einarson's extensive research turned up little more than the fact that Kelly Clark was born on November 11, 1918, in Lenexa, Kansas, and that, according to family lore, there might be Native American blood in the family tree that has been concealed. Or maybe Pop Clark's history is murky for other reasons.

What is known is that Kelly Clark apparently quit high school and went to work for the parks department as a groundskeeper. While tending the grounds at the Milburn Country Club, he met young Jeanne Faherty, who apparently was taken there fairly frequently by her employers—because most wealthy people, it seems reasonable to conclude, take their young servants with them to the country club. After a relatively brief courtship, the two married on May 29, 1941, and promptly started a family.

Bonnie Clark was born on March 13, 1942, just over nine months after the couple exchanged vows. Kelly Katherine was to be the couple's second child, but she was, alas, reportedly stillborn on the summer solstice of 1943. Nothing suspicious about that. Nor about the peculiar fact that, while Gene and other members of the family would be laid to rest in the Sommerhauser family plot at St. Andrews cemetery in Tipton, "Kelly Katherine's is a solitary stone at the far south end of the cemetery," as recounted by John Einarson in *Mr. Tambourine Man*.

A few months after Kelly Katherine Clark's curious death, Kelly George Clark was called up for radio and gunnery school. Following training, he was assigned to a unit that served as General George Patton's mop-up crew. Clark's team landed at LeHavre, France, and steadily made their way towards Germany. By May of 1945, immediately following the fall of the Third Reich, Clark was in Berlin. Meanwhile, the third Clark child, Gene, was born in November 1944. Officially, Jeanne Clark was impregnated while her husband was briefly home on leave, presumably in February 1944, though it seems very unlikely that he would have been at home at that time. In any event, Gene spent the first years of his life in a house at 304 Morgan Street, directly across the street from a funeral home.

Kelly Clark returned home at the end of WWII and promptly impregnated his wife once again; Nancy Patricia Clark was born on July 19, 1946. The family would continue to grow until there were no fewer than ten Clark siblings, all living in a tiny house far off the beaten path. As a former classmate and friend told Einarson, "You had to take a dirt road up and it was the only house back in the woods, way up high. I couldn't believe the first time Gene took me there... It was kind of spooky in a way." As sister Bonnie has acknowledged, the Clarks "were known as a very strange family in the community." That may have had something to do with the family's rather unusual choice of recreational activities, such as throwing knives at laundry detergent boxes: "Gene was very good at it. We both were. This was one of the things we did as a family function," noted Bonnie.

Gene would have a lifelong fascination with knives—and guns. According to friend Joe Larson, after Clark began making money with the Byrds, he "started buying guns." In the cover photo for one of Gene's solo albums, he is sitting on a picnic table. As brother Rick Clark has noted, "there are bullet holes in the table where we would shoot at cans and bottles from the back porch with Gene's guns." One of those guns was an antique rifle given to Gene by fellow gun aficionado David Crosby. Apparently a lot of those peacenik hippie types in Laurel Canyon were packing heat.

Shockingly enough, most of the members of that "strange family" living in the backwoods did not fare so well as they grew into adulthood. As of the time of the writing of Einarson's *Mr. Tambourine Man* (2005), one Clark sibling had been diagnosed as a paranoid schizophrenic, another suffered from severe bouts of clinical depression, another was homeless due to untreated mental illness, another was on psychiatric meds most of her life before dying suddenly in 1987, another was bipolar, and yet another was diagnosed with severe mental retardation. Even more shockingly, mysterious father Kelly Clark was said to be a raging alcoholic who suffered from severe mood swings.

Gene's formal education began in 1949 at a strict Catholic school in Raytown. According to big sister Bonnie, quoted by Einarson, "there were truly some abusive people [there]. I can remember some of those nuns being real nightmares." By 1960, the family had moved to Bonner Springs, Kansas, where Gene attended high school. He was known to hang with a rough crowd during his high school days, and a few of his buddies from those years ended up serving prison time.

On August 12, 1963, Gene Clark, still a few months shy of his nineteenth birthday, was inexplicably offered a spot in the New Christy Minstrels vocal group; he was on a plane to California the very next day. The Minstrels were a very busy touring group, averaging some 300 dates a year, so Gene would spend a lot of time on airplanes during his six-month tenure as a Minstrel. Curiously though, fear of flying would be cited a couple years later as Gene's reason for leaving the Byrds.

One of the gigs the group played, on January 14, 1964, was at the White House as special guests of Lyndon Johnson, who had taken office less than two months earlier following the assassination of John Kennedy. After the performance, Gene and other Minstrels (including Barry McGuire, who, as was discussed previously, released Eve Of Destruction a couple years later) went out on the town and partied with Johnson's two daughters, Lynda Bird and Luci Baines, who were just nineteen and sixteen at the time.

As the story goes, Gene quit the New Christy Minstrels a couple of weeks later, in February of 1964, after hearing the first album released by an upstart British band known as the Beatles. Clark immediately headed out to Los Angeles, as would so many others, where he regularly hung out at the Troubadour, just off the Sunset Strip. It was there that he met one James Joseph McGuinn III, who had, curiously enough, once been in the New Christy Minstrels himself, for exactly one day. The two quickly formed a folk duo and began writing songs, hoping to soon get bookings at the Troubadour and other local clubs. But according to McGuinn, the pair "never got to the stage of performing as a duo... Crosby came along quite quickly."

McGuinn was initially quite wary of the interloper, but the three nevertheless became a trio known at first as the Jet Set. With Crosby, of course, came Jim Dickson, who would transform the trio into the Byrds. According to Vern Gosdin—who, along with his brother, Rex, played with many of the Laurel Canyon musicians—it was Jim Dickson who "put the Byrds together, you might say. If I'm telling the truth, this is what I think: I don't think the Byrds had any ideas whatsoever, and Jim Dickson put it all together for them." Dickson originally envisioned the band as a Beatlesque quartet, with Gene as John (lead vocalist/rhythm guitarist), Roger as George (lead guitar and vocals), and Crosby as Paul (bass and vocals).

This arrangement proved unworkable, however, since Crosby was reportedly unable to sing and play bass at the same time. This then led Dickson to recruit mandolin player Chris Hillman to take over bass duties, leaving Crosby with little to do other than provide harmony vocals. That didn't sit well though with Lord Crosby, so he began a relentless campaign aimed at eroding Gene's confidence in his own guitar playing ability. Crosby's constant ridicule paid off and he soon enough took over rhythm guitar duties. The five-man band was then complete: Gene would provide most lead vocals and bang the tambourine, Jim/Roger McGuinn would provide the band's signature twelve-string guitar sound and harmony vocals, Crosby would provide serviceable (at best) rhythm guitar work and harmony vocals, and Chris Hillman and Michael Clarke would pretend (initially at least) to play the bass guitar and the drums.

The band released its first single as the Beefeaters. The record was produced by Jim Dickson, who would go on to guide the Byrds' career, and Paul Rothchild, who would go on to guide the Doors' career. The single, released by Elektra Records, went nowhere. By November of 1964 though, the band, renamed the Byrds, was signed with Columbia Records. Just two months later they would record *Mr. Tambourine Man* and become huge stars. But there was a hurdle to overcome first; as Einarson notes, "[Gene] had received his draft notice. Roger and Michael had already dodged that bullet; now it was Gene's turn." Not to worry though; Gene was able to dodge that bullet as well. According to Einarson, Gene was deemed unfit for military service due to an "old football disease," identified as "Osgood Schlatter's Disease." Luckily for Gene, it apparently didn't prevent him from playing football but it did keep him out of the service.

Gene Clark was, without question, an astoundingly prolific songwriter. Relatively few of his compositions, however, appeared on Byrds' albums, which instead featured a lot of covers. The truth is that Gene had more than enough songs—and reportedly good songs—to fill the early Byrds' albums. Even Crosby has acknowledged that Clark "was prolific. He would show up every week with new songs and they were great songs." Crosby wasn't so generous though with his assessments of Gene's talents back in the day. According to most accounts, it was the jealousy of Crosby and McGuinn that kept Gene's tracks off the records.

In those days, there wasn't a lot of money to be made by performing and recording music. The real money was in song royalties, so Clark was paid considerably more than the rest of the band. As McGuinn put it, "Gene was into Ferraris and we were still starving." That disproportionate compensation quickly drove a wedge between Clark and the other two thirds of the original trio. At times, Gene even shared writing credits on his songs just to get them onto albums. The classic Eight Miles High, for example, was written by Gene but credited to Crosby and McGuinn as well.

As has been noted previously, Vito Paulekas played a key role in launching the careers of the Byrds. And so it is that we find references to Vito and his entourage in Einarson's telling of the Gene Clark story: "Vito and Carl were legendary hipsters on the LA scene and were into LSD long before anyone else. It was at their studio that Gene believed the Byrds truly found their magic as a group." According to Morgan Cavett, the son of Oscar-winning screenwriter Frank Cavett, "They had this group of hippies before that term came into use. Somehow they had hooked up with the Byrds."

When the band launched its very first national tour in July 1965, "Along for the trip were LA scene-makers Vito and Carl and their entourage of crazed hippie dancers whose uninhibited gyrations caused quite a stir in the heartlands of America." Einarson's account though is not quite accurate; Vito stayed home while first lieutenant Carl Franzoni led the faction of the troupe that hit the road with the Byrds. Assisting Franzoni was Byrds' roadie Brian McLean, who shortly thereafter would beat out Mansonite Bobby Beausoleil for the rhythm guitarist position in Love. As troupe dancer Lizzie Donohue would later recall, many of those in America's hinterlands "thought we were from outer space. In Paris, Illinois, they actually threw us off the dance floor." Gene Clark would later remember that the band "could have played out of tune all day. Nobody ever heard us anyway." According to many accounts, the band oftentimes did play out of tune all day. And all night as well.

When the band followed up its first national tour with a tour of the UK, the Byrds were not well received. Often the band would spend more time tuning their instruments between songs than they did actually playing those songs. And by most accounts, the boys made virtually no attempt to forge a connection with the audience. Gene did though forge a bond with the Rolling Stones' Brian Jones, whose life would be tragically cut short a couple years later.

Sometime after that tour, members of the Byrds famously met with members of the Beatles and they all dropped acid together. Some accounts hold that that meeting took place in the Cielo Drive home where Sharon Tate would later be butchered, but it appears to have actually taken place at another home in Benedict Canyon, one that may have been formerly owned by Zsa Zsa Gabor. Laurel Canyon stalwart Peter Fonda was reportedly in attendance, and legend holds that it was he who supplied a very high John Lennon with the line, "I know what it's like to be dead."

In March of 1966, a press release announced Gene Clark's departure from the Byrds. McGuinn has alleged that Dickson and co-manager Eddie Ticknor encouraged Gene to split from the band so that they could exploit his solo potential. If so, then they must have been greatly disappointed since Clark never came close to living up to that potential.

One of the first offers Gene received upon his departure from the Byrds was from drummer Dewey Martin, who invited Clark to join the newly formed Buffalo Springfield. Clark declined, choosing to form his own band, the first of which was dubbed the Group. As Einarson explains, "Six weeks after rehearsals began, Gene Clark and the Group debuted at the Whisky-A-Go-Go on June 22 for a two-week stand, on the heels of a dazzling six-week stint by new group Buffalo Springfield." Around that same time, Clark began having an affair with Michelle Phillips, who lived with hubby John Phillips just a couple of blocks down the canyon.

Following what were reportedly unproductive recording sessions, Gene's first post-Byrds formation broke up. On July 10, he was signed as a solo artist and he entered the studio the next month accompanied by doomed guitarist Clarence White, Brian Wilson collaborator Van Dyke

Parks, our old friend Glen Campbell, the ubiquitous Chris Hillman, and Vern and Rex Gosdin, who had gotten their start alongside Chris Hillman in the formation known as the Hillmen. In January of 1967, Clark's first solo album was released as *Gene Clark with the Gosdin Brothers*.

Like many of the other records we have stumbled upon while on this journey, some fans and critics regard the record as the first country-rock album (released a year-and-a-half before the country-rock forays by the Byrds and Buffalo Springfield). The album, unfortunately, was quickly overshadowed by the Byrds' own *Younger than Yesterday*, which Columbia released just two weeks after releasing Gene's solo effort.

By March of 1967, Clark had put together a new version of the Group, which debuted at the Whisky with Clark, Clarence White and two members of the Mamas and the Papas' touring group, whom Gene had met through his paramour, Michelle Phillips. At the tail end of 1967, Gene briefly rejoined the Byrds, replacing the fired David Crosby. The reunion lasted only a few weeks but it was long enough for Gene to contribute to *The Notorious Byrd Brothers*, released in January 1968.

When Gene had left the Byrds, it should be noted, he had done so empty handed. Not so with Crosby, who was given a substantial settlement upon his departure. He used that money to purchase a yacht, which he dubbed the Mayan. Crosby thereafter was known to spend extended periods of time aboard the Mayan, sailing to and from various locations. He was not the only canyon musician to own and operate such a vessel; John Phillips had one as well, as did Dennis Wilson. All three of them also had a passion for controlled substances. And guns. Perhaps there is some connection there.

Following his brief reunion with the Byrds, Clark composed the original score for *Marijuana*, a short anti-drug film hosted by Sonny Bono. His next project, dubbed *The Fantastic Expedition of Dillard and Clark*, featured Gene, Doug Dillard (formerly of the Dillards, from whom Buffalo Springfield, it will be recalled, had obtained their instruments), Bernie Leadon (who had been a peripheral member of San Diego's Scottsville Squirrel Barkers, alongside Chris Hillman), and, of course, Chris Hillman.

By that time Gene had married and his wife, Carlie, was an avid reader of occult literature, particularly, as she recalled, "this lady named Madame Blavatsky." Circa 1971, Clark was approached by his friend and fellow Canyonite, Dennis Hopper, to compose songs for the soundtrack to Hopper's *American Dreamer*. Around that same time, according to Einarson, "Gene's running buddies included David Carradine and John Barrymore." That was, to say the least, a rather curious group of friends. According to authors such as Craig Heimbichner, Martin P. Starr, and John Carter, Dennis Hopper and John Carradine (David's dad) were both members of the infamous Agape Lodge of the OTO, alongside doomed rocket scientist Jack Parsons, actor Dean Stockwell, and doppelgängers L. Ron Hubbard and Robert Heinlein. According to Gregory Mank, writing in *Hollywood's Hellfire Club*, John Carradine and John Barrymore were also members of the so-called "Bundy Drive Boys," a group that engaged in such practices as incest, rape and cannibalism. And according to Ed Sanders, among the upscale homes visited by a Process work group "was the John Barrymore mansion, located at 1301 Summit Ridge Drive."

The year 1972 saw yet another brief Byrds reunion, with another record released, this one in February of 1973. Gene next began recording sessions for a new solo project, financed by his friend Gary Legon, the husband of porn star and Ivory Soap model Marilyn Chambers. Joining Gene on some of the tracks was Emmylou Harris, whose hubby Tom Slocum—a descendant of famed explorer Joshua Slocum—was a member of Gene's inner circle.

After briefly relocating to Albion, California with his wife and kids, Clark moved back to Laurel Canyon, where he moved into a home on Stanley Hills Drive with his new girlfriend, Terri Messina. Born into considerable wealth, Messina was the daughter of a prominent area physician. In 1963, she had enrolled in theater arts at UCLA, which quite likely would have placed her in the company of a couple of other UCLA theater arts students named Jim Morrison and Ray Manzarek. Terri and Gene moved in together in the summer of 1977. According to Einarson, Messina "laterally work[ed] in film editing, [but] she was better known in exclusive circles as a supplier of cocaine." And heroin. As has been previously discussed, during that time period the "entire Laurel Canyon lifestyle revolved around cocaine," and "Gene fell into line, becoming a legendary partier."

Canyon resident Ken Mansfield recalled those dark years: "That particular point in my life, and most of us, was the craziest time of all, when we were all into drugs the most. Tommy's [Kaye] house was one of the houses we hung out at a lot. David Carradine was my neighbor in Laurel Canyon. Our two properties were side by side. David had a group called Water. I could tell you some wild canyon stories... Looking back it's not a nice memory. Even though we thought we were having a good time, I don't think we really were. Shortly after Tommy Kaye's little girl, Eloise, died in an unfortunate accident, it just seemed like everybody's life got dark and we all kind of lost hope there for a while."

Kids living in Laurel Canyon apparently had to be particularly vigilant about avoiding tragic accidents.

Circa 1978, Clark teamed with former bandmates Hillman and McGuinn for a contrived reunion tour. An album followed in early 1979, with a second released in early 1980. During that time, according to brother David Clark, Gene "was hanging around with these really gross characters who were just a bunch of burnouts and he wasn't much better. Cathy Evelyn Smith was there." Not long after, Smith would attain a certain amount of notoriety for her involvement in the curious death of John Belushi at the Chateau Marmont. We should then, I suppose, add John Belushi to the Laurel Canyon Death List. And Eloise Kaye as well.

Following the release of the second Byrds reunion album, Clark and a close friend, guitarist Jesse Ed Davis, left LA for Oahu, Hawaii, supposedly to get clean. They returned at the end of 1981, with Gene once again settling into his favorite canyon. Among his close friends at that time were former child star Kurt Russell and his then-wife, actress Season Hubley, who had also taken up residence in Laurel Canyon. Gene's solo career sputtered on for another decade, though fewer and fewer people seemed to be paying much attention.

In January 1991, the original members of the Byrds came together for their induction into the Rock and Roll Hall of Fame. Clark died just four months later, reportedly of a heart attack. He was just forty-six at the time. The circumstances of his death remain murky to this day. As Einarson has noted, "What transpired over the last three days of Gene's life remains clouded by controversy... conspiracy theories abound; accusations have been leveled." For the most part though, Gene has now been all but forgotten. His vast stockpile of unreleased material, however—much of which mysteriously disappeared after his death—likely lives on, albeit credited to others.

According to Einarson, Clark had been fighting to stay sober but it "is agreed that he began drinking again on the evening of Wednesday, May 22... What happened next depends entirely on who is telling the story. [One witness] claims he searched the house for drugs and did not find any—contrary to claims by others that drugs and drug paraphernalia were present in the house... there are those conspiracy theorists who continue to insinuate that drugs and certain characters were, indeed, present that night, and that Gene's death was a result of misadventure, necessitating a panicked clean-up campaign that morning."

There were apparently numerous people present at Clark's home on the morning of May 24, 1991, as Gene lay dead on the living room floor. One of those people was Saul Davis, who "took it upon himself to contact the media with the news, another bone of contention with some, given that Saul was not serving as Gene's manager at the time." Another was the manager of the property, identified as Ray Berry, who had served during WWII in Special Ops. While people milled about the house, "arguing over the spoils... Gene's body continued to lie on the living room floor, face up."

Days later, David Carradine caused quite a stir at Gene's open-casket memorial service. Former bandmate Pat Robinson remembered it well: "When Carradine came up, he wasn't as much drunk as he was on acid, I think, and his girlfriend and business manager at the time was there with him. And we're standing there and Carradine says, 'You cocksucker...' and grabs Gene by the lapels. When you pull somebody up from a coffin and they have nothing inside for guts they bend higher up. It was really shocking to see that. And Carradine goes, 'You pissed on my daughter when she was thirteen.' And he said it pretty loud and then he says, 'I saw him snicker, boys, heh heh.' Oh, man, that was weird."

Perhaps weirder still is that many of those who were in attendance remember hearing something a little different: "You *fucked* my daughter when she was thirteen." Maybe Carradine had mistaken Clark for Roman Polanski. Or maybe that's just what everyone was doing in Laurel Canyon. In any event, none of the original members of the Byrds bothered to attend the service. Afterwards, Gene was laid to rest in tiny Tipton.

It should be noted here, before concluding this chapter, that there were very clear indications that Gene Clark suffered from a rather severe dissociative disorder throughout his adult life. As far as can be determined from the literature, he was never diagnosed as such, but comments made by his bandmates and family members are quite revealing. One such bandmate, Pat Robinson, has described how Clark "used to slip into these dream states, which I thought was really amazing. He'd go into these dream states and lay down on the couch and go, 'I'll be right back, Patrick.'" Another, John York, has said that Gene "had these multiple personalities." Yet another, Bernie Leadon, remembered that Clark would often appear to be completely out of it, and he'd "say, 'Hey, Gene, what are you thinking?' and he would go, 'Huh? Oh,' like he was being brought back to reality."

Gene's sister, Bonnie Clark, has also noted that there was more than one version of the troubled singer/songwriter: "There was this persona and the rest of Gene was somewhere in there. He was hard to get to know... He could be very warm and loving, but that could change in a heartbeat." Chronicler John Einarson offered the following summation: "It is often difficult for those who knew him—even family members—to reconcile the two Gene Clarks: the cheerful, engaging yet shy loner with the vibrant imagination, and the frustrated, moody recluse who was sometimes prone to violence."

18

THE WOLF KING OF LA
"PAPA" JOHN PHILLIPS

"John [Phillips] was the ultimate controller." Mamas and the Papas producer/manager Lou Adler

"She was practically his slave." Michelle Phillips, describing John's relationship with his third wife, Genevieve Waite

THUS FAR ON THIS JOURNEY, WE HAVE SEEN HOW WHAT ARE ARGUABLY THE two most bloody and notorious mass murders in the history of the City of Angels—the murders of the occupants of the home on Cielo Drive in Benedict Canyon, and the so-called Four on the Floor bludgeoning murders of four drug dealers on Wonderland Avenue—were directly connected to the Laurel Canyon music scene. But the city of Los Angeles can boast of one other particularly notorious murder, one that stands to this day as both the most gruesome single-victim murder and the most famous unsolved murder in the city's history.

On January 15, 1947, the mutilated body of aspiring actress Elizabeth Short was found posed in a field. The ritualistically butchered body was nude, sliced cleanly in half, and completely drained of blood. Parts of the body had been removed, after which the corpse had been thoroughly sanitized. Bruising clearly indicated that the young girl had been savagely beaten. Forensic evidence suggested that she had been forced to eat feces during her tortuous ordeal. She was quickly dubbed the 'Black Dahlia' and it is by that name that she is known and written about today.

Much of what has been written about the brief life of Ms. Short is contradictory. Among the facts that seem to be agreed upon are that she had recently worked at a military facility that is now known as Vandenberg Air Force Base, and that she had some kind of close connection to a US Naval hospital in San Diego, where she may have also worked. That is, in any event, what she had indicated in a letter to her mother.

Unlike the Manson and Wonderland murders, the mutilation of the Black Dahlia occurred some twenty years before Laurel Canyon's glory days. There is, nevertheless, a possible connection.

This story begins on August 30, 1935, with the birth of John Edmund Andrew Phillips to parents Claude and Edna Phillips. Claude was a retired Marine Corps officer and engineer. His father, John Andrew Phillips, who had been a prominent and influential architect, one day "mysteriously fell to his death" on a construction site, according to John Phillips' autobiography.

John's mother, Edna, had what most people would consider a decidedly unconventional upbringing. Her mother was a psychic and faith healer, and many of her eleven siblings were well known locally as gunfighters and bandits. When Edna was just a year old, she was purportedly kidnapped by Gypsies! Not to worry though—her father allegedly found her a year later down in Mexico, though how he would have done so will doubtless forever remain a mystery.

Edna was just fifteen when she met and began a relationship with Claude Phillips, who according to legend had supposedly won an Oklahoma bar from a fellow serviceman in a poker game on the way home from France at the close of WWI—which seems, in retrospect, about as credible as various other aspects of Phillips family history as told by John. By eighteen, Edna had given birth to the couple's first child, Rosie Phillips, born on New Year's Eve, 1922. Rosie would later become a career employee of the Pentagon, where John's first wife would also find work. Years later, according to John, Rosie's daughter Patty would be "found dead of an overdose in a girlfriend's apartment in North Hollywood... There were mysterious questions surrounding her death." This kind of thing tends to happen to families in Laurel Canyon.

In the late 1920s, Claude Phillips was commissioned to Haiti, where he remained for four years. He was then sent back to Quantico, then shipped off to Managua, Nicaragua, before finally returning to Alexandria, Virginia, where John Phillips, who would become arguably the most important music figure in the canyon, grew up and went to school. John attended a series of strict Catholic and military schools. He also served as an altar boy, though according to his own account, he also had a darker side which included forays into vandalism, auto theft, breaking and entering, fighting, and other assorted mischief. His mother, meanwhile, routinely cruised for men, when not spending time with a US Army Colonel named George Lacy. John would later be told that his real father was a US Marine Corps doctor named Roland Meeks, who died in a Japanese POW camp during WWII.

Phillips played basketball at George Washington High School, graduating in 1953. He then scored an appointment to Annapolis Naval Academy, but soon dropped out. One of his first paying jobs was working on a fishing charter boat. As John later recalled it, the crew consisted of him, a retired Navy officer, and four retired Army generals. Seems like a perfect fit for one of the future guiding lights of the hippie movement. Phillips also, for a brief time, tried his hand at selling cemetery plots.

As noted at the beginning of this odyssey, John's first wife was the aristocratic Susie Adams, a direct descendent of President John Adams and an occasional practitioner of voodoo. The couple's first son, Jeffrey, was born on Friday the 13th in December of 1957. Shortly after that, John found himself in, of all places, Havana, Cuba, just as the Batista regime was about to fall to the revolutionary forces of Fidel Castro. According to Phillips, he and his traveling companions "were once whisked off the street by a director, straight into a TV studio to appear on a live Havana variety show." Many of you, I'm sure, have had a similar experience.

Some months later, in 1958, Phillips flew to Los Angeles and began performing on amateur nights at Pandora's Box on the legendary Sunset Strip. His first band, the Journeymen, featured Phillips, Scott McKenzie and Dick Weismann. It was while touring with this formation that John Phillips met a very young Holly Michelle Gilliam. Michelle was born November 10, 1944, in Long Beach, California, to a father variously described as a merchant marine, a movie production assistant, and a self-taught intellectual. When Michelle's mother, a Baptist minister's daughter, reportedly died of a brain aneurysm when Michelle was just five, Gardner "Gil" Gilliam took his daughters and promptly relocated to Mexico, ostensibly to attend college on the GI Bill. They remained there for several years. Upon their return to Southern California, Gil found work as an LA County probation officer. According to John, Gil's work "often required him to go out of town," though one would think that that would make it rather difficult for him to keep tabs on his charges.

In 1958, while future husband John was vacationing in war-torn Cuba, Michelle found a new mother figure in twenty-three-year-old Tamar Hodel. Tamar's father, Dr. George Hodel, was described by *Vanity Fair* in December 2007 as "the most pathologically decadent man in Los Angeles" and "the city's venereal-disease czar and a fixture in its A-list demimonde." Also noted in the article was that "George Hodel shared with Man Ray a love for the work of the Marquis de Sade and the belief that the pursuit of personal liberty was worth everything." In other words, Hodel embraced that all-purpose Luciferian creed, "Do what thou wilt."

According to the same article, Tamar and her siblings had "grown up in her father's Hollywood house, which resembled a Mayan temple, was designed by Frank Lloyd Wright's son, and was the site of wild parties, in which Hodel was sometimes joined by director John Huston and photographer Man Ray." The luxurious home reportedly features, among other amenities, a subterranean walk-in vault, which is always a nice thing to have around. Within the walls of that singularly odd Hollywood Hills home, which lies about three miles due east of the mouth of Laurel Canyon, Tamar has talked of how she "often 'uncomfortably' posed nude... for 'dirty-old-man' Man Ray and had once wriggled free from a predatory John Huston." Her own father, not so shockingly, "had committed incest with her. 'When I was eleven, my father taught me to perform oral sex on him.'" Her father also "plied her with erotic books, grooming her for what he touted as their transcendent union," and freely shared her with his wealthy and influential friends.

"To the girl's horror, she became pregnant" at the tender age of fourteen—with her father's child. "To her greater horror, she says, 'my father wanted me to *have* his baby.'" A friend, nevertheless, took her to get an abortion. Dr. George was so incensed that, according to Tamar, he "struck her on the head with his pistol," prompting her stepmother (who also happened to be John Huston's ex-wife) to assist her in going into hiding. Dr. George Hodel was arrested and charged with, among other things, offering his young daughter to several friends at an orgy. The sensational 1949 incest trial featured a witness who took the stand to describe being hypnotized by Hodel at a party.

Allegations that the rich and powerful were dabbling in incest, hypnotism, pedophilic orgies and Luciferian philosophies must surely have been shocking to Angelenos in the 1940s, as they would still be to most Americans today. Perhaps that is why the jury chose not to believe Tamar and instead acquitted Dr. Hodel. Of course, it should probably be factored in that Tamar was roundly vilified by both the Jerry Giesler-led defense team and the local press.

Far more shocking than the allegations aired at trial was the then-unknown fact that, even while Hodel was standing trial on the sensational charges, he was, and still is today, a prime suspect in the Black Dahlia murder case! There have been, to be sure, numerous suspects identified in the case, including actor/director Orson Welles. But George Hodel does seem to be a much more likely suspect than most of those who have been identified. And his possible guilt, it should be noted, does not exclude others from likely complicity as well. The mistake that virtually all investigators of this case have made is assuming that there was only *one* culprit. It is entirely possible that Hodel committed the crime in conjunction with various others in his Luciferian social circle. Photographer Man Ray, for example, is a compelling suspect given that the posing of Ms. Short's body appeared to mimic the Minotaur, one of his better-known photographs.

It seems unlikely that the fourteen-year-old daughter of a lowly probation officer would fall into the orbit of the daughter of the very wealthy and well-connected George Hodel, but not any more unlikely, I suppose, than numerous other aspects of the Laurel Canyon saga. Tamar, who has been described by Michelle as "the epitome of glamour," quickly took the youngster under her wing, buying her clothes, enrolling her in modeling school, teaching her to drive, and providing her with a fake ID and a steady stream of prescription drugs—obtained, one would presume, from her father. According to Michelle, "Tamar put on perfect airs around my dad and when it became necessary she would sleep with him." That perhaps explains why, in early 1961, Gil didn't have a problem with allowing his underage daughter to move to San Francisco with her surrogate mom.

Soon enough, Tamar found herself in a relationship with Journeyman Scott McKenzie, and bandmate John Phillips began coming by Tamar and Michelle's room on a nightly basis. It wasn't long before Michelle, still just sixteen, was romantically involved with twenty-five-year-old Phillips, despite the fact that John was still married to and living with Susie Adams, with whom he by then had two children, Laura MacKenzie Phillips having been born on November 10, 1959 in, naturally enough, Alexandria, Virginia. Father Gil, who had recently taken a sixteen-year-old bride of his own (one of a string of six wives), still wasn't concerned. And it's probably safe to assume that Phillips' father, who had pursued his bride when she was just fifteen, wouldn't have been too concerned either.

In October 1962, a year or so after meeting Michelle, John curiously found himself in Jacksonville, Florida, alongside Naval Air Station Jacksonville and Naval Station Mayport for "two weeks of rest and rehearsal" that just happened to coincide with the Cuban Missile Crisis. For a guy who, in his own words, "never felt comfortable with political advocacy," John seems to have had a keen interest in Cuban affairs. Two months later, on New Year's Eve 1962, Holly Michelle Gilliam became John Phillips' second wife. She also joined his reconfigured band, as did Canadian Denny Doherty, who had formerly been with the Mugwumps alongside Cass Elliot. This new lineup was dubbed the New Journeymen.

The newly formed trio promptly embarked on a drug-fueled Caribbean adventure, arriving first at St. Johns, where John claimed that they "snorkeled on acid" for several weeks. They next ferried over to St. Thomas, where they set up camp at a dive beachfront boardinghouse known as Duffy's. Soon enough, Ellen Naomi Cohen, better known as Cass Elliot, showed up with John's nephew, who was a childhood friend of hers. Cass had been born in Baltimore but had grown up in Alexandria, where, like Phillips, she had attended George Washington High School. As the legend goes, Cass waited tables at the dive while the trio performed folk songs. During their time there, "The town was," according to Phillips, "crawling with drunken Marines and sailors on their way home from Vietnam."

Moving on from the boardinghouse, the group next took over an unfinished home on Creeque Alley, where, according to John, they were known as "the island's open house and everyone was welcome to our commune." At some point though the governor supposedly ordered them off the island "because he thought his nephew was doing drugs with the crazies at Creeque Alley." The band had formalized its new lineup of John Phillips, Michelle Phillips, Denny Doherty and Cass Elliot, and they had a whole album's worth of material written. That first album would feature such enduring classics as California Dreamin' and Monday, Monday. On none of the band's subsequent albums would they produce anywhere near the level of songwriting that they were somehow able to achieve on that Caribbean adventure.

Though isolated on St. Thomas, the songs the group brought back to LA with them just happened to be of the previously unheard but soon-to-emerge folk-rock variety. In his autobiography, *Papa John*, Phillips quotes Doherty as saying that everyone was "evolving toward the same sound at the same time without really communicating with each other about it." It was, I suppose, just the way things were fated to be—another one of those amazing serendipities!

To be sure, Phillips told a number of different versions of the story of the origins of the songs on that first album. One version had California Dreamin' being written in a New York hotel room in the middle of the night, with assistance from Michelle. Another version held that the tune was composed on the drive to LA from New York. Yet another version had the song dating back to 1963. Phillips also claimed at times that the song wasn't even written for the Mamas and the Papas but rather for Barry McGuire, who was a hot commodity following the 1965 release of Eve Of Destruction.

Within a month of arriving in LA, the band had a producer/manager (Lou Adler, a Jewish kid who had grown up in a tough, Hispanic section of East LA) and a record deal, and John and Michelle were at home in a comfortable house on Lookout Mountain in Laurel Canyon. They would soon be able to afford to purchase Jeanette McDonald's former Bel Air mansion at 783 Bel Air Road, which featured "hand-carved wooden gargoyles" and "a walk-in vault beneath the house," which, as I already mentioned, is a very handy feature. Sitting on five acres, the lavish home, with five Rolls-Royces in the driveway, was the site of virtually nonstop partying.

The new lineup, of course, needed a name, and John pushed hard for the occult-based Magic Cyrcle, a name by which the band was briefly known before ultimately settling on the Mamas and the Papas. They proved to be a rather short-lived band, recording and performing only from 1965 to 1968, with a brief reunion in 1971 to satisfy contractual obligations to their record company. During that time, the band produced five albums and eleven top forty singles. To date, the lineup has sold nearly 100,000,000 albums.

The Mamas and the Papas' freshman album, *If You Can Believe Your Eyes and Ears*, was released in early 1966 and rose to the very top of the charts. It was all downhill from there. While recording their second album in June 1966, Michelle was discharged from the band due to the fact that she was having an affair with Denny Doherty, which was causing severe friction in the group. By August though she was back, which didn't prevent the group's second album from performing rather poorly. The third, recorded in 1967 and entitled *Deliver*, failed to live up to its name. Then in June of that year, the Mamas and the Papas delivered a closing set at the Monterey Pop Festival that almost everyone agrees was pretty wretched.

Two months after Monterey, the band made their final television appearance on the *Ed Sullivan Show*. Two months after that, the quartet headed off to Europe while recording their fourth album, *The Papas and the Mamas*. Shortly thereafter, the band broke up. John tried his hand at a solo career with the unsuccessful release of *John Phillips, the Wolf King of LA*, which bore the logo of his own Warlock Records. To satisfy record label demands, the group then briefly reformed for their fourth album, *People Like Us*. Following that unsuccessful venture, the band once again dissolved.

During the heyday of the Mamas and the Papas, John and Michelle Phillips knew, and regularly played host to, virtually everyone of importance in the canyons. In addition to all the singers and musicians living in Laurel Canyon, the power couple's circle of friends included Warren Beatty, Peter and Jane Fonda, Jack Nicholson, Terry Melcher and girlfriend Candice Bergen, Marlon Brando, Roman Polanski and Sharon Tate, Abigail Folger and Voytek Frykowski, soon-to-be-dead gossip columnist Steve Brandt, Larry Hagman, presidential brother-in-law Peter Lawford (fresh from his alleged involvement in covering up the murder of Marilyn Monroe), Dennis Hopper, Ryan O'Neal, Mia Farrow, ethereal Freemason Peter Sellers, and Zsa Zsa Gabor. And a short, scraggly singer/songwriter by the name of Charles Manson.

There were, to be sure, numerous ties between the Mamas and the Papas and Charles Manson. And between the Mamas and the Papas and the Cielo Drive victims. John Phillips, for example, had invested $10,000 in Jay Sebring's business venture, Sebring International, which was rumored to have been a front for various illegal activities, including drug trafficking. Michelle Phillips had a brief affair with Roman Polanski in London while Polanski was married to the soon-to-be-murdered Sharon Tate (during that same sojourn to London, Tate was reportedly initiated into the practice of witchcraft). Mama Cass, as previously noted, lived just across the road from the house at 2774 Woodstock Road occupied by Folger and Frykowski. Both homes were frequently visited by known drug dealers. Regulars at Cass' home included Pic Dawson (also a regular at the Frykowski/Folger home and at the Tate/Polanski home), the son of a US State Department official who, according to John Phillips, was suspected by authorities "of using diplomatic pouches to move drugs between countries," and Billy Doyle, a local dealer who Dennis Hopper claimed was filmed while being flogged at the Tate/Polanski house just three days before the murders. Another regular was Bill Mentzer, later convicted of the brutal murder of Cotton Club producer Roy Radin. The LAPD once described Mentzer as a member of "some kind of hit squad."

So dark was the scene at the home of the 'Lady of the Canyon' that, according to journalist Maury Terry, four of the LAPD's initial prime suspects in the Tate killings were drug dealers associated with Cass Elliot. And yet, curiously enough, many of the canyon's peace-and-love spewing musicians were regulars at Mama Cass' home as well. As *Rolling Stone* noted in its fortieth anniversary edition, "'Mama' Cass Elliot's cozy canyon house functioned as a sort of rock salon." In a similar vein, Barney Hoskyns wrote in *Hotel California* that "Cass kept permanent open house." Also noted in Hoskyns' tome was that the Laurel Canyon scene "all spun around him and Cass," with the "him" in this case being David Crosby, who, like Cass, had an insatiable appetite for potent pain killers like Demerol, Dilaudid and Percodan. Crosby was one of many Canyonites who regularly dropped by Cass' place to hang out and engage in impromptu jam sessions, and to mingle with some seriously disreputable characters.

Also a regular at Cass' place, by some reports, was Charlie Manson himself. According to Ed Sanders, it was at Cass' home that Charlie first met her neighbor, coffee heiress Abigail Folger (who helped finance Kenneth Anger's films, like the one that was supposed to star Godo Paulekas but instead starred Mansonite Bobby Beausoleil). According to Maury Terry, the rather notorious Process Church of the Final Judgement—which evidence suggests had deep ties to the Manson, Son of Sam and Cotton Club murders—also came knocking on Cass' door, actively seeking to recruit her as well as John Phillips and Terry Melcher.

Terry has written that the Manson Family's iconic bus was seen parked at the home of John and Michelle Phillips in the fall of 1968. Some reports also hold that Manson attended a New Year's Eve party at the couple's home on December 31, 1968, just months before the murders began. So close were the ties between the Mamas and the Papas and the Manson clan that both John Phillips and Mama Cass were slated to appear as witnesses for the defense at the Family's trial, though neither was ever called. For a band that sang about being "safe and warm, if I was in LA," the members of the Mamas and the Papas kept some pretty dangerous company in the City of Angels.

Speaking of dangerous company, not long after the band hit the charts, Tamar Hodel received a postcard from Michelle Phillips asking her to watch their scheduled performance on the *Ed Sullivan Show* and to then meet the group at San Francisco's Fairmont Hotel before a scheduled concert. Tamar showed up with father George at her side—the two, as with Gram and Robert Parsons, apparently still maintaining a close relationship—and Tamar, George, John, Michelle, Denny and Cass embarked on a drug-fueled pre-show odyssey.

By 1970, John and Michelle had divorced. Many years later, Michelle would reveal that their time together had included at least one episode of domestic violence, one that she was still reluctant to discuss: "It was serious. I ended up in the hospital. That's all I'll say about it." The union had yielded John a second daughter, Gilliam Chynna Phillips, born February 12, 1968, in Los Angeles. On January 31, 1972, John Phillips married for the third time, to actress and Crowley aficionado Genevieve Waite. On the wedding guest list were soon-to-be-governor Jerry Brown and soon-to-be-lieutenant-governor Mike Curb.

The couple's time together would be marked by wildly out-of-control drug consumption and the birth of two more offspring: Tamerlane, whose name is perhaps in part an homage to Tamar Hodel, and Bijou Lilly, who was taken away and placed in foster care in Bolton Landing, New York, after her drug-addled parents were deemed unfit to raise her. In June 1972, shortly after marrying Waite, Phillips moved into a canyon home at 414 St. Pierre Road that had been built by William Randolph Hearst. The Rolling Stones had just vacated the property and their trusty sidekick, Gram Parsons, was still hanging around and would grow very close to John Phillips. Parsons though would soon turn up dead, while John would head off to London where he reportedly planned to record a solo album with assistance from Mick Jagger and Keith Richards. That project never got off the ground, however, as Phillips' addictions rendered him impossible to work with.

Cass Elliot turned up in London the very next year, but unlike her former bandmate, her trip abroad was to be one-way; on July 29, 1974, she was found dead in occasional Canyonite Harry Nilsson's London flat. Ms. Elliot, it seems safe to say, knew a little too much about the dark side of Laurel Canyon.

Following the dissolution of the Mamas and the Papas, Cass had gone on to a successful solo career and had become a familiar face on American television screens. In addition to hosting two primetime network specials, she had guest-hosted the *Tonight Show* and had appeared on such popular early 1970s shows as *The Red Skelton Show* and *Love, American Style*. She had been married twice, first in 1963 to vocalist Jim Hendricks in what was reportedly a platonic arrangement aimed at getting Hendricks a draft deferment. During that first marriage, which was annulled in 1968, Cass had given birth to a daughter, Owen Vanessa Elliot, born on April 26, 1967. Hendricks, however, was reportedly not the father and Cass steadfastly refused to reveal who Owen's true father was. In 1971, following the breakup of the band, Cass married again, to Baron Donald von Weidenman, a wealthy Bavarian heir. That marriage collapsed after just a few months though and Cass was single when she died just a few years later. Owen, already fatherless, was just seven.

Denny Doherty, meanwhile, went on to host a popular variety show in Canada, as well as perform in various formations of the New Mamas and the Papas. He passed away on January 19, 2007, reportedly due to kidney failure.

Michelle Phillips released an unsuccessful solo album and then switched gears and went on to a successful acting career, gracing the small screen in such hit shows as *Knot's Landing*, *Hotel*, and *Beverly Hills, 90210*. She continued to have numerous flings and has married several more times. She is currently the only living member of the original Mamas and the Papas.

As for John Phillips, in 1975 he sobered up enough to put together the soundtrack for the film *The Man Who Fell to Earth*, a surreal venture featuring the talents of fledgling actor David Bowie and director Nicolas Roeg, who had previously collaborated with Crowleyite Donald Cammell on *Performance*. At that same time, Phillips was working on completing a horrifically bad, Andy Warhol-produced stage musical entitled *Man on the Moon*, which closed just two days after opening. Phillips at one time had Don "Miami Vice" Johnson in mind to play the lead in his space opera. Like the rest of the Hollywood notables in this story, Johnson was a canyon dweller at the time. His next-door neighbor happened to be a guy by the name of Chuck Wein, an avid occultist and buddy of Warhol who, in addition to managing bizarre nightclub acts, directed the 1972 documentary *Rainbow Bridge*. Wein shared a curious nickname with fellow Canyonite Charlie Manson: The Wizard.

For the remainder of his career, Phillips' musical output consisted primarily of occasionally writing songs for and with others, his most well known contribution being his co-writing duties on *Kokomo*, recorded and released by the Beach Boys.

In 1981, Phillips found himself facing charges of trafficking large quantities of narcotics. By his own account, he had an arrangement with a pharmacy that allowed him to obtain large amounts of narcotics without prescriptions (daughter Bijou would later say that he had actually purchased the pharmacy, guaranteeing virtually unlimited access). The charges were quite serious; in Phillips' own words, he "was looking at forty-five years and got thirty days." He began serving his sentence, appropriately enough, on April 20 and he was released just three-and-a-half weeks later. It never hurts to have friends in high places.

Phillips' circle of friends in the post-Mamas and the Papas years included J. Paul Getty, Jr., Bobby Kennedy, Jr., and Princess Margaret. Getty and Kennedy, both plagued by demons of their own, were likely being supplied by Phillips. Another name in Phillips' Rolodex was Colin Tennant, the wealthy heir of a massive petrochemical conglomerate in the UK. Tennant owned a private island in the British West Indies where wealthy friends like John Phillips and Mick and Bianca Jagger could engage in unknown activities in complete seclusion.

Upon being released from his preposterously short period of confinement, Phillips put together a version of the Mamas and the Papas that included daughter Mackenzie Phillips and original lead vocalist Denny Doherty. Scott McKenzie, who had summoned all the runaways across the country to come to San Francisco with flowers in their hair, later replaced Doherty. Laurie Beebe subsequently replaced Mackenzie Phillips, after which Doherty returned once again to replace John Phillips. The band finally called it quits in 1994.

Phillips had divorced Waite in 1985. In 1992, he received a liver transplant and a new lease on life. Just months later, he was photographed drinking in a bar in Palm Springs. In 1998, Phillips and the other surviving members of the Mamas and the Papas were inducted into the Rock and Roll Hall of Fame. Three years later, on March 18, 2001, Phillips died of heart failure. The saga wasn't quite over, however; Phillips' daughters would carry on with the family tradition—while spilling some dark family secrets along the way.

Oldest daughter Mackenzie began her acting career at the tender age of twelve when she landed a role in what was to be George Lucas' breakthrough film, *American Graffiti*. Just a few years before, it will be recalled, Lucas had been an unknown cameraman at the Rolling Stones' notorious Altamont concert. During the filming of *Graffiti* in 1972, John Phillips, who I'm sure had lots of important business to attend to and therefore little time to look after his daughter, signed over legal guardianship of Mackenzie to producer Gary Kurtz. A few years later, in 1975, Mackenzie landed a role on what would quickly become a hit television series, *One Day at a Time*. During the third season, however, Mackenzie was arrested for public drunkenness and cocaine possession, after which her substance abuse problems continued to spiral out of control, causing frequent problems and considerable tension on the set of her hit show.

Providing a template for Charlie Sheen to later follow, she was fired from her show in 1980. After two nearly fatal overdoses, she was invited back by producers in 1981. The following year she collapsed on the set and was once again fired. What had once seemed a very promising acting career was over as quickly as it had begun. From the late 1980s through the early 1990s, she performed intermittently with the reformed Mamas and the Papas. In 1992, she reportedly entered a long-term rehab program that she didn't emerge from for nine months. Following that, she kept a low profile for many years. In August 2008, however, she was arrested at LAX for heroin and cocaine possession and on Halloween day 2008, she entered a guilty plea and was once again sent to rehab.

A year later, in September 2009, Mackenzie released her tell-all memoir, *High on Arrival*, which painted a disturbing picture of her late father. In addition to introducing her to drugs at the age of eleven by injecting her with cocaine, Mackenzie claimed that Papa John had raped her on the eve of her first marriage and had engaged in an incestuous affair with her that spanned a decade and ended only when she became pregnant and did not know who the father was—a scenario, it should be noted, with remarkable parallels to the ordeal endured by Michelle's surrogate mother, Tamar Hodel.

John Phillips' memoir covering the time period in question made no mention of the illicit relationship with his daughter. He did though claim that Mackenzie was once raped at knifepoint by an unknown assailant. He also noted, shockingly enough, that Mackenzie's "house in Laurel Canyon was destroyed by fire." That, as we all know, hardly ever happens.

The year after dropping her bombshells, Mackenzie appeared on what is arguably the most appalling 'reality' show to ever hit the airwaves, *Celebrity Rehab*, in a role far removed from her glory days on a hit primetime show. That same year, sister Chynna Phillips entered rehab as well, though she was reportedly seeking relief from "anxiety." Chynna first captured the spotlight in 1990 as one-third of the vocal group Wilson Phillips, alongside Carnie and Wendy Wilson, offspring of reclusive Beach Boy Brian Wilson. That group though proved to be very short-lived, as did Chynna's musical career. In 1995, Chynna married actor William Baldwin. In 2003, she became what *Vanity Fair* described as a "fervent born-again Christian. She was baptized in brother-in-law Stephen Baldwin's bathtub." The magazine also quoted Chynna as saying that "being a mom is challenging for me—my perspective is warped."

Like her older sisters, Bijou Lilly Phillips—born April 1, 1980, just a year before her father was harshly punished for running a major narcotics trafficking operation—merged into the fast lane at a very young age. Her mother was addicted to heroin while carrying her and Bijou has candidly described herself as a "crack baby." Raised partially in a foster home, she was reunited with her father by the courts when in the third grade. That wasn't necessarily a good thing.

Described by *Index* magazine as "a wild child who, through fate and circumstance, was somehow allowed to partake of New York's nebulous nightlife at an age traditionally more suited to playing with dolls," Bijou was a cover model from a very young age. She was also the fourteen-year-old star of a Calvin Klein ad campaign that many people (as well as the US Justice Department) considered to be bordering on child pornography, and that Bijou herself has referred to as "the kiddy porn ads."

Bijou told her interviewer from *Index* that coaching her and creepily lurking behind the scenes of that notorious Calvin Klein photo shoot—I'm guessing as a technical adviser—"was this porn guy." The interviewer identified that "porn guy" as Ron Jeremy, who is not your run-of-the-mill "porn guy," and not just because he is arguably the world's most famous porn star. He is also a very well-connected porn star. His mother, for example, was an asset of the OSS, precursor to the CIA. His uncle had ties to notorious gangster Benjamin "Bugsy" Siegel. And he attended high school with none other than future CIA director George Tenet.

Bijou has alluded to the fact that Mackenzie was not the only Phillips daughter to receive unwanted attention from Papa John. In her music can be found lyrics such as "he touched me wrong." Asked directly about such references, she told an interviewer that she had "made this decision not to talk to the press about anything that's gone on in my life, but just to write music about it. They can interpret it themselves," though she then quickly added, "It's blatantly obvious." The youngest of the Phillips clan also acknowledged that she has a "Daddy" tattoo on her rear. "That was [done] during a time," she said, "when I was a pretty sick puppy."

Bijou made her film debut in 1999 and has had a number of low-profile film and television roles since then. Most recently, she has had a recurring role on the television series *Raising Hope* as, of all things, a serial killer. She is currently an avid Scientologist. Many of the problems she has faced, she ultimately realized, stem from the fact that she'd "never been shown respect by my parents. I'd always been treated like an object, not like a human."

19

HUNGRY FREAKS, DADDY FRANK ZAPPA

"The fact that Frank Zappa was one of the most prominent rock-star residents of Laurel Canyon didn't change the fact that he viewed the flower-power underground with amused contempt." Barney Hoskyns, author of Hotel California

"Frank openly made fun of the very counterculture he was helping to sustain." Jefferson Airplane vocalist Grace Slick

FRANK ZAPPA WAS BORN ON THE FIRST DAY OF WINTER IN THE YEAR 1940 IN Baltimore, Maryland. Precisely sixty-four years later, on the winter solstice of 2004, his first grandchild, Mathilda Plum Doucette, would be born to daughter Moon Unit Zappa.

Zappa's father, Francesco Vincenzo Zappa, hailed from Partinico, Sicily, described by Zappa biographer Barry Miles as "the Mafia heartland." Francesco was of Greek and Arab ancestry, while his wife Rose Marie was a blend of Italian and French. Many of Francesco and Rose Marie's siblings seem to have lived very short and tragic lives, including Francesco's twin sisters who perished in a train crash. Rose Marie had one sister who died at birth, another (Margaret) who only made it to the age of two, and a third who died shortly after Margaret. She also had a brother who simply vanished at the age of nineteen and was never seen or heard from again.

Francesco Zappa arrived in America in 1908, settling with his parents in the city of Baltimore, Maryland, just outside of Washington, DC. He attended the city's Polytechnic High School and then the University of North Carolina, after which he spent the rest of his life in the employ of the US military intelligence establishment. He and Rose Marie had four offspring, the oldest of whom was Francis Vincent, better known as Frank.

Frank's first schooling was at the Edgewood School, part of the Edgewood Arsenal complex where his father worked and the family lived. Edgewood was, for the uninformed, the longtime home of US chemical warfare research, as well as being, by the government's own admission, the site of human mind control experimentation in the post-WWII years. At some point in the 1940s, the Zappa clan relocated to Florida for a short time for unknown reasons, but they soon returned to Baltimore and the Edgewood Arsenal. In 1951, father Francesco was offered a position at Dugway Proving Ground in Utah, but he chose instead to head further west and relocate the family to Monterey, California. While there, he taught classes at the Naval Postgraduate School.

After a couple years in Monterey, the Zappas relocated once again, first briefly to Claremont before moving on to the San Diego area, the current home of the world's largest naval fleet. While there, Francesco put his skills to work on the Atlas Missile Project, a program that would produce America's very first intercontinental ballistic missiles. Zappa's area of expertise would tend to indicate that the US was looking into developing chemical warheads for those ICBMs; that though is impossible to determine since Zappa's work in San Diego and elsewhere was classified.

In the summer of 1956, the Zappa family hit the road once again, this time landing in Lancaster, California, right alongside Edwards Air Force Base. Frank Zappa wouldn't be the only rising star to later arrive in Laurel Canyon by way of the sparsely populated wasteland of Lancaster; joining him would be tragically short-lived Byrd Clarence White, America vocalist Dewey Bunnell, and the indescribably bizarre Don Vliet, better known as Captain Beefheart.

Shortly before the move to Lancaster, there was an unusual event in Frank's life. According to the Zappa biographies, to celebrate his fifteenth birthday his mother arranged for her son a personal phone call to famed composer Edgard Varese, who at the time was out of the country and unable to take the call. Frank did though speak with the composer's wife and later received, by various accounts, either a letter from Varese or a personal phone call. None of those accounts offer any clue to how Rose Marie Zappa had ready access to someone of Varese's stature.

In Lancaster, Frank attended Antelope Valley High School where he began experimenting with 8mm film and met and befriended Vliet, who would later change his surname to Van Vliet. The two graduated together in 1958, with Frank receiving a diploma despite the fact that he was short on credits. In 1959, at the tender age of eighteen, Frank moved into his own apartment in Echo Park and began attending Pomona College, where he met Kathryn "Kay" Sherman. Frank's brother Bobby Zappa, meanwhile, enlisted in the US Marines.

On December 28, 1960, just a week after Zappa's twentieth birthday, Frank and Kay were married and Frank began working in advertising. The marriage would last just four years. Not long after marrying Sherman, Zappa became involved with character actor Timothy Carey's bizarre underground film project known as *The World's Greatest Sinner*. Zappa provided the soundtrack for Carey's experimental film, which remained largely unseen for decades after its completion in 1962. The occult-based plot revolved around star Carey's metamorphosis from insurance salesman to rock star to cult leader to self-proclaimed god.

At around that same time, Zappa met and played occasional gigs with Terry Kirkman, who would later form yet another Laurel Canyon-affiliated band, the Association. He also began writing songs for other up-and-comers and forged a friendship and working relationship with Paul Buff, owner of the independent Pal Recording Studio in Cucamonga, California. Buff had studied aviation electronics in the US Marines, where he graduated top in a class of 500. Following his time in the service, he secured a job at General Dynamics where he engineered parts for guided missiles. He eventually left that job to, of all things, open his own recording studio. It was in that studio that Buff taught Zappa how to multi-track and overdub. At a time when most independent recording studios featured just mono or, at best, two-track recording capabilities, Buff's studio featured a custom-built five-track tape recorder.

In March of 1963, Zappa famously appeared on *The Steve Allen Show* to 'play' a bicycle as a musical instrument. That same year, Herb Cohen, who would become the manager of Frank Zappa and fellow canyonites Linda Ronstadt, Alice Cooper, Lenny Bruce and Tim Buckley, returned to Los Angeles. After conveniently being in the Congo at the time of the CIA-sponsored coup that toppled (and led directly to the execution of) Patrice Lumumba, the country's first legally elected prime minister, Cohen had spent time in Copenhagen, Denmark, where he functioned as an international arms dealer.

In 1964, Zappa's marriage to Sherman collapsed and he moved into friend Paul Buff's Pal Studio, which he quickly took over and renamed Studio Z. Not long after, in a curious incident in March 1965, Zappa was charged with 'conspiracy to commit pornography' after accepting an offer to produce erotic audiotapes in his studio/home. He was sentenced to a six-month stint in jail, but all but ten days were suspended.

A year later, in June 1966, Frank Zappa and his recently formed band, the Mothers of Invention, released the groundbreaking album *Freak Out!* It was, depending upon who is telling the story, either the first or second double rock album. (Bob Dylan's *Blonde on Blonde* was scheduled to be released a month before *Freak Out!*, but Dylan's album was apparently delayed.) It was also the first rock 'concept album' and the first to print lyrics on the album sleeve. During the recording of the album—which featured contributions from Vito's troupe, Bobby Beausoleil, Frank's ever-present groupies, and various other hangers-on—Zappa moved into a Laurel Canyon home on Kirkwood Drive with Pamela Zarubica, also known as Suzy Creamcheese.

In the spring of 1967, Frank signed a contract to play at the Garrick Theater in New York, an engagement that would last six months. On one notable occasion, Zappa invited active-duty Marines onto the stage and handed them a doll, which he instructed them to pretend was a "gook baby." The GIs happily obliged the request and gleefully dismembered the doll while Frank looked on. Though Marines weren't normally part of the show, concerts by the Mothers often included the "hurling of severed baby-doll heads into the crowd of gaping groovers," as former GTO Pamela Des Barres remembers it in her book *I'm With the Band*. It was a practice that Zappa protégé Alice Cooper would greatly expand upon.

On the autumnal equinox of 1967, Zappa married Navy brat Adelaide Gail Sloatman, who was then working as former cop/gangster Elmer Valentine's personal assistant, overseeing the operations of the Whisky-A-Go-Go and the Trip. Just one week later, on September 28, 1967, daughter Moon Unit Zappa was born. She would ultimately be joined by three siblings, each bearing a progressively more bizarre name: Dweezil Zappa, Ahmet Emuukha Rodan Zappa, and Diva Thin Muffin Pigeen Zappa. All would be pulled out of school at the age of fifteen and their father would refuse to pay for any of them to attend college.

The Zappas soon returned to Laurel Canyon and took up residence in what had already become the community's most notorious commune, the iconic Log Cabin. Des Barres described the living conditions for her and other future members of the GTOs: "Lucy and Sandra shared the vault in the basement of the log cabin that Tom Mix built... Directly across from the vault was a large closet where Christine Frka privately resided." The basement featured a second walk-in vault that was frequently occupied by Carl Franzoni, to whom the Zappa song Hungry Freaks, Daddy was dedicated. People lived in every nook and cranny of the property, as well as on the grounds, which came "complete with a stream and minilake, caves, hideaways..."

Also at that time, Zappa and manager Cohen jointly launched two new record labels, Bizarre Records and Straight Records. Along with a recording of comic Lenny Bruce's last live performance, the labels would deliver to the world some of the oddest and most outrageous acts ever committed to vinyl, including the partially underage GTOs, shock-rocker Alice Cooper, Captain Beefheart and his Magic Band, and Larry "Wild Man" Fischer.

When discovered and signed by Zappa, Fischer was a self-styled 'street singer' with a colorful history and a noticeable lack of songwriting and vocal talent. Born on November 6, 1944, Larry lost his father when he was quite young and his mother was described as being emotionally distant and verbally abusive. Larry had no friends during his childhood and he was reportedly thrown out of high school. At the age of sixteen, he was institutionalized after attacking his mother with a knife. He later made two additional attempts to kill his mother and attacked his brother on at least one occasion as well.

In 1963, he was institutionalized once again, at Camarillo State Hospital, where he was subjected to repeated electroshock 'treatments.' "They did all kinds of things to me," Fischer once said, "like I was like a guinea pig." He was released in 1964 but was committed again two years later, in 1966. Accounts vary as to whether he was released or whether he escaped in this instance. One way or another he was back out in 1968, although he was never welcomed home again and so took to the streets, singing for change. It was there that he was discovered by Zappa, who released Fischer's first single in October 1968 on, appropriately enough, the Bizarre label.

Fischer's magnum opus, *An Evening with Wild Man Fischer*, hit record stores on April 28, 1969. The double album, produced by Zappa, featured Fischer on the cover holding a knife to a maternal figure. Later that year, Zappa got Fischer a booking on *Rowan and Martin's Laugh-In*. It wasn't long though before Larry had bitterly parted ways with Zappa following an incident in which Fischer angrily threw a bottle that narrowly missed hitting infant Moon Unit. Larry thereafter dropped out of sight for several years, surfacing again in 1975 when he wrote and sang a jingle for the newly launched Rhino Records.

In 1977, Rhino returned the favor by releasing Fischer's second album, *Wildmania*, to less than critical acclaim. Billy Mumy, yet another former child actor, co-produced Fischer's third and fourth albums, *Pronounced Normal* (1981) and *Nothing Scary* (1983), both on the Rhino label. Though Mumy maintained a close relationship with Fischer, Wild Man once pulled a gun on the former *Twilight Zone* and *Lost in Space* star, who Larry suspected of being involved in a bizarre conspiracy involving Weird Al Yankovic and Dr. Demento.

A few years after the release of *Nothing Scary*, Mumy recorded a duet featuring the unusual pairing of Fischer and Rosemary Clooney. After that, Wild Man Fischer largely drifted back into obscurity. By 2004, he was living anonymously in an assisted care facility. On June 16, 2011, his tragic life came to an end, reportedly due to a heart condition. Six months earlier, on December 17, 2010, another decidedly offbeat onetime member of the Zappa inner circle, Captain Beefheart, had also passed away.

Don Glen Vliet, born on January 15, 1941, in Glendale, California, was one of Zappa's earliest musical collaborators. Vliet, who moved to

Lancaster as a pampered young teen in 1954, was a child prodigy by some reports. He was also the grandson of a second cousin to accused Nazi sympathizer Wallis Simpson, wife of King Edward VIII.

Beefheart first professionally collaborated with Zappa at Pal Studio in 1963, but the demos produced from those sessions were unsuccessful. Vliet then worked for a while as a door-to-door salesman, during which time, if legends are to be believed, he sold a vacuum cleaner to psychedelic pioneer Aldous Huxley. If so, then Huxley must not have gotten much use out of it, since he passed away later that year, just hours after the assassination of John F. Kennedy on November 22, 1963.

By 1965, Beefheart had formed the Magic Band, which would release thirteen albums between 1965 and 1982, albums on which Vliet would play harmonica and saxophone as well as provide his distinctive lead vocals. The first of those albums was *Safe as Milk*, released in 1967, followed by *Strictly Personal* in 1968. The band's third album, 1969's *Trout Mask Replica*, was released by Zappa's Straight Records and is considered to be Beefheart's signature work. To this day, the disc is regarded by some as one of the greatest rock albums of all time, though others have described Vliet's work in considerably less flattering terms.

Whether Vliet was the musical genius some view him as is a topic for others to debate; what is of far more interest here is how that music was created. *Trout Mask Replica* was recorded in a tiny two-bedroom house with blacked out windows in Woodland Hills. It was there that Beefheart's band members were essentially held prisoner for eight months, with the Captain in total control of everything, including the band members' eating and sleeping schedules. The drummer, John French, has described the atmosphere in that house as "cultlike" and has made ominous references to "brainwashing sessions."

The musicians were restricted from leaving the house and were forced to rehearse for fourteen hours every day. They were subjected to both sleep deprivation and food deprivation, and they were actively encouraged to physically attack each other. Beefheart would frequently utilize physical violence to keep the others in line; French wrote in his memoirs of being "screamed at, beaten up, drugged, humiliated, arrested, starved, stolen from, and thrown down a half-flight of stairs." They lived in poverty and squalor, with public assistance the band's only income. For one full month, the abused musicians had to survive on a single cup of beans each per day. Arrests for shoplifting were not uncommon.

Beefheart also assigned new names to all the band members, "loosening," as Barry Miles wrote, "their hold on their old identities." John French, for example, became Drumbo. So strong was Vliet's hold on his bandmates that though a couple were able to escape the deplorable conditions, they ultimately returned to an environment that was, according to a friend of the band, "positively Mansonesque." For their efforts, the musicians were paid little or nothing. And Beefheart claimed sole credit for composing and arranging the album, though it was in fact a collaborative effort. Later albums would follow much the same patterns.

There certainly doesn't appear to have been any shortage of "Mansonesque" characters populating Laurel Canyon circa 1969, and they mostly seem to have been clustered around Frank Zappa. We have already seen how Vito Paulekas, who ran the Mothers' freak sideshow, had clear parallels to Manson and was even described by those close to him as being very Manson-like. Now we see that Beefheart as well seems to have attended the Manson school of cult leadership. And Zappa himself had some rather Mansonesque qualities, including a dictatorial, autocratic style; a penchant for surrounding himself with an endless stream of very young, impressionable girls; some peculiar ideas about child sexuality; his self-assignment as the leader of a commune; and a fondness for handing out offbeat names.

It should also be mentioned here, I suppose, that Manson associate Phil Kaufman served as Zappa's road manager for a time. And according to Ed Sanders, "In early May [1969]... Beausoleil went to Frank Zappa, the brilliant composer and producer, and wanted Zappa to come to the ranch to hear the music," an invitation that was reportedly declined. Less than two months later, Beausoleil would conspire to murder musician Gary Hinman.

Nineteen-sixty-nine was also the year that Zappa dissolved the original Mothers of Invention. Together for just five years, there had always been tension within the band, owing primarily to Zappa's dictatorial style. Frank was viewed by many as a "control freak," and he was widely seen as being cold and emotionally distant, even with his immediate family (he chose to spend the vast majority of his time alone in his home studio, where it was understood that he was never to be disturbed). He was also viewed by band members and others as elitist, owing in part to his habit of staying at a different hotel than the rest of the band while on the road. David Anderle of MGM Records perhaps summed up Zappa best: "I always felt there was something a little totalitarian about Frank... I was awed by the clarity of the vision and his ability to make it happen... but it was without warmth."

Some viewed with suspicion Zappa's fondness for taking out full-page ads in the local *LA Free Press*, ostensibly to report on band news. According to Miles, "there were dark mutterings about Frank's attempt to control the Freak scene." The freak scene, that is, that he openly disdained and yet still sought to control. "The other Mothers," notes Miles, "were concerned by Frank's somewhat messianic diatribes."

Around that same time, Zappa gave up his role as ringleader of the Log Cabin and bought a house high up in the hills of Laurel Canyon, on Woodrow Wilson Drive. In stark contrast to his readily accessible prior lodgings, the new home was isolated and security was very tight, including a guardhouse and a closed-circuit television system. It was there that Zappa would live out the remainder of his years. The Log Cabin, meanwhile, was taken over by Eric Burden of British rock band the Animals. The cabin had by then become a mandatory stop for all visiting 'British Invasion' bands. According to biographer Barry Miles, the cabin's new ringleader didn't much care for working with the former occupant, comparing working with Zappa to "working with Hitler."

Zappa's move, and his newfound obsession with security, was said to be prompted in part by a curious visit to the Log Cabin in the summer of 1969—the summer of the Tate/LaBianca murders. A man identified only as "the Raven" arrived wielding a gun. Little else seems to be known about the incident but it is interesting to note that just a few years earlier, a guy who was very fond of that moniker had arrived in California. Also known as the Reverend Jim Jones of the People's Temple, he would become a rather infamous figure.

Frank Zappa remained an enormously prolific composer, arranger and performer of music throughout his life, sometimes playing with various incarnations of the Mothers. Although never a huge commercial success and almost never heard on the radio, his immense body of work is widely respected among fellow musicians and is considered to be hugely influential. What is of far more interest here though are some specific events from Zappa's later years.

On July 14, 1982, while Zappa was performing on his father's home turf in Palermo, Sicily, a war broke out between tear-gas wielding police and inexplicably armed audience members. According to Miles, the concert was held at the "mafia-controlled Stadio Communale La Favorita and all the security appeared to be made men." The Italian army was soon called in to restore order. Had Zappa's father been alive and in attendance, he might well have joined in the gunplay; he reportedly owned a handgun that he at times threatened to use, and he also was said to enjoy a good brawl now and then.

In September 1985, Frank testified before the Senate Commerce, Technology and Transportation Committee, taking Tipper Gore's PMRC committee to task over the issue of record album labeling. This is said to have ignited in Zappa a passion for politics, to such an extent that he dabbled with the idea of running for president. What he ultimately decided to do instead was serve as something of a front man for organizations like the World Bank, the International Monetary Fund and the World Trade Organization.

In 1990, he visited Czechoslovakia at the request of newly installed president Vaclav Havel, who asked him to serve as a consultant on trade and tourism. Zappa was treated by the new Czech administration (which wasn't nearly as popular at home as it was in the West) as though he was making an official state visit. He announced that he had "come to Czechoslovakia to see Communism die... I have been an enthusiastic capitalist for years." He also announced his intention of starting up an international consulting firm aimed at breaking down barriers to Western trade and investment. Toward that end, he began meeting with multinational corporate entities that had an interest in investing in Czechoslovakia.

The man who had, as Miles has noted, refused during the Vietnam era "to be drawn into anti-war protests or demonstrations," and who had his whole life been "more content to mock hippies and groupies than to criticize the Vietnam War, the American overthrow of democratic governments in Chile and Iran, or any of the other excesses committed in his name by his government," had now "internalized the whole Time-Life anticommunist line." Following his escapades in Czechoslovakia, Zappa made a number of trips to Russia to facilitate business deals through what he dubbed his "international licensing, consulting and social engineering" business enterprise.

Zappa's role as unofficial front man for the World Bank came to a premature end when he died of prostate cancer on December 4, 1993, just a couple weeks short of his fifty-third birthday. Rather bizarrely, he was laid to rest in an unmarked grave following a private ceremony less than twenty-four hours later. And it was not until the next day, December 6, 1993, with the body already safely in the ground, that his death was announced to the world.

In 2001, son Ahmet began dating actress Rose McGowan (no relation), whose colorful history included spending part of her childhood in the pedophilic Children of God cult. Her father ran a chapter of the sect, which also bequeathed to Hollywood the Phoenix brothers, Joaquin and River, the latter of whom died under mysterious circumstances at the tender age of twenty-three outside the Viper Room, very near the mouth of Laurel Canyon, on Halloween night, 1993. McGowan's previous paramour had been shock-rocker Brain Warner, better known as Marilyn Manson. A fourth cousin of bellicose political commentator and onetime presidential candidate Pat Buchanan, Warner, whose stage surname is an homage to—who else?—Charles Manson, has proudly served as a high priest in Anton LaVey's Church of Satan.

20

BORN TO BE WILD JOHN KAY

"I have an explosive temper if someone aggravates me... I have been known to put my fists through one or two walls." Steppenwolf vocalist John Kay

"John had a hell of a temper when he was doing drugs." Steve Palmer, a member of one of many incarnations of Steppenwolf

OF ALL THE SINGERS, SONGWRITERS AND MUSICIANS TO ANSWER THE PIED Piper's call summoning them to Laurel Canyon, none took a longer route there than John Kay, the enigmatic frontman for the band Steppenwolf. Kay, as it turns out, came all the way from Nazi Germany, by way of Toronto, Canada and Buffalo, New York, as did his wife and one of his bandmates.

Kay was born Joachim Fritz Krauledat on April 12, 1944, in East Prussia, a province of Germany before 1914 that was separated from the rest of the country by provisions of the Treaty of Versailles, though it remained a German-speaking province. After the plunder and annexation of Poland by the Nazis, it once again became a part of the German state, but only for the next five years. After the fall of Nazi Germany, East Prussia ceased to exist, with the northern portion being absorbed by the USSR into Byelorussia and the southern portion placed under the Polish flag.

Kay was born in Tilsit to Fritz and Elsbeth Krauledat. Fritz had enlisted in the German army in 1936 and decided to make a career of it, eventually rising to the rank of *Oberwachtmeister*, which roughly translates to Brigade Sergeant Major. He was on hand for the invasion of Poland in 1939 and the plunder of France in 1940. With the launch of Operation Barbarossa on the summer solstice of 1941, Fritz was sent to the Russian front. He last saw his wife at Christmastime in 1943. In March of the following year, she received notification of his death.

Between late July and early August of 1944, the widowed Elsbeth left Tilsit with her infant son. It was a fortuitous exit given that the Red Army almost immediately thereafter began bombing the region into oblivion. Elsbeth had been issued a permit that allowed her to travel anywhere in Germany and she used it to move herself and Joachim to Arnstadt, crossing the pre-Berlin Wall border in the process. Upon arrival in Arnstadt, Elsbeth and Joachim were taken under the wing of the Kranz family, who put a roof over their heads and became their benefactors. Soon enough, Elsbeth met Gerhard Kyczinski, a former German soldier and POW who was a mason by trade. In August 1950, Gerhard and Elsbeth married. For the next eight years, they would share a home in Arnstadt with Joachim.

During those years, young Joachim twice vacationed with his mother in the resort town of Travemunde, which Kay later described as "a very popular vacation spot with white beaches and fancy hotels." He also attended the Freie Waldorf Schule, an exclusive private school with a perpetual waiting list. Mother, son and stepfather seemed to travel rather freely, twice crossing over into East Germany and back to visit Gerhard's family. Also while still in Germany, Joachim acquired his first radio and began listening to US Armed Forces Radio, where he first heard an early idol, Little Richard. He also acquired a record player and began collecting albums by Little Richard and others, including Elvis and the Everly Brothers. He also attended screenings of rock'n'roll themed Hollywood films, like Elvis' *Love Me Tender*. At the age of thirteen, not long before leaving Germany, he acquired his first camera.

It would appear then that Kay experienced a rather privileged upbringing for a young war refugee.

In March of 1958, Gerhard, Elsbeth and Joachim packed up and headed off for Toronto, Canada, where several members of the Krauledat and Kyczinski families had already relocated. The trio opted to travel by plane rather than ship, even though flying was a decidedly luxurious mode of travel in those days. Joachim Krauledat, who would soon become John Kay, entered the Canadian school system in the ninth grade. It is said that he knew virtually no English upon arrival, but within mere months he was reportedly speaking it fluently.

The family quickly acquired a late model Chevy and John acquired his first acoustic guitar—and a reel-to-reel tape recorder. He also discovered that Toronto had far more radio stations playing rock'n'roll music than Germany had had to offer. He discovered other strains of American music as well, including gospel and country. Before long, he would have an electric guitar and an amplifier and speaker, along with a better acoustic guitar.

In April of 1963, Gerhard and Elsbeth relocated once again, this time to Buffalo, New York. John stayed behind in Toronto to finish up high school, joining his parents a couple months later. As recounted by Kay in his autobiography, in Buffalo the family rented "a luxurious main floor flat in a stately old house on Woodward Street out towards Williamsville." Gerhard, according to John, "started his own import-export business," a pretty impressive accomplishment for a guy who had just entered the country.

The family didn't stay long in Buffalo, choosing instead to pull up roots once again and relocate, this time all the way across the country to Los Angeles, California. Elsbeth immediately landed a job at the upscale Bullocks department store in Westwood. Within just a few years, she was named manager of her department. Gerhard, meanwhile, quickly "found the job of his life, working for the German consulate in Los Angeles as the Consul General's chauffer," a job he held from 1964 until 1978. As always, John and his family lived charmed lives; not only did the parents both quickly land good jobs, but the aspiring-rock-star son had the good fortune to land in LA at the dawn of a music revolution!

John lost no time forging a friendship with Morgan Cavett, who was already introduced to readers as the son of Oscar-winning screenwriter Frank Cavett. At the time, Cavett was working as the manager of the New Balladeer coffeehouse. Morgan also happened to be the godson of poet and writer Dorothy Parker, who had been born Dorothy Rothschild and who had herself lived for many years at the mouth of Laurel Canyon, at the famed Garden of Allah apartments (where she attempted more than once to kill herself). Morgan had also gone to school with doomed canyon musician Lowell George and he was a close associate of the Vito Paulekas dance troupe. Kay began regularly sleeping on the floor of Cavett's large home, which sat at the mouth of Laurel Canyon directly behind the Chateau Marmont.

Cavett quit his job at the Balladeer soon enough and Kay took over as manager of the popular club. Among the regulars at the time were soon-to-be-Byrds David Crosby, Roger McGuinn and Gene Clark, and Bryan MacLean, who would become a member of Love. In his off hours, Kay also began hanging out at the Troubadour and was soon working there as a self-styled floor manager. There he met Van Dyke Parks, who was known at the time for hosting drug-fueled parties attended by the likes of David Crosby and Beach Boy Brian Wilson. By that time, Morgan had rented an apartment in Laurel Canyon and John regularly camped out there, sleeping in a large walk-in closet. Kay also became a regular at Ciros and was there, along with Vito and his crew, when the Byrds hit the scene and ignited the folk-rock revolution.

Having quickly formed connections to some of the key players in the nascent Laurel Canyon scene, Kay made the rather bizarre decision to leave Los Angeles and his family behind and return to Toronto, hitch-hiking there by way of Buffalo. By then, Toronto's Yorkville district had a flourishing folk scene featuring soon-to-be-stars like Gordon Lightfoot, Neil Young and Joni Mitchell. It was almost as if Kay had been dispatched back to Canada to point the other artists there in the right direction, which is exactly what he seems to have done.

According to Kay's autobiography, "within a day or two of [his] arrival" in Toronto, he met the manager of a local club and promptly got a booking that lasted several weeks. He was also offered the basement of the club to sleep in. John Kay, it appears, just had a knack for immediately establishing himself in a new town. He quickly joined a band that would come to be known as the Sparrow, which was known for swapping members with another local band known as the Mynah Birds, fronted by Rickey James Matthews. The Mynahs were bankrolled by a local businessman named John Craig Eaton. At the height of their power, the immensely wealthy and influential Eaton family, which is often referred to as 'Canada's Royal Family,' was worth some $2 billion.

Kay recruited bassist Bruce Palmer but then traded him to the Mynah Birds for Nick St. Nicholas, who, like John, had begun life in Nazi Germany. St. Nicholas was born Klaus Karl Kassbaum on September 28, 1943, but, as with John, Kassbaum's family had emigrated to Toronto in the 1950s. Also joining Kay was keyboardist John Raymond Goadsby, another former Mynah Bird who went by the name Goldy McJohn. Rounding out the band were drummer Gerard McCrohan, known as Jerry Edmonton, and his songwriter brother Dennis McCrohan, who also adopted the surname Edmonton before later settling on the name Mars Bonfire.

Mynahs Neil Young and Bruce Palmer soon found their calling and rode out of town for their magical meeting with Stephen Stills. Joni soon headed west as well. Kay, meanwhile, married Jutta Maue, with whom he had much in common. Maue was born in Nazi Germany in February 1944, just a couple of months before John was born. Her father was killed on the Eastern Front in May 1944, not long after Kay's father was likewise killed. After the war, Maue and her family emigrated to Toronto, a seemingly popular destination for German families in the 1950s.

With his new band in tow, Kay soon headed out of town as well—the first destination being New York City, where the group cut three tracks before returning to Toronto. They were soon back in New York though with a lengthy club booking and a recording contract that kept them there for an extended period of time in 1966. During that time, according to Kay, the band started listening to Edgard Varese, a favorite pastime of future Laurel Canyon musicians.

Later that same year, bookings at the Whisky-a-Go-Go and the club formerly known as Ciros brought the band out to Los Angeles. After about a month though the boys ran out of gigs and Kay resumed his habit of sleeping at Morgan Cavett's apartment. Things were not looking good for the band in LA at that time; they had run out of work and most band members had expired work visas and were in the country illegally. But John Kay, as we have already seen, seems to have had a guardian angel: "It was like a fairy tale. Here I was, no work, no money, a pregnant wife and no prospects, then in walks this guy living next door, from a successful record label, saying he thought I might have a shot at a contract if I could get a band together. It seemed almost like it was all meant to be. Everything seemed to fall into place at the right time."

Kay quickly began putting together a new band. For guitar duties, strangely enough, he recruited a local high school kid with the rather provocative name of Michael Monarch. According to Monarch himself, quoted in Kay's *Magic Carpet Ride*, when he joined the band he "had only been playing for less than two years." According to legend, Monarch was just sixteen when he laid down the lead guitar track for Born To Be Wild and just seventeen when he did the same for Magic Carpet Ride.

Through posted notices advertising the band's need for a bass player, John met and hired John Russell Morgane, also known as Rushton Moreve. Jerry Edmonton on drums and Goldy McJohn on keyboards completed the new ensemble, which took the Germanic name Steppenwolf—inspired by the occult-influenced novel of the same name by Herman Hesse—and signed with ABC Dunhill. This formation would not last long though. Over time, Kay, whom Nick St. Nicholas has referred to as "the Führer," would fire nearly every one of the original band members. And some of their replacements.

The fledgling band rehearsed through the summer of 1967 in a rented garage. By December 1967, though they had been together just a matter of months, ABC decided the band was ready to cut an album. That self-titled debut was recorded in just four days at a cost of just $9,000 and released the very next month. On April 4, 1968, just a few months after the release, Steppenwolf had their national television debut on *American Bandstand*, lip-syncing to their monster hit, Born To Be Wild.

The week before the band was beamed into America's living rooms, Jutta gave birth to what would be John Kay's only offspring, Shawn Mandy Kay, on March 29, 1968. Growing up, Shawn's circle of friends and classmates would include Carnie and Wendy Wilson (daughters of Beach Boy Brian Wilson), John Phillips' daughter Chynna, Zappa offspring Moon Unit and Dweezil, Ethan Browne (son of Jackson Browne), and Phil Spector's son Donte. Shawn Kay would later recall that she was intimidated by her father when she was young, adding that, "when he was around, there was a certain amount of tension in the air."

In October 1968, Steppenwolf dropped its second album, unimaginatively entitled *The Second*. That disc contained the band's second monster hit, Magic Carpet Ride, based on an unfinished song brought to the band by bassist Rushton Moreve. It was to be the band's last top-ten single. It was also, given that Born To Be Wild was donated to the band by the aforementioned Mars Bonfire, the only hit single written by a band member (a lesser hit, The Pusher, was penned by Hoyt Axton, who also wrote Three Dog Night's Joy To The World, and who was both a resident of Laurel Canyon and the son of a US Navy officer).

It makes perfect sense then, I suppose, that following the release of that second album, Moreve was unceremoniously fired by Kay and replaced with Nick St. Nicholas. According to Kay, Moreve had been "becoming increasingly paranoid of the police and would relate to us these wildly imaginative tales of being arrested and beaten." Moreve, it should be noted, was the boyfriend of 'Animal' Huxley, the only granddaughter of the very same Aldous Huxley who had been sold a vacuum cleaner by Captain Beefheart. As Goldy McJohn recalled it, just before being let go, Moreve and Huxley (who was name-checked on the cover of Zappa's *Freak Out!* album) packed up their belongings and left the state out of fear that there was going to be a massive earthquake that would cause California to sink into the ocean. When that failed to materialize, Moreve ultimately returned to the LA area but was never asked to rejoin the band. He was later killed in a motorcycle accident on July 1, 1981, in Santa Barbara, California at the age of thirty-two.

Steppenwolf released their third album, *At Your Birthday Party*, in March 1969. The cover art featured a photo of the band taken at the burned-out remains of Canned Heat's former Laurel Canyon home. The disc yielded no top ten singles and was largely a commercial failure. Just a few months later though, the band's career got a massive boost with the release of the film *Easy Rider* on July 14, 1969. With a soundtrack that prominently featured Born To Be Wild and The Pusher, both pulled from Steppenwolf's debut album, the film gained the band a worldwide audience. It also solidified their image as a Hell's Angels/outlaw biker band. Kay, who fancied himself to be a tough guy, actively embraced that image, frequently appearing with his band at biker rallies and routinely appearing on stage and in publicity photos clad in black leather and with a perpetual scowl.

As 1969 came to a close, Kay and the band released their fourth album, *Monster*, which sold somewhat better then its predecessor. The band also launched a successful tour in 1970, which included a stop at the Bath Festival of Blues in the UK alongside fellow Laurel Canyon acts the Byrds, Canned Heat and the Mothers of Invention. Another Laurel Canyon band, Three Dog Night, which already had three top ten singles by 1970, tagged along for part of the tour.

Steppenwolf released two more instantly forgettable albums before Kay officially retired the band in 1972. He had already fired Nick St. Nicholas, in part because, as Kay noted in his autobiography, he and the rest of the band "weren't sure what Nick's sexual orientation was or had become." That is apparently a problem when one wants one's band to project a tough, macho image.

Kay had been hinting since the release of Steppenwolf's second album that he had aspirations for a solo career. His first two solo efforts though, released in 1972 and 1973, failed to attract much attention, with the latter of the two stalling out on the charts at number 200. Not surprisingly then, it didn't take Kay long to decide to get the band back together, initially including original members Edmonton and McJohn. Goldy though, whom Kay claimed "had a lot of demons buried deep in his psyche," was fired after the first of three albums the new lineup released, leaving drummer Jerry Edmonton as the only original band member to not be discharged. With the albums failing to gain much traction on the charts, Kay once again retired the band in 1976.

A new version of Steppenwolf soon emerged, however, this one put together by fired former members Goldy McJohn and Nick St. Nicholas. That development though did not sit well with Kay, who felt that he alone had the moral right to use the Steppenwolf name, though he did not have exclusive legal rights to it. Kay would later write that St. Nicholas and McJohn were "both lucky to be alive today after what they did. I knew people who in turn knew people who, for a price, would put a serious hurt on someone with no questions asked." As I may have mentioned, Kay likes to think of himself as something of a bad-ass.

Kay quickly engaged his attorneys in some legal maneuvering to strongarm McJohn and St. Nicholas into signing over all their future royalties to he and Edmonton. He then set about putting together his own version of Steppenwolf, this time leaving out even Edmonton. Kay had decided that, this time around, he alone would cash in on the Steppenwolf name. The reconstituted band embarked on a low-budget tour that featured small venues where band members had to set up and tear down their own equipment. It was a far cry from the band's heyday in the late 1960s and after two failed albums, the second of which was not even released in the US, the band once again called it quits in 1984.

It wasn't long though before Kay, in his own words, "received an offer to tour jointly with the Guess Who, a reconstituted lineup fronted by their original bass player." Kay readily accepted the offer and by doing so lent his tacit approval to a version of the Guess Who that included only one original member. This was, of course, the very same John Kay who had used every means available to prevent his own bass player and keyboardist from using the name Steppenwolf.

The new Steppenwolf lineup released two instantly forgettable albums in 1987 and 1990 before Kay once again retired the band name. He continues to occasionally put out relatively obscure solo efforts, including live albums in 2004 and 2006. Others connected to the band have not fared so well. Steppenwolf's original producer, Gabriel Mekler, who also produced Three Dog Night, died in a motorcycle accident sometime in 1977. Rushton Moreve, as already noted, also perished in a motorcycle accident, in July 1981. Drummer Jerry Edmonton died in a car accident on November 28, 1993. Nick St. Nicholas and Michael Monarch, meanwhile, play in an all-star band dubbed the World Classic Rockers.

And Born To Be Wild and Magic Carpet Ride continue to be played daily on classic rock radio stations.

21

A WHITER SHADE OF PALE
ARTHUR LEE AND LOVE

"We definitely started what became the Hippie movement and it spread from there up to Haight-Ashbury and the Fillmore in San Francisco, and then all across the nation." Arthur Lee, vocalist for the band Love

"Arthur was the whitest black guy I knew. He didn't live the black lifestyle, always liked the white way of life, and liked white girls." Producer Skip Taylor

OF ALL THE BANDS TO POUR OUT OF LAUREL CANYON DURING ITS HEYDAY, none is more shrouded in mystery and rumor than Love, fronted by one of the most talented and troubled figures on the Sunset Strip, the menacingly charismatic Arthur Lee. Though Lee and his bandmates never achieved the sales figures of contemporaries like the Doors, the Byrds, and the Mamas and the Papas, the band's body of work continues to be hugely influential and its album *Forever Changes* is widely considered to be among the greatest rock albums of all time.

Arthur Porter Taylor was born in Memphis, Tennessee, on March 7, 1945. His mother, Agnes Porter, was the daughter of Ed Porter, a white man, and Malvise "Mal" Mosley, a very fair-skinned black woman. Throughout her life, most of Agnes' friends and acquaintances assumed she was white. Chester Taylor, a black cornet player, was Arthur's father, but Arthur only saw him a few times throughout his life and he consequently never knew whether he had any half-siblings on his father's side.

Arthur's early years were spent in Memphis, where he was raised by his doting—though authoritarian—mother and her sister Vera, who frequently babysat while Agnes worked. Vera was a heavy drinker and smoker who Arthur credited with starting him on cigarettes when he was just three. According to Arthur, Aunt Vera died young from ingesting rat poison, which must have had a considerable impact on the young boy.

Growing up just one block away was friend and classmate Johnny Echols, two years younger than Arthur. In 1952, Agnes and then seven-year-old Arthur uprooted and moved to Los Angeles. The next year, Johnny Echols and his family decided to move to LA as well, strangely finding a home just two doors down from Arthur's new family home. Agnes soon met Clinton "C.L." Lee, whom she married on April 23, 1955. Five years later, C.L. legally adopted Arthur, who would from then on be known as Arthur Lee.

Clinton had served in the military during WWII before settling in Los Angeles in 1946. Arthur's authorized biography provides the following description of C.L. Lee's postwar employment: "Skilled at masonry, he prospered during LA's postwar construction boom. Arthur would often point to the sculptures that adorned buildings along Wilshire Boulevard as evidence of his stepfather's handiwork." Many of those adornments, as with those on the monuments of Washington carved by Carl Franzoni's ancestors, are loaded with Masonic symbolism.

Arthur's LA neighborhood was filled with musical influences. Little Richard, who had such a profound influence on John Kay, was a neighbor, as was singer Bobby Day. Ray Charles had a recording studio nearby. Attending Dorsey High School with Albert were Billy Preston and future Beach Boy Mike Love. And Arthur, unlike other kids in the neighborhood but very much like other future Laurel Canyon stars, had musical instruments and a reel-to-reel tape recorder, as well as a television. He was also known for always having money in his pocket.

Lee was a naturally gifted athlete who served as the captain of Dorsey High's basketball team. He was also known as a tough kid who didn't shy away from a fight. In the late 1950s, legendary fighter Sugar Ray Robinson lived around the corner and Arthur entertained thoughts of becoming a boxer. Instead he opted to pursue a musical career, dropping out of high school during his senior year. Arthur had formed his first successful band while still in school. Dubbed Arthur Lee and the LAGs, their first professional gig was at an exclusive Beverly Hills country club, right across the street from future bandmate Bryan MacLean's family home. The LAGs' unscrupulous manager/agent routinely booked them as the Coasters, or the Drifters, or whoever else had a current hit on the charts. Lee and the rest of the group were, though quite young, very accomplished musicians who could mimic the sound of numerous other bands.

While still a minor, Lee recorded his first single, The Ninth Wave, for prestigious Capitol Records. The release received little promotion though and failed to chart. Also while still a minor, he received a brand new Corvair Monza, courtesy of step-dad Clinton. In 1964, he wrote the song My Diary for vocalist Rosa Lee Brooks. The guitar work on the single was supplied by an unknown musician named Jimi Hendrix, who had never before set foot in a recording studio. That same year, Lee disbanded the LAGs and formed the American Four with longtime friend and classmate Johnny Echols. They soon added acclaimed local drummer Don Conka. The group was essentially a top forty cover band, once again good enough to sound like anyone they chose to mimic, though they did release an original single, Luci Baines, named for the First Daughter who had spent a night out on the town with Gene Clark.

One figure on the canyon scene who would prove to be hugely influential on young Arthur was club owner and former cop/gangster Elmer Valentine. Arthur would later write that "Elmer Valentine was not only a good friend, he was like a father figure to me." Another major influence was the emergence of the Byrds and the human circus surrounding them. As Echols would later recall, "What impressed us when we saw the Byrds were the people in the audience—what the *Los Angeles Times* called the 'Sherwood Forest People'—because they looked like something out of Robin Hood. It was this huge, fascinating group of eclectic people, all dressed totally bizarrely, with long, long hair. These were the leftovers from the Beat era. They followed the Byrds around."

Those Sherwood Forest people were, of course, the Vito Paulekas crew. And they would soon be following Arthur and his band around as well.

When the band had worked its way up from playing a bowling alley to playing the Brave New World club, they changed their name to the Grass Roots. They also added a rhythm guitarist by the name of Robert Kenneth Beausoleil. Shortly thereafter, they added a second rhythm guitarist, Bryan MacLean, who had grown up amid considerable wealth—his father was an architect for the rich and famous. As Bryan later acknowledged, he "knew everyone in Hollywood." Bryan had been a regular at the New Balladeer club, along with Gene Clark, Roger McGuinn, David Crosby, Michael Clarke, and John Kay. He had dropped out of high school at seventeen to pursue an art career, but had decided to focus on music instead, unsuccessfully auditioning to be one of the Monkees. Soon after, he met Arthur and Johnny and gave up his temporary employment as the Byrds' road manager.

For a brief time, both Bobby and Bryan filled the rhythm guitar position, making it a six-piece band. However, Arthur soon found that the band wasn't earning enough to carry both of them and so Beausoleil was let go. Bryan was chosen over Bobby in part because MacLean had a connection to the Vito crew, guaranteeing the fledgling band a lively audience and a lot of buzz on the Strip.

Beausoleil would later migrate to the San Francisco area for the famed Summer of Love, moving into the former Russian Embassy with filmmaker and occultist Kenneth Anger, who—according to Bobby, quoted in John Gilmore's *Garbage People*—"had this contact with this group called 'The Process.'" Anger was also, not too surprisingly, yet another son of the military/intelligence complex; his father, Wilbur Anglemyer, had been an engineer who developed machineguns for Kellogg during WWII and later went to work for Douglas Aircraft.

Beausoleil played in a number of long-forgotten bands, many bearing names with obvious occult overtones. While playing with a lineup known as Orkustra, Bobby once shared a stage with Stephen Stills, Neil Young and the rest of Buffalo Springfield. Another formation he briefly joined was known as the Magick Powerhouse of Oz.

Beausoleil returned to LA in October 1967 following a split with Anger. Meanwhile, Charles Manson, released from prison on March 21, 1967, established his first roots in Los Angeles around December 1967 at a notorious home in Topanga Canyon known as the 'Spiral Staircase,' which by some reports was a cult gathering spot. It was there that Bobby first met Charlie and the two aspiring musicians quickly formed a bond, with Bobby agreeing to join Charlie's band, the Milky Way. That supergroup broke up after only one gig, however, though Bobby and Charlie remained close.

Beausoleil—who, according to John Gilmore's *Garbage People* was chronically abused as a child by an aunt and uncle, with a former girlfriend describing it as "typical of the worst of the sexual and other abuse brought down on a little kid"—had a brief film career as well, appearing as Lucifer in Anger's *Invocation of My Demon Brother* (though the footage was originally shot for *Lucifer Rising*), and as Cupid in Robert Carl Cohen's *Mondo Hollywood*. Later, as previously noted, Beausoleil would compose, perform and record the soundtrack for *Lucifer Rising* from a prison cell, with help from fellow Mansonite/musician Steve "Clem" Grogan.

At the time he met Manson, Beausoleil was living with musician Gary Hinman, as was Mansonite Mary Brunner; Hinman's Topanga Canyon home reportedly featured a basement drug lab. By 1968, Bobby had his own place in Topanga Canyon, at 19844 Horseshoe Lane. By early 1969, he was living in an apartment in Laurel Canyon. In July of that year, Bobby, Brunner and Susan Atkins murdered Hinman in his home, reportedly on the orders of Manson. Bobby was arrested on August 6, just two days before the carnage at Cielo Drive. But here, I suppose, I may have digressed just a bit.

Love's initial lineup of Arthur Lee on vocals, Johnny Echols on lead guitar, Bryan MacLean on vocals and rhythm guitar, John Fleckenstein on bass and Don Conka on drums would not last long. Actually, as was true with Steppenwolf, none of the configurations of Arthur's band would last long. In those early days, Lee and Echols were still living at home with their parents. Bryan though had moved into the upper loft of the Vito Clay Studio; on the lower level was the Byrds' rehearsal space. By the end of summer 1965, Arthur and Johnny had moved in as well.

As John Fleckenstein recalled, "Vito and those guys were like our groupies. They trailed us everywhere we played and brought their whole scene with them." But unlike the other group with whom Arthur's band shared both groupies and rehearsal space, the Grass Roots were considered to be a great live band, arguably the best that Laurel Canyon had to offer. The band though had a slight problem—the name Grass Roots was already taken by another band. So in the fall of 1965, Arthur's band became Love, claimed by some to be an homage to departed guitarist Bobby Beausoleil, whose nickname was Cupid.

With the name change came a new venue, Bido Lito's, yet another of the small clubs lining the Sunset Strip during its glory days. Vito and company, of course, came along for the ride. Kenny Forssi, who had arrived in LA in 1964, was recruited as the band's new bass player, replacing Fleckenstein. Forssi's roommate, Swiss-born Alban "Snoopy" Pfisterer, was subsequently hired to fill in on drums for the frequently absent Conka. Don was, by all accounts, a much more proficient drummer than Snoopy, but his prodigious drug intake made him extremely unreliable.

In January 1966, the band was signed by Jac Holzman to his Elektra Records label. Holzman's was, to say the least, an unlikely success story. Between the years 1950 and 1955, over 1,000 record labels were reportedly launched in the US. Only two survived, one of which was Atlantic Records. The other was Jac Holzman's Elektra Records, launched, as industry legend is written, while Holzman, the son of a Harvard-educated doctor, was a nineteen-year-old student living in the dorms at St. John's College in Annapolis, Maryland. The venture was purportedly financed with just $600, half from Holzman's Bar Mitzvah and the other half from a classmate's veteran's bonus.

As part of Arthur's deal with Holzman, he was given his own publishing company, Grass Roots Records. Publishing royalties were paid through Third Story Music, a company controlled by the shadowy Herb Cohen and his brother. Arthur also had a signed personal management contract with Cohen.

Once signed, the band quickly got to work recording their self-titled debut album. Snoopy laid down all the drum tracks for the perpetually AWOL Conka. And in a strange turn of events, Echols, Forssi, and MacLean actually played their own instruments in the studio, though Lee did fill in at times. It is said that Lee could play any band member's instrument better than they could, with the notable exception of guitar virtuoso Johnny Echols. And all of the band members, needless to say, could play better than the guys in the band they shared rehearsal space with.

Elektra staff producer Paul Rothchild—who would play a key role in shaping the sound of the second rock band signed by Elektra, the Doors—was doing prison time on a minor drug charge so Holzman and various others filled in as producers on the disc. Released just a few months after the band was signed, the album featured cover art photographed at—where else?—the ruins of a fire-ravaged home in Laurel Canyon.

On June 18, 1966, the band made its first television appearance on Dick Clark's *American Bandstand*. Also appearing was the Bobby Fuller Four, performing their hit song I Fought The Law. Exactly one month later, on July 18, 1966, rising star Bobby Fuller would be found dead in his car, the victim of a very obvious homicide that was treated by the LAPD as a suicide. At about that same time, Arthur moved into what was known as The Castle, a massive estate that occupied a full city block and that was, by some reports, the onetime home of Bela Lugosi. Lee had previously been living on one floor of a large home owned by Elmer Valentine.

It is said that the members of the Doors, and Jim Morrison in particular, idolized Love and its leader, Arthur Lee. The Doors' long, improvisational songs like The End and When the Music's Over were directly inspired by Love's long, improvisational jams, as Ray Manzarek has freely admitted. And Arthur often claimed that Morrison would camp out outside Lee's Laurel Canyon home waiting for a chance to hang out with his label mate. For a time in the mid-1960s, Lee dated Pamela Courson, who would thereafter become Morrison's frequent companion and, upon his death, the sole heir to his sizable estate. Courson was with Morrison when he died under what remains to this day a shroud of mystery. She herself was dead less than three years later, on April 25, 1974, allegedly of a self-administered heroin overdose.

Before recording sessions began for the band's sophomore album, Michael Stuart joined as the group's new drummer, with Snoopy moving over to keyboards. Arthur also added John Barbieri, also known as Tjay Cantrelli, on saxophone and flute. Little is known about the mysterious Cantrelli other than that he apparently hailed from Compton,

California. The new additions made Love, for a brief time, a seven-piece band, which Arthur felt was necessary for the intricate arrangements that were to be featured on the album.

Stuart's father worked in the aerospace industry, first in Texas and then in the military town of San Diego, where various other Laurel Canyon notables spent time during their formative years. Stuart scored a scholarship to Pepperdine, followed by a stint at UCLA. Before joining Love, he played with the Sons of Adam, yet another band that had a communal home in everyone's favorite canyon. The Sons had gotten their start in Baltimore, just outside Washington, DC, where they were known as Fender IV. Their new name had been bestowed upon them by Vito associate Kim Fowley.

Da Capo, Love's second album, was produced by Paul Rothchild, who had, as previously noted, been a fixture at Club 47 in Cambridge in the Boston Strangler days. Rothchild's parole officer, ever accommodating, had signed off on him venturing out to California. The cover art for the new disc was once again photographed at a fire-ravaged home in Laurel Canyon, though the sound of the record was much different than the first, fusing jazz with psychedelic rock.

Around the time of the *Da Capo* sessions, Arthur vacated The Castle and moved into what was dubbed the 'Trip house' on Kirkwood Drive in Laurel Canyon, so named in honor of the fact that the film of that name was shot there. About that very same time, Peter Fonda, star of *The Trip*, decided to more fully immerse himself in the folk-rock scene by recording an entire solo album that, perhaps mercifully, was never to be released. The disc contained a single penned by up-and-comer Gram Parsons.

As was true of virtually all of Laurel Canyon's stars, the members of Love were of military draft age. As John Einarson's biography of Arthur Lee notes, "Unless you were able to secure a college deferment or a coveted 4-F ineligibility rejection, the draft (compulsory military service) was a cold, looming reality for every adolescent male... [and] black Americans found themselves drafted in disproportionate quantity." And yet, shockingly enough, every member of every incarnation of the band, black and white alike, deftly avoided military service. Arthur is said to have fooled the draft board by pretending to be gay. Snoopy supposedly did so by showing up sleep-deprived and unwashed. And so on.

Soon after the recording of *Da Capo*, Arthur dropped Snoopy and Tjay from the roster and Love once again became a quintet. The pared down band quickly got to work on the material for what is widely regarded as their masterpiece and essentially their swan song, *Forever Changes*. Recording sessions began at the dawn of the Summer of Love. The band Love, meanwhile, made the dubious decision to pass on the Monterey Pop Festival.

Arthur initially brought in Hal Blaine and the rest of the Wrecking Crew for the *Forever Changes* sessions, which he later described as a ploy to motivate the band. By that time, Echols, Forssi, MacLean and Stuart all had serious heroin habits. Arthur was shooting up as well, but his drug of choice was cocaine. He was also a prolific smoker of hash and an acid head. In any event, the ploy reportedly worked and the band pulled it together enough to complete the sessions, but it was the last time they would record together.

Though now considered one of the finest collections of songs ever pressed on vinyl, *Forever Changes* received a lukewarm reception when released in November 1967, topping out at number 154 on the charts. Though a local favorite, Love had never established a strong national presence. And by 1968, local gigs were drying up and band members weren't above pawning their instruments for drug money. Arthur decided to let Bryan go. Around that same time, road manager Neil Rappaport returned home from a Miami gig and promptly turned up dead. Dark rumors circulated suggesting that band members had murdered Rappaport in a dispute over drugs and money. Years later, Arthur claimed that he "still [didn't] know what happened to him." Some of the rumors circulating suggested that he had been hanged. Snoopy told an interviewer that, "Neil and Johnny [Echols] became shooting partners. And then one day, Johnny fixed Neil a little too much—can you dig it? Technically you could call it murder, but each guy prepares his own needle."

By mid-1968, Love had ceased to exist as a band. There hadn't been any formal breakup—Arthur had simply stopped calling the others, who were rapidly descending into a downward spiral of heroin addiction. Forssi was living in the converted garage of a home in Laurel Canyon, with his accommodations, according to Arthur, painted entirely black, including the windows. By late summer 1968, Lee had assembled a new band he was calling Love, though it didn't contain any of the eight musicians who had previously played under that name (John Fleckenstein, Don Conka, Johnny Echols, Kenny Forssi, Bryan MacLean, Snoopy Pfisterer, Tjay Cantrelli, and Michael Stuart). Arthur served as singer, songwriter, manager, booking agent, arranger and producer.

Circa 1969, Lee sold the 'Trip house' and moved to a more secluded, secure location off Coldwater Canyon. There he would become something of a recluse, though stepdad C.L., who handled maintenance of the property, was a frequent presence. That same year, Arthur declined an invitation to play at Woodstock, just as he had done with Monterey. He did though release two new Love albums in rapid succession, just three months apart at the tail end of 1969. Neither gained any traction on the sales charts. A year later, in December 1970, he tried again with an album entitled *False Start*. The disc generated a certain amount of buzz owing to the fact that the first track on the album featured the lead guitar work of Jimi Hendrix, who had also helped arrange the song. It was the first release of new music by the guitar legend since his tragic death just three months earlier, on September 18, 1970. The album, nevertheless, failed to sell.

Shortly before his death, Hendrix had talked to Lee about putting a new band together, which was to feature the two of them and Steve Winwood. Arthur had another curious connection to Hendrix; both had been lovers of Devon Wilson, who had been one of the last people to see Hendrix alive and who died in a mysterious fall at the Chelsea Hotel just five months after the death of Hendrix. And so it was that Arthur Lee was romantically linked to two women, Courson and Wilson, who in turn were romantically linked to two legendary rock stars, Morrison and Hendrix, with all four of them subsequently turning up dead in a span of just three-and-a-half years, from September 1970 through April 1974.

Lee released his first solo album, *Vindicator*, in late 1972. It was poorly reviewed and failed to generate much in the way of sales, so Arthur put together a new version of Love and came back with *Reel to Real* in 1975. No one seemed to really care. Rumors soon began to circulate that Arthur was reduced to working as a house painter or, worse yet, was panhandling on Sunset Blvd. If true, it was a remarkable fall from grace for a guy accustomed to such luxuries as getting his clothes custom-made. He would remain a rather elusive enigma for the next several years, and then begin a series of incarcerations. Meanwhile, in 1980, his uncle, Johnson Porter, was gunned down on the mean streets of Los Angeles.

In December 1983, Lee was arrested and charged with arson, a crime that he did time for at the California Institution for Men in Chino, California. Upon his release, he left LA for Memphis, returning to LA in 1988, only to soon be arrested and charged with auto theft, a crime for which he briefly served more time. Upon his release this time, he moved into his girlfriend's apartment in Valley Village, just north of Coldwater Canyon. A year-and-a-half later, in March 1991, he sold fifty percent of his song publishing catalog to raise cash.

One year later, Arthur released what was to be his last album of new music, *Arthur Lee and Love*. Once again, it was not well received by fans or critics. After remaining largely out of sight for the next three years, Lee was arrested on June 10, 1995, for discharging a firearm off his balcony. He was also found to be in possession of a cache of armor-piercing Teflon bullets and, of course, drugs. Like many of his contemporaries in the peace-and-love crowd, Arthur had a longtime fondness for guns. Less than three weeks later, he was arrested once again for a domestic violence incident.

On June 27, 1996, Lee was convicted on the weapon and drug charges, a 'third strike' under California law that resulted in a twelve-and-a-half year prison sentence. At the end of 2001, he was granted an appeal and released to face a new trial; at retrial he was convicted of lesser charges and sentenced to time served. Arthur was a free man once again, but that freedom proved to be rather short-lived; on August 3, 2006, Lee passed away in Memphis after a battle with leukemia.

Arthur was not the only member of the band to spend time in a California correctional facility. Don Conka, the band's original drummer, though he never actually played on any Love records, reportedly served ten years or more on drug-related charges. In latter years, he rejoined Arthur in reformulated versions of Love, though nothing that came from those sessions and performances was recorded. Conka died on September 24, 2004; many who knew him were surprised that he hadn't died years earlier.

Bryan MacLean initially walked away from the music business following his discharge from the band. As one might expect from a kid born into a life of privilege, he dabbled for a time in the world of high finance, trading in stocks and real estate before suffering a nervous breakdown and then finding his salvation in the mid-1970s with an Evangelical Christian ministry. He then returned to the music industry, focusing largely on Christian music and collaborating at times with his half-sister, Maria McKee, vocalist for the short-lived band Lone Justice. On Christmas Day 1998, MacLean was dining with writer Kevin Delaney at a Los Angeles eatery when Bryan excused himself to use the restroom, where he promptly collapsed and died of a reported heart attack at the relatively young age of fifty-two. Delaney had been working on a book about the legendary band, but that book never materialized.

The fate of Tjay Cantrelli is one of many lingering mysteries that surround the band. It is generally assumed that he died sometime in the early 1990s, but no one really knows for sure. Alban "Snoopy" Pfisterer and Michael Stuart, now known as Michael Stuart-Ware, both reportedly disappeared for varying lengths of time but both eventually resurfaced, with Stuart-Ware publishing a biography of the band in 2003 and Snoopy releasing an obscure solo album in 2008.

Another enduring mystery surrounds the post-Love activities of Johnny Echols and Ken Forssi, both of whom dropped out of sight for an extended period of time. According to persistent rumors, the pair were reduced to holding up donut shops to get drug money, resulting in lengthy prison sentences following convictions on multiple counts of armed robbery. Echols has claimed the rumors are untrue, but he has acknowledged that the pair were arrested outside an LA donut shop, and the fact remains that the two disappeared for nearly twenty years.

Forssi, who showed quite an aptitude for aerospace engineering before embarking on a music career, died of a brain tumor on January 5, 1998, the same year as MacLean's curious death. It is said that he had been obsessed with the notion of global political conspiracies in his final years. His alleged partner-in-crime, Johnny Echols, is currently living in the 'New Age' mecca of Sedona, Arizona.

Ken Forssi was not, it should perhaps be noted, the only Laurel Canyon local with prior connections to the aerospace industry; at least two of Charlie's girls had such connections as well. Nancy Pittman, who was introduced to the Manson Family by actress Angela Lansbury, was the daughter of an aerospace engineer who designed missile guidance systems. And 'Squeaky' Fromme, childhood friend of actor/comedian Phil Hartman, was the daughter of yet another aerospace worker, one who has been described as being abusively authoritarian.

Arthur Lee also had, by numerous accounts, an authoritarian streak of his own. According to drummer Snoopy, Lee was "a megalomaniac; extremely authoritarian." Record producer David Anderle noted that he didn't "want to say that Arthur was demonic, but he was very manipulative and destructive." Lee also had undeniable charisma and a commanding, and somewhat menacing, stage presence. Michael Ware has written that, "Arthur had... an aura of calm, quiet power... he seemed better than 'regular' human beings. More capable. Everyone looked up to him and respected him, and feared him."

Like others in this saga, Arthur Lee also appears to have suffered with a rather pronounced dissociative disorder. Drummer Gary Stern once said that he believed "there were two Arthurs, as if he was schizophrenic." Rock'n'roll photographer Herbie Worthington described Arthur as "a walking contradiction. He could be the sweetest person one minute and then his mind would click and he could be an asshole." Worthington's take on Lee, needless to say, sounds hauntingly like Bonnie Clark's take on brother Gene: "He could be very warm and loving, but that could change in a heartbeat."

22

ENDLESS VIBRATIONS
THE BEACH BOYS

"Dennis Wilson was killed by my shadow because he took my music and changed the words from my soul." Charles Manson

ARTHUR LEE WAS CERTAINLY NOT WITHOUT RIVALS FOR THE TITLE OF 'MOST talented yet troubled musician on the Sunset Strip' in the 1960s. Many would argue that the rightful holder of that crown was the man whose eccentricities are the stuff of legend—Brian Wilson, the primary creative force behind the spectacular rise and enduring success of the Beach Boys.

The Beach Boys were somewhat unique among the bands calling Laurel Canyon home back in the day. For starters, they dropped their first album before there *was* a Laurel Canyon scene, and before there was a British Invasion as well. And their squeaky clean, all-American public image was seriously at odds with the look favored by their long-haired, bearded peers. Their music as well, initially focused almost exclusively on surfing, cars and girls, seemed far removed from the folk-rock revolution swirling around bands like the Byrds and Buffalo Springfield.

Some readers may be inclined to dismiss the Beach Boys as being roughly on par with that other much-maligned Laurel Canyon band, the Monkees. But as was true of Mickey Dolenz, Peter Tork and Mike Nesmith, the Wilson brothers and their bandmates were very much welcomed as peers by the rest of the canyon community. Brian Wilson was, in fact, looked upon as an almost God-like figure, regarded as arguably the finest musician, songwriter, producer and arranger of his era. No less a figure than David Crosby has said that, in the 1960s, "Brian was the most highly regarded musician in America, hands down."

The story of the Beach Boys begins in the late 1700s, when the Wilson clan first ventured across the Atlantic and put down roots in New York. Henry Wilson, born in 1804, was the first American-born member of the family. He moved to Ohio where, according to Peter Carlin, "he worked as a stonemason." Not unlike Carl Franzoni's father. And Arthur Lee's stepfather. And John Kay's stepfather. There might be a pattern developing here.

In the late nineteenth century, William Henry Wilson moved to Kansas to try his hand at farming, but soon lost interest in that and went into the industrial plumbing business instead. Again according to Carlin, he soon scored "contracts to work on the state's new reformatory system." There was, no doubt, lots of money to be made in the prison-building business. Some of that money was invested in ten acres of prime farmland in Escondido, California, where he arrived around 1904. By 1905 though, he was back in Kansas in the plumbing business. William Henry's son, William Coral "Buddy" Wilson, set out for California a decade later, in 1914.

Buddy has been described by Carlin as "Moody and scattered, plagued by searing headaches and a self-destructive thirst for whiskey... Often awash in alcohol and self-pity, Buddy's bile regularly boiled over into violence, directed most often at [wife] Edith. But he could also turn his fists on his children." One of those children, who came to blows with his dad on more than one occasion, was Murry Gage Wilson, born July 2, 1917. Murry reportedly despised his abusive father and after the death of his mother never saw or spoke to him again.

Murry left school in 1935, at the height of the Great Depression, and, though many Americans were struggling to eke out a living any way they could, he had no trouble finding work as a clerk with the Southern California Gas Company. On March 26, 1938, he married Audree Korthof, with whom he would have three boys, two of them born in curious proximity to the summer and winter solstices: Brian Douglas Wilson, born June 20, 1942; Dennis Carl Wilson, born December 4, 1944; and Carl Dean Wilson, born December 21, 1946.

By 1942, Murry had landed a better job as a junior administrator at Goodyear Tire and Rubber Company. A few years later, he took a foreman's position at AiResearch, an aeronautics firm tasked with manufacturing parts for Boeing civilian and military aircraft. He next decided to go into business for himself, opening an industrial equipment rental company in South Gate that he called ABLE Machinery.

Like his father before him, described by Steven Gaines in *Heroes and Villains* as having an "explosive temper," Murry was widely regarded as being volatile and prone to violence. Son Dennis would say that he and his brothers had "had a shitty childhood. Our dad used to whale on us... That asshole beat the shit out of us." The chronic abuse, he noted, led to both of his brothers being bed-wetters into their teens. Gaines wrote that, "on many occasions [Murry's] punishments went beyond simple beatings into the realm of the sadistic." It is said that Dennis, the most rebellious of the three boys and therefore the most frequent target of Murry's wrath, was on various occasions beaten with a 2 x 4 and burned with matches. One particularly savage beating delivered to brother Brian when he was just two left him nearly deaf in his right ear.

Even more disturbing if true was another aspect of the boys' childhoods that Dennis would later allude to when he would tell people cryptic stories about being raped by black men.

Murry's younger sister Emily had also married in 1938, to Milton Love, whose family owned a thriving Los Angeles-area sheet metal business. Milton and Emily lived in a luxurious 5,000 square foot villa in Baldwin Hills with their six offspring, the oldest of whom was Mike Love. The couple were said to be rather rigid disciplinarians.

Following his graduation from high school, Brian began taking music and psychology classes at El Camino Junior College. It was at that time that the Beach Boys, conceived as a family business, came into being. Brian was joined by brother Dennis, who would evolve into the band's drummer, and brother Carl, who would become the group's lead guitarist, as well as cousin Mike Love and neighbor/classmate Al Jardine. Dennis, the only real surfer in the band, is credited with suggesting the group's musical direction. The band's first single, Surfin', was recorded in September 1961 and released December 8 of that same year. The song quickly climbed to numbers two on the local charts and seventy-five on the national Billboard charts. Brian promptly dropped out of college to devote his undivided attention to music. Dennis was just seventeen at the time and Carl was not quite fifteen. They were, it appears, getting into the music business at the right time—in the decade from 1955 to 1965, record sales increased tenfold, from about $60 million annually to $600 million.

Murry almost immediately appointed himself the band's manager and producer, while assigning Audree bookkeeping duties. He then formed the Sea of Tunes publishing company to handle Brian's songs, granting himself controlling interest. He also got the boys a contract with prestigious Capitol Records. The Beach Boys offices, fortuitously enough, would end up being located right across the hall from the offices of master publicist Derek Taylor, so they would naturally become clients. Taylor would arrive in Los Angeles seeking work as an independent press agent just in time to take on the Byrds as his star clients. But first he would make quite a name for himself in the UK by generating a media firestorm around a fledgling band known as the Beatles.

Throughout his life, Brian worked with a series of collaborators, many of them with interesting connections. His first such collaborator was Gary Usher, an aspiring twenty-year-old musician who, according to industry legend, happened to be walking down a Hawthorne, California, street while visiting a relative when he heard the Boys in their home studio working on the song Surfin' Safari and, intrigued, knocked on the door. Usher is credited with starting what would become a Beach Boys trademark—songs about cars.

On June 4, 1962, with Dennis and Carl still just seventeen and fifteen, Capitol released the Beach Boys' first major label single, Surfin' Safari, backed by one of Usher's automotive songs, 409. Both songs soared up the charts, leading to a summer tour and a commitment from Capitol for a full album. By October, *Surfin' Safari* the album had debuted and Murry had the band booked at Pandora's Box. He also managed to convince Capitol to give up producing duties to Brian. Though just twenty years old, Brian Wilson was granted unprecedented artistic control, serving as the band's songwriter, producer and arranger. He would prove to be amazingly proficient at those duties, putting out an astounding ten albums in just over three years, beginning with *Surfin'*

USA in March of 1963, which climbed to number three on the Billboard charts, and carrying through to the groundbreaking *Pet Sounds* in May of 1966. Along the way, Brian wrote and recorded for other artists as well. After *Pet Sounds* though, following the much-publicized failure-to-launch of *Smile*, his output became considerably more erratic and of decidedly variable quality.

Back in those early days at Pandora's Box, Brian met and was immediately drawn to Marilyn Rovell, who, along with her sister Diane, made up two-thirds of the vocal group the Honeys. The Rovell family home on Sierra Bonita Drive soon became Brian's favorite hangout, despite the fact that he was twenty and the object of his affections was just fourteen. The pair quickly fell into an illicit romantic relationship, as Carlin writes, "seemingly with the knowledge and permission of [Marilyn's parents], who were sleeping under the same roof at the time."

In the fall of 1964, Brian moved into his own apartment on Hollywood Blvd., where Marilyn, still just fifteen, was a frequent guest. The two were married by the end of the year. Brian though was not the only Beach Boy with a preference for very young girls. Brother Dennis would later begin an affair with Carole Freedman, who, though just sixteen, had already been married and was the mother of a one-year-old son (rumored to have been fathered by Jim Morrison). Brother Carl would marry barely sixteen-year-old Anne Hinsche, the daughter of a wealthy casino owner from the Philippines. Mike Love's second wife would be seventeen-year-old Suzanne Belcher. In the summer of 1968, also known as the summer of Manson, Dennis would begin an affair with fifteen-year-old Diane Adams. And shortly before his death, Dennis would marry Shawn Love, who, in addition to being only fifteen when she moved in with Dennis, then well into his thirties, was by most accounts the illegitimate daughter of first cousin and bandmate Mike Love!

The lyrics to some of the Beach Boys' songs also at times revealed a taste for underage girls, which is often the case in rock'n'roll records. This was particularly evident in tracks such as I Wanna Pick You Up and Hey Little Tomboy. And Brian once shared with an interviewer some disturbing observations concerning his then three-year-old daughter Carnie. After describing her sexual experimentation, which he attributed to her having picked things up from observing her parents, he concluded: "It just goes to prove that if you don't hide anything from kids, they'll start doing things they normally wouldn't do until much later."

Around the time that Brian married Marilyn, he fell into the social circle of Loren Schwartz and Tony Asher, best friends from their days together at Santa Monica High School. Asher, the son of silent film star Laura LaPlante and movie producer Irving Asher, had grown up in a sprawling Westside mansion, surrounded by Hollywood luminaries. Schwartz was yet another former child actor whose home functioned as the gathering spot for the clique, which also at times included Stephen Stills, Chris Hillman, David Crosby, Roger McGuinn and Van Dyke Parks. It was at Loren's place that Brian was first introduced to pot and acid.

In 1965, Brian and Marilyn bought their first real home, on Laurel Way, where Schwartz was a regular visitor. By then, Brian had been heavily influenced by the work of deranged producer Phil Spector, having repeatedly sat in on Spector's recording sessions with the Wrecking Crew, who became the musicians featured on most of the classic Beach Boy recordings. Brian was also by that time regularly getting his hair styled at the salon of a guy named Jay Sebring, who Sammy Davis, Jr. credited with having introduced him to Satanism.

Two of the guys from Schwartz's social circle, Tony Asher and Van Dyke Parks, would later become Brian's two most acclaimed collaborators, Asher on Pet Sounds and Parks on the legendary lost album, *Smile*. Parks was the son of a Jungian psychiatrist as well as being, as previously noted, another former child actor. A few years before the *Smile* sessions, Van Dyke's older brother, Benjamin Riley Parks, was killed in unusual circumstances in Frankfurt, Germany, while on an unspecified assignment for the US State Department. According to Richard Henderson, writing in *Van Dyke Parks' Song Cycle*, Benjamin had been the "youngest member of the State Department to date" and a "pall of uncertainty surrounded the tragedy, as evidence suggested that his brother could have been a casualty of the Cold War." That, of course, would seem to suggest that Parks was, in reality, doing intelligence work under State Department cover.

Though Wilson and Parks were previously acquainted through Schwartz, Terry Melcher is credited with getting the pair together as a songwriting team; Melcher reintroduced the two at a party at his 10050 Cielo Drive residence and they got to work soon after that at Brian's home studio on Laurel Way. Melcher had recently been one half of the vocal duo Bruce & Terry; the other half had been Bruce Johnston, who in 1965 became a touring member of the Beach Boys, replacing Glen Campbell.* Both were replacements for Brian, who was always far more comfortable in the studio than on the stage.

By 1967, Brian and Marilyn had relocated to Bellagio Road in Bel Air, to a home reportedly once owned by Edgar Rice Burroughs. According to Gaines, "The house boasted... a hidden study that could be entered by a secret door behind a bookcase." Around that same time, Brian developed a ravenous appetite for Desbutals, a potent combination of methamphetamine and pentobarbital that was, remarkably enough, legally available with a prescription at the time. His bedside reading material in those days included the novels of Hermann Hesse, who inspired the name of John Kay's band, and literature on the Subud philosophy, which inspired Jim/Roger McGuinn's name change.

Also in 1967, Brian made the decision, just two weeks before show time, to cancel the Beach Boys' booking for the Monterey Pop Festival. Wilson was of the opinion that his band wouldn't quite fit in with the likes of Jimi Hendrix and Janis Joplin, and he was probably correct. By the next year, 1968, the Boys were clearly out of step with popular youth culture.

Around that time, Brian took on a side project—building a band around his good friend Danny Hutton. Born in Ireland in 1942, Hutton had moved to the US as a child and grown up in Los Angeles. Before hooking up with Wilson, he had produced tunes and done voiceover work for Hanna-Barbera and had also, like many of his peers, auditioned to be a Monkee. With Wilson's help, he joined with Cory Wells and Chuck Negron to form a vocal trio originally named Redwood. Their first singles were recorded and produced by Brian in his home studio.

Wells was born Emil Lewandowsky in 1942 in Buffalo, New York, where he was raised by his mother and a violently abusive stepfather. He joined the US Air Force right out of high school, in large part to escape his home life. After being discharged, he formed the Enemies and

* Campbell, a former member of the Wrecking Crew, was another member of the Laurel Canyon community with curious views on the war and the draft. He told *Variety* magazine back in the 1960s that protestors who were burning their draft cards "should be hung... if you don't have enough guts to fight for your country, you're not a man."

soon relocated to Los Angeles, just in time to join the emerging scene and become the house band for a time at the Whisky. Negron was also born in 1942, in New York City. Raised in the Bronx, Negron was a high school basketball star who had been recruited to play for a college in California. He would later become a raging heroin addict for some twenty years and make three-dozen failed rehab attempts before finally getting clean.

Brian Wilson wanted to sign the new band to the Beach Boys' Brother Records, but that idea was vetoed by Brian's brothers and cousin. It was probably not the best financial decision by the other Beach Boys given that the new band, renamed Three Dog Night, quickly became one of the most successful recording acts of the era, selling millions of albums and releasing a long string of hit songs, many of which, including Harry Nilsson's One, Paul Williams' Just An Old Fashioned Love Song, and Randy Newman's Mama Told Me Not to Come, were written by other famous Laurel Canyon residents.

Nineteen-sixty-eight proved to be a rather strange and eventful year for many of the Beach Boys. Mike Love, who had bought a house in Coldwater Canyon in the summer of 1967, ventured off to India to visit the personal compound of Maharishi Mahesh Yogi and engage in some Transcendental Meditation. Perhaps he was seeking a little anger management. In *Catch a Wave*, Carlin notes that "barely harnessed rage was a recurring feature of Mike's public persona." In *Heroes and Villains*, he is described as "a pretty evil guy, kind of like a secret service agent, with a real military attitude." Joining Love at the compound were all four Beatles, singer/songwriter Donovan, and Mia and Prudence Farrow.

Brian, meanwhile, found himself committed to a mental hospital in 1968, which very likely means, given the era, that he was subjected to electroshock 'therapy' and heavy doses of anti-psychotic drugs. In February 1970, cousin Mike Love would also find himself committed to a mental hospital, but only, according to Carlin, after "a long, high-speed car chase through Hollywood as he attempted to evade cars driven by his father and brothers." Love was taken away in a straightjacket for involuntary treatment.

It was Dennis Wilson though who would later have the most memorable 1968 stories to tell, though he would claim to have virtually no memories of that time. Early in the year, he moved to Will Rogers' former home at 14400 Sunset Blvd., at the mouth of Rustic Canyon. It was there that, through the summer of 1968, he played host to Charles Manson and a number of his followers. Wilson not only provided the Family with food and very comfortable accommodations, he also picked up the tab for their medical expenses and allowed Charlie and Co. the use of his expensive vehicles, at least one of which, a Ferrari, was wrecked by aspiring musician Steve "Clem" Grogan, who was barely sixteen at the time.

Through Dennis, Manson met and gained the admiration of various other Laurel Canyon regulars, including Terry Melcher and Gregg Jakobson. Dennis also took Charlie on several occasions to record some of his songs at brother Brian's home studio, where Manson met Brian and his then-collaborator, Van Dyke Parks, and where Redwood was also recording at the time. No recordings from those sessions have ever seen the light of day, though one of Manson's songs, Cease To Exist, was essentially stolen by Dennis and renamed Never Learn Not To Love.

On November 22, 1968, the fifth anniversary of the assassination of JFK, the Beatles released what is known as "the White Album" (*The Beatles*), which would allegedly inspire the 'Helter Skelter' Manson murders. Just days after the Beatles' release, the Beach Boys released the single Bluebirds Over The Mountain backed by the Manson b-side Never Learn Not To Love. The next year, Dennis told an interviewer that, "Sometimes the Wizard frightens me—Charlie Manson, who is another friend of mine, says he is God and the devil! He sings, plays and writes poetry." Wilson added that Brother Records would likely be releasing an album by the aspiring singer/songwriter. But Manson, like Three Dog Night, ended up taking his talents elsewhere.

By 1969, Brian appeared to have lost interest in making music and was selling vitamins out of a health food store in West Hollywood. In November of that year, Murry sold Brian's Sea of Tunes song catalog to A&M, with Brian reportedly not seeing a penny of the proceeds. The next year, the band hired a new publicist, former radio newsman Jack Rieley, who many considered to be something of a huckster. According to Gaines, a "report claimed that Jack was in the employ of a Washington, DC, right-wing conservative organization called the Stern Concern."

As the early 1970s rolled around, Brian took to hanging out at Danny Hutton's house, which was, not surprisingly, on Wonderland Avenue in Laurel Canyon. The home's most compelling feature was the 'party room' with blacked-out windows, where piles of cocaine could usually be found. Wilson wasn't the only regular visitor—Ringo Starr was known to hang out there as well, as was John Lennon and his sidekick Harry Nilsson. Keith Moon, who would soon turn up dead in Nilsson's home, was a regular as well.

The world barely bothered to say goodbye to Murry Wilson, who passed away on June 4, 1973 after suffering a massive heart attack. So loathed was he that neither Brian nor Dennis bothered to show up for his funeral.

Around the time of Murry's death, Brian began working with Tandyn Almer, one of the more curious figures circulating around the Sunset Strip scene. Almer's biggest claim to fame was penning the song Along Comes Mary, which was a massive hit for the Association in 1966. The following year, Almer appeared on a CBS special entitled *Inside Pop: The Rock Revolution*, hosted by Leonard Bernstein. Showcasing the best of the new acts, the show also featured Frank Zappa, Hollie Graham Nash, Byrd Roger McGuinn, and Beach Boy Brian Wilson. Tandyn Almer was clearly expected to be the next big thing, but that never came to pass.

The project that Brian initially sought Almer's help with was a bizarre one—writing new lyrics for his beloved old songs. That project was ultimately aborted though and Wilson instead penned some new songs with Almer, including the 1973 hit Sail On, Sailor. Around 1974, after completing his work with Brian, Almer left LA and disappeared. For decades, no one knew his whereabouts and there was much speculation that he was dead. Not known until his actual death, on January 8, 2013, was that he had been alive and well and living a reclusive life in and near Washington, DC for nearly forty years! He died in a nondescript basement apartment in, of all places, McLean, Virginia. What he was doing for all those years living in the CIA's backyard will likely forever remain a mystery.

On June 24, 1974, the Beach Boys released *Endless Summer*, a double album of their early hits, and for the first time in years they were back on the charts and drawing huge crowds at their concerts. The record spent three full years on the charts and sold more than three million copies. With Brian Wilson once again a valuable commodity, Stan Love—younger brother of Mike, former NBA player, and at 6' 9" a physically imposing figure—was assigned as a full-time minder and bodyguard for the perpetually troubled songwriter.

By 1975, Stephen Love, another brother, had taken over as the band's manager and the wildly controversial Eugene Landy had replaced Stan Love as Brian's minder. Landy preached the gospel of complete control over his patients' personal, professional, social, financial and sexual lives. Employing an army of minions, he monitored, recorded and controlled every aspect of Brian's life, with strong indications that he also kept him heavily drugged. Wilson was treated like a child and constantly humiliated by his coterie of handlers.

Landy's outlandish and ever-escalating fees led to his ouster by the rest of the Beach Boys the following year. He was replaced with a brawny trio of bodyguards/minders: towering Stan Love, former professional football player and *Playgirl* model Rocky Pamplin, and Steve Korthoff, another Wilson cousin and a former US Marine. Brian also retained a new psychiatrist, Steve Schwartz, but as Carlin reveals, Schwartz didn't last long: "One day the phone rang and a strange doctor asked Brian to come see him; when Brian arrived at the office, he was told that Dr. Schwartz had been in a terrible camping accident and had fallen off the side of a mountain to his death." Wilson had apparently picked an unacceptable handler.

In late summer 1978, Brian and Marilyn separated, ending their troubled marriage amid allegations that Brian had supplied drugs to his two very young daughters. Around that same time, Brian spent several months in the Brotman Memorial Hospital's psychiatric ward.

The summer before, Dennis had released the first solo album by a Beach Boy, the critically acclaimed but now largely forgotten *Pacific Ocean Blue*. The album was co-written and co-produced by fellow Manson fan Gregg Jakobson. By the end of the year, Dennis was living in Coldwater Canyon with Christine McVie of Fleetwood Mac, a British band that had been transformed into a Laurel Canyon band following the mid-1970s addition of Lindsey Buckingham and Stevie Nicks. Wilson lived with McVie for more than two years, during which time the home's pool house burned to the ground.

As 1980 rolled around, the Beach Boys could be found playing a benefit concert in support of the presidential campaign of former spymaster George H.W. Bush. Early the next year, they played one of the inaugural balls for the incoming administration, putting their stamp of approval on the Reagan/Bush era. It wasn't the first time the Reagan and Wilson families had crossed paths; Dennis had once had a brief affair with Reagan daughter Patti Davis, who also had a relationship with Eagle Bernie Leadon. The Boys later played a private birthday bash for then-Vice President Bush.

Around the time of the Reagan inauguration, Stan Love and Rocky Pamplin invaded the home of Dennis Wilson, who by then was said to have a serious alcohol addiction, and savagely beat him. Wilson was reportedly kicked, stomped, bludgeoned with a telephone receiver and thrown through a plate glass window. The assault, later described by Love as "one of the most brutal beatings ever," left Wilson in the hospital with broken ribs and a battered face. Love and Pamplin were served with restraining orders and received fines and probation for the attack, which was allegedly motivated by the desire to prevent Dennis from supplying drugs to Brian. It seems likely though that it was actually motivated by Mike Love's rage over Dennis' affair with his illegitimate and underage daughter.

After having a son together in September 1982, Dennis and Shawn were married on July 28, 1983. The marriage though was a violent and turbulent one, with divorce papers filed just four months later, in November 1983. The divorce case never made it to court though because Dennis allegedly drowned in thirteen feet of water in a Marina Del Rey boat slip the next month, on December 28, 1983. At the time, he reportedly had no home of his own and had taken to crashing at friends' houses. He was largely estranged from his brothers and cousins, once telling an interviewer that if "there wasn't the Beach Boys and there wasn't music, I would not even talk to them."

Dennis was known throughout his adult life for living life in the fast lane, with a fondness for fast cars, faster women and mass quantities of controlled substances. He was married five times in his brief thirty-nine years on this planet, a record bested by cousin Mike Love, who according to Carlin had already been married and divorced six times by 1981. One of Dennis' paramours, according to a court filing, was one of Love's wives. Another, as previously stated, was Mike's daughter. Dennis was also known for having expensive tastes and for being generous to a fault. He was said to be obsessed with sex and to at times refer to himself as 'The Wood.' All of which, along with his obvious interest in music, made Dennis an ideal companion for Charlie Manson, who continued to see Dennis from time to time after the summer of 1968, even turning up at his door a day or two after the Cielo Drive murders.

A year before Dennis' untimely death, Eugene Landy had reentered Brian's life. He would remain in control of Wilson this time for nearly a decade, pocketing millions of dollars in fees along the way. The California Board of Medical Quality Assurance ultimately filed charges against Landy, leading to him surrendering his license to practice psychology in the state. That did not, however, end his complete control over Brian's life; Landy soldiered on, claiming that Brian was no longer his patient and that the two were now creative and business partners.

In May 1990, Stan Love filed to be Brian's legal conservator, igniting a battle over, quite literally, the control of Brian Wilson. That battle came to an end on February 3, 1992, when Landy was ordered by the courts to permanently remove himself from Brian's life. Wilson remained curiously conflicted about his longtime therapist/controller, claiming at one time that he slipped so far into the abyss under Landy's care that he attempted suicide in 1985, but also contending that Landy's death on March 22, 2006 left him devastated.

A few years after Brian was liberated from Landy's control, he married Melinda Ledbetter, with whom he adopted five kids. A couple years later, in December 1997, Audree Wilson, matriarch of the clan, passed away at the age of eighty. Carl Wilson succumbed to cancer just two months later, on February 6, 1998, leaving Brian as the last Wilson brother standing, an outcome that few in the 1960s and 1970s would have likely predicted. Following Carl's death, Mike Love, ever the authoritarian control freak (because every Laurel Canyon band had to have one), worked diligently to oust Al Jardine from the touring band, leaving himself in complete control of a band that featured him as the only original member.

Brian, meanwhile, finally completed the long overdue *Smile* project. He debuted the work live from the stage in 2004, and followed with an album in September of that same year, nearly forty years after the album's originally intended release date.

As with various other artists profiled herein, there is little question that Brian Wilson has throughout his life suffered from a serious dissociative disorder. He has at times complained of hearing disembodied voices. His biographers have frequently described what the psychiatric community would identify as 'fugue states.' Gaines, for example, has written that, "Often Brian would disappear," turning up days later "penniless in Watts or East LA." Carlin has likewise described an incident that involved Brian going missing for days before turning up in a gay bar in San Diego happily playing the piano for drinks. Carlin also provided a revealing description of Brian's writing technique: "While composing, Brian appeared strangely absent, as if he were functioning less as a conscious artist than as a kind of antenna."

23

THE GRIM GAME HOUDINI

"What struck both of us was that there were huge gaps in Houdini's life story and some puzzling inconsistencies. So we embarked on a journey to discover the real man. Early on, we discovered an important connection that most biographers seemed to miss." From the Introduction to The Secret Life of Houdini, by William Kalush and Larry Sloman

THERE IS CONSIDERABLE DEBATE OVER THE QUESTION OF WHETHER HARRY Houdini ever lived in the Laurel Canyon home known locally as the 'Houdini House.' Even if Houdini did live in the home that now lies in ruins, his story would seem to have little relevance here. After all, Houdini, widely considered to be the consummate entertainer of his era, reached the peak of his career long before there was a Laurel Canyon—before there was even that magical place known as Hollywood. But perhaps there is still something to gain through an examination of the life of the famed magician.

What are generally claimed to be the basic details of Harry Houdini's life can be found in several published biographies. Born Erik Weisz in Budapest, Hungary, on March 24, 1874, he was the fourth of seven children born to Rabbi Mayer Samuel Weisz and the former Cecelia Steiner. The family later changed the spelling of their names and Houdini became Ehrich Weiss, known by friends and family as "Ehrie," which ultimately became "Harry." His stage surname was an homage to famed

French magician Robert Houdin.

In mid-1878, Rabbi Mayer, with his five sons and pregnant wife in tow, set sail for America, arriving on July 3, 1878. The family first put down roots in Appleton, Wisconsin, before later moving, in 1887, to New York City. Four years later, Houdini launched his career as a magician, at first performing basic card tricks. He had little success and at times would make ends meet by performing in freak shows. In 1893, he met singer/dancer Wilhelmina Beatrice Rahner, known as "Bess," who would become both his wife and lifetime stage assistant. The pair though, performing as "The Houdinis," continued to find success an elusive goal.

To say that Houdini's fortunes changed in 1899 would be a bit of an understatement. As recounted by Kalush and Sloman, "Within months, he had gone from cheap beer halls and dime museums to the big-time—vaudeville. In one year's time, he had gone from literally eating rabbits for survival to making what today would equal $45,000 a week." After finally hitting it big, however, Houdini then did something rather inexplicable—he abruptly sailed off to England to begin a lengthy European tour. Kalush and Sloman pose the obvious question: "Why would someone who had finally made it big risk everything and leave behind lucrative contracts to go to England with no real prospects in sight?" Why indeed? Such a move in those days would normally be an act of career suicide, but things worked out a little differently for Houdini; everywhere he went—first in England and then in Scotland, Holland, Germany, France and Russia—he was lauded by the press and quickly catapulted into the national limelight.

After a four-year absence, Houdini returned to the US in 1904 and resumed his lucrative career. For many years he was the highest-paid performer on the vaudeville circuit and would frequently perform to huge crowds in stunts that were sometimes arranged with corporate sponsors to promote their business. In 1912, he introduced what would become his most famed escape act, the Chinese Water Torture Cell.

In 1918, Houdini decided to try his luck with the fledgling new entertainment medium known as motion pictures, starring first in a multipart serial and then in *The Grim Game* (1919) and *Terror Island* (1920). It was during this time that he is said to have taken up residence in Laurel Canyon, at the corner of Laurel Canyon Boulevard and Lookout Mountain Avenue. Following that, he moved to New York and started up his own production company, the Houdini Picture Corporation, which released *The Man From Beyond* (1921) and *Haldane of the Secret Service* (1923), after which Houdini gave up his less-than-successful film career.

For the last few years leading up to his death on October 31, 1926, Houdini primarily focused on debunking psychics and mediums, leading some to speculate that the spiritualist movement may have been behind his untimely demise. To this day, séances are regularly held around the world in attempts to contact the famed magician and escape artist.

And that, in a nutshell, is the Harry Houdini story as it is usually told. But telling stories as they are usually told is a rather boring pursuit, so we are going to take a slightly different approach to see if maybe there isn't an entirely different story hidden in the obscure details of Houdini's life—beginning with his sudden rise to fame after wallowing in obscurity for years. As noted by Kalush and Sloman, "The young Houdini... couldn't make enough money to succeed at magic. Hungry and crestfallen, he was ready to give up his dream, until he walked into a Chicago police station and met a detective who would change his life. Immediately after this fateful encounter, his picture graced the front page of a Chicago newspaper. That picture catapulted him to renown." Within months, Houdini was arguably the most famous entertainer in the country.

The detective with whom he had that fateful encounter was John Wilkie, a major player in the formation of the International Association of Police Chiefs, which was founded in Chicago in 1893, at the outset of what has been dubbed the Decade of Regicide (which set the stage for WWI). Wilkie also had a hand in the formation of the ominously titled National Bureau of Identification, and he ultimately became the chief of the US Secret Service, America's premier intelligence operation during that era. It should probably be noted here that one of Houdini's nephews, Louis Kraus, worked for the Treasury Department, overseer of Wilkie's Secret Service.

Authors Kalush and Sloman are of the opinion that, "It was forward-thinking for the chief of America's only intelligence operation to be using entertainers for covert activities in 1898." Maybe so, but the authors duly note that such actions were not unprecedented; nearly four decades earlier, Abraham Lincoln had recruited an eighteen-year-old magician named Horatio G. Cooke to serve as a Civil War spy. Lincoln and Cooke were close enough that he was reportedly present at the president's deathbed. Later, near the end of his life, Cooke became a close friend of Harry Houdini. An entertainer of a different variety, stage actor John Wilkes Booth, also appears to have served as an intelligence operative during the Civil War.

There are indications that the practice of using entertainers to carry out covert operations dates back to well before the 1860s. If researchers Graham Phillips and Martin Keatman are to be believed, the most acclaimed entertainment figure of all time, poet/actor/playwright William Shakespeare, was part of a spy ring serving under Sir Francis Walsingham, head of the Elizabethan Secret Service. So too were Christopher Marlowe and various other of Shakespeare's contemporaries. As Phillips and Keatman point out, spymaster Walsingham chose "the best possible recruits—poets and dramatists, whose lifestyles were ideally suited to his purpose. They had the perfect cover, travelling widely and receiving welcome everywhere, and since many were also actors, role playing was often second nature... many knew foreign languages. Furthermore, as the usual social barriers were often dropped for poets, they were equally at home in back street pubs or in the palaces of the mighty. They were thus in the privileged position of having their eyes and ears everywhere."

It appears then that the practice of utilizing entertainers for covert operations didn't begin with Wilkie, who was himself a magician and a disciple of escape artist R.G. Herrmann. In addition to Houdini, Wilkie recruited other magicians as well, including Herrmann, Louis Leon, and heavyweight prizefighter/magician Bob Fitzsimmons. In addition to Wilkie, another of Houdini's covert backers was Senator Chauncey Depew, an uncle of magician Ganson Depew and a former mentor to then-Vice President Theodore Roosevelt (who would be catapulted into the presidency by the assassination of William McKinley, one of the final victims of the Decade of Regicide). Houdini soon gained another hidden backer—William Melville, the head of Scotland Yard's Special Branch and the most visible law enforcement official in the UK. Melville would ultimately become the first chief of Britain's MI5, assuming essentially the same position filled more than three centuries earlier by Walsingham. As Kalush and Sloman discovered, "Within days of arriving in England, Houdini met with a prominent Scotland Yard inspector and once again, his career took off." That inspector was Melville, whom Houdini secretly met with on June 14, 1900, five days after arriving on England's shores. He had left the US on May 30 using a passport issued just two days earlier—a passport that contained more than its fair share of anomalies.

The document listed Houdini's birthday as April 6, though his actual birthday is said to be March 24. It claimed that he was born in 1873, making him one year older than he actually was. Most curiously of all, the document indicated that Houdini was a native-born citizen, though he most assuredly was not. For reasons that no one seems able to explain, he had been allowed to surrender his previous passport, issued to a naturalized citizen, in exchange for the officially issued but clearly fraudulent passport that he used to tour Europe.

Given his background as both a magician and a Mason (by his own account), it goes without saying that secrecy, deception, and illusion were second-nature to Houdini. He also, as Sloman and Kalush noted, had the unusual "ability to interact with a country's police officials and do demonstrations inside their jails," and he was known to be rather proficient at the art of breaking-and-entering. Needless to say, these abilities would have served Houdini well in the world of espionage. So too would many of the devices he boasted of inventing. Again according to Kalush and Sloman, Houdini "told the *New York Herald* that he invented rubber heels and cameras that work only once. The *Boston Transcript* reported that he invented 'an envelope which cannot be unsealed by steam without bringing to light the word 'opened' and a wash which will remove printer's ink from paper'... In his own *Conjurer's Monthly*, he touted the use of chloride of cobalt for sending invisible messages."

A friend of Houdini's, fellow magician Billy Robinson, was also well-versed in the tradecraft of the intelligence community. In his book *Spirit Slate Writing and Kindred Phenomena*, Robinson "detailed thirty-seven methods for secret writing [which] would play an important part in spy communication during World War I." He also "detailed how to read other people's letters without opening the envelopes by using alcohol to render them temporarily transparent," and offered readers "subtle methods to share information while being closely scrutinized." Kalush and Sloman share what became of Robinson not long after penning the book: "Then, virtually overnight, he changed his name and appearance, left the country, and broke many of his connections. Years later, his only brother wouldn't even be able to find him." Robinson died in 1918 while performing a bullet catch trick that he had performed many times before. Houdini would write that "it seems as if there were something peculkar [sic] about the whole affair."

In addition to possessing skills and knowledge that were ideally suited to the spook trade, Houdini also ran what could best be described as his own personal spy ring; in addition to an unknown number of fulltime confederates (mostly young women, including one of his nieces), "Houdini employed female operatives on an *ad hoc* basis when he came to town." Probably the most important of his operatives was a young fellow magician named Amedeo Vacca, whose relationship with Houdini was unknown to virtually everyone throughout the escape artist's life. So secret was the close relationship between the two that even Harry's wife, as well as his brother, magician/confederate Hardeen, were unaware of it.

Houdini was a man for whom secrecy seems to have been something of an obsession. His home was said to be laced with secret passageways and hidden rooms, and his desk contained hidden compartments. There are indications that, while on the road, he would frequently maintain, for unknown purposes, a second hotel room in a different hotel. A man named Edward Saint (aka Charles David Myers), who was close to Bess, once claimed that Houdini "had safes and vaults in his home, and vaults in banks that his lawyers had access to; but one secret, now made public for the first time, is the fact that Houdini had one safety deposit vault in a bank or trust company in the East under some familiar name other than Houdini, and of which the secret location rested only in Houdini's brain. In this vault was kept highly secret papers." As far as is known, no one—not even Geraldo Rivera—has located that secret vault.

With his espionage tradecraft and dubious passport in tow, Houdini traveled to Germany in September 1900 after taking the British Isles by storm. As was the case in England and Scotland, the press immediately showered the visiting entertainer with accolades. There was one key difference in the German press coverage though: "The newspaper accounts of Houdini's demonstrations at German police stations portray him as a police consultant rather than a mere entertainer... For a vaudeville performer, Houdini seemed to spend an inordinate amount of time and have unprecedented access at the Berlin police station."

As he had in the US and the British Isles, Houdini established some unusual connections in Germany for a stage performer. One associate of his in Germany was a chemist named Hans Goldschmidt, who had patented an incendiary compound known as thermite. "Houdini noted that he was in Berlin when Goldschmidt performed his first test on a safe. He didn't explain why a stage escape artist would be at such a demonstration."

Houdini continued his pre-WWI tour by visiting France and Russia. Curiously, the countries that Houdini visited on his unusual tour—Russia, Germany, France and England—would have the distinction of being the major players in the soon-to-unfold Great War, but that's probably just a bizarre coincidence. In Czarist Russia, "the magician had official permission to appear in any city in Russia, an extraordinary set of circumstances that bespeaks the close relationship between Superintendent Melville and the Okhrana, the imperial Russian secret police." Houdini's Russian tour was booked by a guy named Harry Day, "a mysterious expatriate American who changed his name and met Houdini in London around the same time as Houdini's first meeting with Melville... [Day] eventually became a member of Parliament and did overseas espionage for the British government." For many years thereafter, the shadowy Day would handle Houdini's European bookings.

Following his lengthy tour of prewar Europe, Houdini returned to America with much press fanfare. One of his most high-profile stunts upon his return was escaping from the heavily fortified Cell #2 at the United States Jail in Washington, DC—the cell that had famously housed Charles Julius Guiteau, convicted assassin of President James Garfield, prior to Guiteau's hanging at the facility. Guiteau, who, like his father, was closely affiliated with a religious cult known as the Oneida Community, shot Garfield on July 2, 1881, having learned how to use a handgun just a few weeks earlier. He claimed to be acting on orders from God.

Houdini, needless to say, succeeded in escaping from Guiteau's former cell—and also rearranged all the prisoners residing on the jail's fabled 'murderer's row.' To do so, of course, he would have needed a master key, which someone clearly provided to him. But why? Such were the perks provided an entertainer who appeared to be "working as an agent for US government agencies, international police associations, and a special branch of Scotland Yard."

A couple years after his escape from the US Jail, there was an unusual incident at the Houdini household. On October 25, 1907, an intruder made a concerted effort to kill the performer, slashing at the sleeping figure more than 100 times with a razor. Harry Houdini, however, was not home at the time. Had he been, there might have been a different outcome, given that some reports contend that the escape artist carried a handgun at all times. The victim of the attack instead was his brother Leopold, who closely resembled Harry. Household servant Frank Thomas was arrested and charged with the attack, though there was scant evidence linking him to the crime and no known motive. Indeed, Thomas had arrived the next morning for work seemingly unaware the attack had taken place. Remarkably, Houdini was able to keep his name out of all press accounts of the crime and trial despite the fact that the attack occurred at his home, he appears to have been the intended victim, and the alleged assailant was his own servant.

On November 26, 1909, Houdini became the first man to successfully fly a powered craft on the Australian continent. He cheerfully dispatched publicity photos featuring him in a plane surrounded by German soldiers—a move he would soon regret when those German soldiers found themselves on the opposite side of the battlefields of WWI (following America's entry into the war, Houdini would attempt to destroy all photographs documenting his training of German pilots). That first flight and all subsequent Australian flights were arranged by Lieutenant George Taylor of the Australian Intelligence Corps. Curiously, despite Houdini's avid early interest in aviation, he did not, as far as is known, ever fly again after leaving Australia.

On April 29, 1911, Houdini debuted his famed Chinese Water Torture Cell escape in Southampton, England, though he had perfected and copyrighted the act well over a year earlier. The inherently dangerous stunt caused quite a sensation: "Just the sight of the apparatus was enough to give you shivers and make you believe, as one critic noted, that you were about to witness a ritual sacrifice." Around that same time, Houdini was, for reasons unknown, busily buying mothballed electric chairs at auctions across the country.

In 1913, Houdini's beloved mother passed away, which apparently resulted in Harry learning some deep family secret. Following her death, Houdini sent the following cryptic note to one of his brothers: "Time heals all wounds, but a long time will have to pass before it will heal the terrible blow which Mother tried to save me from knowing." The meaning of this rather provocative note remains a mystery. Houdini, by the way, was in Denmark when his mother died and he requested a delay of her funeral to allow himself time to return to the States. Despite strict prohibitions in Jewish law, the entertainer's request was granted.

In December 1914, just a few months after the provocation that allegedly triggered WWI, Houdini was summoned to the nation's capitol for a private audience with then-President Woodrow Wilson. It is anyone's guess what business the two men discussed but it probably had little to do with stage tricks. A year-and-a-half later, on that most notorious of dates, April 20, an estimated 100,000 people gathered in Washington, DC to watch Houdini perform a straightjacket escape. Other than for a presidential inauguration, it was said to be the largest crowd ever assembled in downtown Washington. One year later, in April 1917, the US declared war on Germany.

For the duration of the United States' involvement in the war, Houdini spent a considerable amount of time aiding the war effort, both through fundraising and by frequently visiting the front lines, where he ostensibly went from camp to camp providing entertainment for the troops. Houdini's Hollywood career also began just as the US was entering the war. It has often been said that one of his first credits was as a special-effects consultant on the *Mysteries of Myra* cliffhanger serial, though others have claimed that Houdini had no involvement in the production. Curiously, the real consultant for the project is said to have been occultist/intelligence asset Aleister Crowley.

Houdini's first feature-length film, *The Grim Game*, opened to rave reviews. Ensconced in Hollywood, Houdini quickly made friends with mega-stars Charlie Chaplin and Roscoe "Fatty" Arbuckle, both of whom would soon be caught up in scandals—a career-ending one in Arbuckle's case. The fledgling actor next began work on *Terror Island*, filmed largely on Catalina Island. Unlike his feature debut, *Island* opened to poor reviews, leading a discouraged Houdini to launch his own production company to create his own starring vehicles.

Just after completing *Terror Island*, in December 1919, Houdini was involved in yet another bizarre incident. Having injured his ankle performing the water torture escape, he paid a visit to a doctor who examined the performer and pronounced him in imminent "danger of death." Houdini nevertheless lived on for several more years; the doctor, meanwhile, turned up dead within two weeks.

By the end of 1921, the Houdini Picture Corporation had two feature-length films in the can—*The Man From Beyond* and *Haldane of the Secret Service*. The first, co-written by Houdini himself and released on April 2, 1922, featured a strange plotline revolving around a man found frozen in arctic ice and brought back to life, a case of mistaken identity, confinement in a mental institution, escape from that same institution, and an abduction. *Haldane*, released the following year, was Houdini's first attempt at directing himself. It featured the magician as his real-life alter ego, but its performance at the box office signaled the end of Houdini's film career.

For the rest of his years, Houdini devoted a considerable amount of time to investigating and debunking the spiritualist movement, which flourished in the post-WWI years as legions of fake 'mediums' preyed upon the grief of those who had lost loved ones in the war. By design or otherwise, Houdini's crusade served primarily to publicize the movement, which included among its members a number of Harry's friends, most notably and prominently Sir Arthur Conan Doyle, creator of fictional detective Sherlock Holmes and possible perpetrator of the infamous Piltdown Hoax of 1912. Both Doyle and Houdini also had connections to Le Roi and Margery Crandon, and that is where this story takes a decidedly dark turn.

Margery, born Mina Stinson in Canada in 1888, had moved with her family to Boston, Massachusetts, at a young age. As a teenager, she is said to have been a musical prodigy and to have played various musical instruments in local orchestras, while later working as an actress, secretary and ambulance driver. In 1917, the then-married Mina was hospitalized and operated on by Dr. Le Roi Goddard Crandon, a man who occupied a prestigious position in Boston society. Crandon was a direct descendent of one of the original twenty-three Mayflower passengers and a member of the Boston Yacht Club. He had graduated from Harvard Medical School and had also obtained a master's degree in philosophy from Harvard, where he also served as an instructor. Just before meeting Mina, he had served as a Naval officer and as head of the surgical staff at a US Naval hospital during WWI.

Shortly after meeting the doctor, Mina divorced her first husband and, in 1918, became the much older Le Roi Crandon's third wife. The two seemed hopelessly mismatched, she being young, vivacious and, by all accounts, very attractive, while he was said to be rather arrogant, unpleasant and antisocial. Nevertheless, the pair quickly became the talk of Boston's high society, particularly after the summer of 1923 when they began holding regular séances in their home. One member of the couple's inner circle was a fellow by the name of Joseph DeWyckoff, a wealthy steel tycoon born in Poland and educated in England and Czarist Russia before settling in America to practice law. He was jailed in Boston on embezzlement charges, later fleeing to Chicago after embezzling yet more money. He soon turned up in, of all places, Havana, Cuba, where, according to Kalush and Sloman, "in 1898 he was recruited by John Wilkie, the Secret Service chief, as a co-optee and was involved in spying for the United States during the Spanish-American War."

That would be, needless to say, the very same John Wilkie who had kick-started Harry Houdini's career that very same year. As a reward for his service, DeWyckoff, who "had a history of violence," "was given the contract to salvage the Battleship Maine in the Havana Harbor." The Maine had been sunk in what appears to have been a false-flag operation carried out by US intelligence operatives to justify launching a bloody colonial war.

Although fragmentary, there is clear evidence that Le Roi and Mina Crandon, in conjunction with DeWyckoff and various others, began sometime soon after getting married to 'adopt' an untold number of children who subsequently went missing. A number of letters that Dr. Crandon penned on the subject and dispatched to his buddy Doyle appear to have gone missing as well. As Kalush and Sloman note, "Strangely, many of the letters regarding the investigation into the boys have been expunged from Crandon's files." In one surviving letter, sent on August 4, 1925, Crandon notes that "about December first I had Mr. DeWyckoff bring over a boy from a London home for possible adoption... In April 1925, our Secret Service Department at Washington received a letter saying that I had first and last sixteen boys in my house for ostensible adoption, and that they had all disappeared."

Four years earlier, a Boston newspaper had reported that two boys had been rescued from a raft; one, eight-year-old John Crandon, was Margery/Mina's son from her previous marriage; the other, a ten-year-old English 'adoptee,' was reportedly so unhappy at the Crandon home that he was frantically attempting an escape, with the younger boy in tow. "Two years later, when Margery began her mediumship, there was no trace of that boy in the household." Perhaps he was the 'homeless' boy whose dead body was reportedly found on the outskirts of Joseph DeWyckoff's large estate in Ramsey, New Jersey, during that time period.

By 1924, Dr. Crandon was openly asking his many friends in the British spiritualist movement to "be on the lookout for suitable boys to adopt." Around that same time, as another associate noted in a letter, Crandon was "being sued for $40,000 for operating on a woman for cancer, when she was simply pregnant, and destroying the foetus... A highly incredible story which persists is that a boy who was in his family some weeks mysteriously disappeared. He claims that the boy is now in his home in England, but still official letters of inquiry and demand are received from that country. This is no mere rumor, for I was shown some of the original letters... The matter has been going on for more than a year. It is very mysterious."

In response to questions raised about the disappearance of one particular boy, Margery/Mina complained that "people wrote asking his whereabouts, and the prime minister of England cabled to ask where he was and demanded a cable reply. Why people even said Dr. Crandon committed illegal operations on little children and murdered them." According to Margery, "the poor little fellow had adenoids and had to be circumcised," so Crandon opted to perform the surgery at home. It was widely rumored that the good doctor had performed another procedure at home as well—surgically altering his wife's vaginal opening to allow her to 'magically' produce various items at séances.

On one occasion, Margery opened a closet in her home and showed an associate a collection of photos of well over 100 children, "most of them really lovely." Margery told the woman that, "Those are Dr. Crandon's caesareans—aren't they sweet? All caesareans." Given that Crandon wasn't known for delivering babies at all, the notion that he had delivered over 100 of them via caesarean was an absurdity. Who then were all these children and why had Dr. Crandon photographed them? Such are the questions raised by the fragmentary evidence trail indicating that an untold number of young boys fell into the nefarious hands of a cabal of wealthy individuals with connections to the intelligence community. Not to worry though—the disappearances were investigated by John Wilkie's Secret Service and a British MP by the name of Harry Day.

Not long before his death, Houdini, who had an extensive library of literature on the occult, began working with horror writer and occultist H.P. Lovecraft on various magazine articles. In 1926, he hired Lovecraft (who could, like Crandon, trace his lineage to the Massachusetts Bay Colony) and Clifford Eddy, Jr. (another occultist and horror writer and one of Houdini's covert operatives), to co-write a book debunking superstition. According to Kalush and Sloman, "Shortly after meeting with Eddy and Lovecraft, Bess was stricken with a nonspecific form of poisoning." Indeed, there is evidence suggesting that both Harry and Bess Houdini suffered from some form of poisoning prior to Harry's death. In addition, Houdini is said to have exhibited severe mood swings and had some "aggressive confrontations" in the weeks leading up to his death, both of which were out of character for the illusionist (though Bess is widely reported to have suffered from extreme mood swings throughout her life).

As the story goes, Houdini, who prided himself on being able to take a punch from pretty much anyone, was sucker-punched in his dressing room by a McGill University student, causing his appendix to burst and ultimately leading to his death on October 31, 1926. Houdini's physicians dutifully swore out affidavits certifying the cause of death to be "traumatic appendicitis," though the medical community now acknowledges that such a medical condition has never existed. No autopsy was performed. Joscelyn Gordon Whitehead, the guy credited with sucker-punching Houdini, had some rather provocative connections. His father, for example, was a British diplomat serving in the Orient. After Houdini's death, Whitehead is said to have become a recluse living something of a hermetic existence. He did have at least one close associate though—Lady Beatrice Isabel Marler, a wealthy heiress and the wife of Sir Herbert Meredith Marler, a prominent Canadian politician and diplomat who once served as Canada's ambassador to the US.

The mid-1920s were not a good time for the Houdini/Weiss brothers. Brother Gottfried Weiss, born two years before Harry, died in 1925. Harry followed suit the next year. Brother Nathan Weiss, born four years before Harry, died soon after, in 1927. On June 22, 1927, Houdini's European booking agent, Harry Day, reported that his apartment had been ransacked. That day would have also been Houdini's wedding anniversary—assuming, that is, that Harry was actually legally married to Bess, which may not have been the case. Two months after the break-in at Day's apartment, Theodore 'Hardeen,' one of Houdini's two surviving brothers—the one who had inherited all of brother Harry's props, effects and papers—reported that his home had also been broken into while he had been on the road.

After Houdini's death, it was widely rumored that Bess—who in addition to suffering from wild mood swings was also an alcoholic and a drug addict who was occasionally suicidal—ran an illegal speakeasy/ brothel in conjunction with a woman named Daisy White, said to have been Harry's mistress. Nothing unusual about that.

In mid-1945, Theodore 'Hardeen' checked into Doctor's Hospital for a scheduled operation. On June 12, 1945, Hardeen left that hospital in a body bag. It was reported at the time that Hardeen had been planning to pen a book on his brother and had begun work on the project before checking into the hospital. Nearly two decades later, on October 6, 1962, Leopold Weiss—Harry's last living sibling and the one who had been brutally attacked in his brother's home—is said to have jumped off a ledge and fallen six stories to his death. The last of Houdini's secrets went to the grave with him.

It has often been noted that Houdini took far longer to perform many of his stage escapes than was actually necessary and that he was frequently out of view of the audience during such times. This has generally been assumed to have been for dramatic effect. Authors Kalush and Sloman though offer a far more compelling possibility: "One explanation is that such challenges gave Houdini both the opportunity and an alibi to conduct a mission while he was performing." It was, in other words, the perfect cover, for how could a man be responsible for something that occurred elsewhere when he was performing on stage for a captive audience at the time? There are, it should be noted, clear parallels here to the story told by Chuck Barris, who has claimed that he was similarly slipping off to conduct covert missions while performing his duties as a chaperone for *The Dating Game*.

Of course, no one took Barris seriously because we all know that such things don't really happen in the real world—or at least not in the world that most of us think we live in.

24

WON'T GET FOOLED AGAIN
PUNK AND NEW WAVE ARRIVE

"He seriously thought that Miles, Stewart and I were part of some conspiracy hatched by my father and backed by the CIA." Ian Copeland, referring to Bernie Rhodes, onetime manager of the Clash

As the 1970s wore on, the sounds emanating from Laurel Canyon began to be replaced by a new genre of rock music. What was initially dubbed "punk rock" was soon transformed into the less raw version known as "new wave," and both were sold to the masses as a new form of rebellion against the status quo.

The new scene was populated with a new batch of rising stars, bands and artists with names like Sex Pistols, the Clash, Buzzcocks, the Cramps, Generation X, Cherry Vanilla, General Public, the (English) Beat, Public Image Ltd., the Fleshtones, the B-52s, the Cure, the Police, Blondie, Television, REM, Patti Smith, Lou Reed, John Cale, Magazine, Simple Minds, the Specials, Wall of Voodoo, the Go-Gos, the Bangles, Joan Jett & the Blackhearts, Echo and the Bunnymen, the Psychedelic Furs, Joy Division, Bow Wow Wow, Gang of Four, Squeeze, Siouxsie & the Banshees, Oingo Boingo, Adam Ant, Gary Numan, the Smiths, the Fixx, A Flock of Seagulls, Bananarama, Sting, Thompson Twins, Katrina and the Waves, Lords of the New Church, Midnight Oil, Steel Pulse, Dread Zeppelin, Social Distortion, Human League, Soft Cell, Timbuk 3, Camper Van Beethoven, Circle Jerks, dada, the Alarm, the Jesus and Mary Chain, the Plimsouls, the Ramones, the Stranglers, UB40, Suburban Lawns, Stan Ridgeway, XTC, Concrete Blonde, Ultravox, and the Fine Young Cannibals.

All of the acts listed above had something in common: In addition to being among the most critically acclaimed and commercially viable of the new artists, all of them owed their success at least in part to their association with one or more members of the Copeland clan.

The patriarch of that clan, Miles Axe Copeland, Jr., born in 1916, was something of a legend in Western intelligence circles. At the outbreak of WWII, the former working musician was magically transformed into one of the founding members of the OSS. During the war years, while he was stationed in the UK, he met Elizabeth Lorraine Adie, a British intelligence asset then assigned to the Special Operations Executive (SOE). Lorraine's brother, Ian Aide, was also a highly placed British intelligence operative.

Miles and Lorraine, he the son of a doctor and she the daughter of a prominent neurosurgeon, were married in the UK on September 25, 1942. After the war, the two moved to Washington, DC, where Miles worked alongside other intelligence heavyweights like "Wild Bill" Donovan to form the Central Intelligence Agency. For the next several decades, Copeland would play key roles in various nefarious activities throughout the Middle East, Africa and Asia. In 1947, he was dispatched to Damascus, Syria to serve as the CIA station chief and to orchestrate a series of coups that resulted in power being consolidated in the military and national security sectors. These were the first coups orchestrated by the newly formed CIA, but they would certainly not be the last. Along for the adventure was firstborn son Miles Copeland III, who had been born in London on May 4, 1944. On April 25, 1949, second son Ian, born just outside of Damascus, joined the family.

The Copeland family thereafter alternated between various posts in the Middle East and their sometime home in Washington. On July 16, 1952, third son Stewart was born in Alexandria, Virginia. That same month, the senior Copeland worked with Gamal Nasser to organize a coup in Egypt. In 1953, Miles worked closely with Archibald and Kermit Roosevelt to orchestrate the coup that toppled Iran's democratically elected Prime Minister Mohammed Mossadegh and consolidated the power of Shah Reza Pahlavi. That same year, the Copeland family was dispatched to Cairo, Egypt, where Miles was tasked with creating the Mukhabarat, Egypt's version of the CIA, for soon-to-be President Nasser. Copeland stayed on for four years, becoming Nasser's top Western adviser and the country's CIA station chief. While there, Lorraine developed a keen interest in archeology and thereafter worked as, or at least posed as, an archeologist. And a very young Miles Copeland III became friends with Colonel Hassan Touhaimi, described in a web-posted bio of Copeland as "Nasser's machine gun toting bodyguard who lived next door." Every pre-pubescent boy, I think we can all agree, needs friends like that.

From 1957 through 1968, the Copeland clan was stationed in Beirut, Lebanon, where Miles, Sr. served as that country's CIA station chief. In his memoirs, son Ian has described Beirut at that time as a "center of intrigue and espionage." During the early years of that assignment, Copeland worked closely with such intelligence community luminaries as Secretary of State John Foster Dulles and CIA chief Allen Dulles. Also during those years, the Copeland sons attended the American Community School in Beirut, where Miles III served as the president of his senior class. When he was just sixteen, Miles also obtained a license to teach judo to the Lebanese Army. Of those years spent in Lebanon, Ian Copeland has written that he "grew up thinking we were stinking rich. We certainly lived like we were." Ian has attributed that lavish lifestyle to his father's rather lucrative expense account.

Following his stint in Beirut—during which time he had frequently been on assignment in various hotspots throughout the Middle East, northern Africa and Asia—Copeland played a more low-profile role in US intelligence operations. In 1988, he penned an article entitled "Spooks for Bush" that argued that the intelligence community heartily backed the presidential bid of former spymaster George H.W. Bush. Three years later, Miles Axe Copeland, Jr. passed away, survived by his wife, daughter and three sons.

From fall 1962 through 1966, Miles Copeland III attended Birmingham Southern College, spending one semester at the American University in Washington, DC. After that, he was off to Lebanon to attend the American University of Beirut, where he spent three years. During that time, he formed his first business partnership with, again according to his online bio, "his close friend, Amr Ghaleb, son of Egypt's ambassador to Lebanon (known to run the largest spy network in Lebanon)." While at work at the business entity he dubbed Middle East Security Consultants, Copeland was reportedly fond of answering the phone with the greeting: "CIA, how can we help you?"

After graduating from the university in 1969, Miles joined the rest of the family in the UK, where he quickly began serving as a manager for the band Wishbone Ash and signing other new musical acts, including Joan Armatrading, Al Stewart and the Climax Blues Band. By 1974, he had launched his first record label, British Talent Managers (BTM), become a partner in a concert-booking agency and started a music industry magazine, *College Event*. As Ian later recalled, "When [Miles] found it difficult to get press on some of his bands, he simply determined to start his own magazine." He also joined with then-unknown attorney Allen Grubman to form what would become the most powerful music industry law firm in the country.

It was, needless to say, a natural progression for a kid who had grown up immersed in the world of covert operations and whose first business venture had been a security consulting firm co-owned by the son of another powerful figure in the intelligence community. The publication *College Event*, not surprisingly, employed some classic spytrade subterfuge: Copeland kept his name off the publication by employing a frontman editor so that he could then write glowing endorsements of his own bands, disguised, of course, as objective reviews.

In 1976, Miles gave up the magazine, record company and booking agency partnership and started over as an agent, manager, producer and record company for numerous new punk and new wave acts that would soon emerge as some of the very brightest stars on the new musical horizon. Copeland launched several new record labels—including Illegal Records, Deptford Fun City Records, Step Forward Records and New Bristol Records—and executive produced the first film dedicated to promoting the new scene, *Urgh! A Music War*. His office soon became the headquarters for the most influential fanzine of the era, *Sniffin' Glue*. In 1979, Copeland and Jerry Moss, the head of AMC Records, launched International Records Syndicate, Inc., better known as IRS Records. The label quickly became home to many of the most influential new wave acts. In 1983, Miles became the only music producer to be given his own show on the upstart MTV network, *IRS Records Presents The Cutting Edge*, which ran through 1987 and served to, not surprisingly, primarily promote Copeland's acts.

Copeland was also given his own prime-time television show in the UK, *Miles Copeland's England*. The program was widely viewed as being pro-Conservative Party and pro-capitalist and was reportedly a favorite of then-Prime Minister Margaret Thatcher. A repeat showing of the short-lived series was cancelled amid complaints that it would have undue influence on pending elections in the country.

Meanwhile, younger brother Ian Copeland had become quite a mover-and-shaker in the music industry as well. His self-professed wayward youth in Lebanon had included joining an older 'outlaw' biker gang after acquiring his first motorcycle at the age of fifteen. His memoirs are filled with other tales of bold adventures—including running away from home as a minor and making his way through several countries—but most of them seem rather apochryphal. He claims that his first business enterprise, when he was still quite young, was "basically running a whorehouse" servicing the US Marines called into the country by his father. He also claims to have helped a friend flee the country after said friend had likely killed a cop.

On September 19, 1967, at the height of the increasingly unpopular Vietnam War, while other kids were desperately trying to avoid the draft, Ian voluntarily enlisted in the US Army. As he emphasized in his memoirs, he "*wanted* to go to Vietnam." Assigned to the 1st Infantry Division, also known as the Big Red One, he arrived 'in country' just after the Tet Offensive of 1968. As recounted in his tome, his unit would soon find itself "banned from Saigon... following numerous complaints alleging brutality." Ian also writes approvingly of his unit's habit of "randomly bombard[ing] places around the country where we suspected Charlie might be," blithely ignoring the fact that those places likely harbored mostly noncombatants. Of his time in Vietnam, Copeland has written that he "loved it—not all the time, but enough to have seen me through it all, and to have mostly fond memories as I think of Vietnam." His fond memories are no doubt influenced by the fact that, as someone cleared to handle sensitive communications, he was given a considerable amount of autonomy: "Since we handled messages classified as Confidential, Secret and Top Secret, we were able to close off our area with barbed wire and make it off-limits to absolutely everyone, including officers."

While just nineteen, Ian Copeland was promoted to the rank of sergeant, becoming, by his account, the youngest US serviceman ever to achieve that rank. He has credited that promotion in part to the fact that he rode as a bodyguard for an unnamed lieutenant who was heavily involved in black market operations. What Copeland fails to mention is that black market operations in Vietnam were mostly run by our own CIA. Copeland also was awarded a Bronze Star, a Good Conduct Medal, four campaign medals, a National Defense Service Medal, a Vietnam Service Medal, and a Republic of Vietnam Commendation Medal.

Following his tour of duty in Vietnam, Ian was assigned to Fort Lee, Virginia, just outside Washington, DC. There he was tasked with providing riot control training to troops being prepped to police the May Day peace march on Washington. He subsequently volunteered for a second tour of duty in Vietnam, but soon found himself facing drug charges in the UK. He was ultimately found "not guilty" of the charges, owing largely to the fact that his father secured representation for him from a member of the Queen's Counsel. His time spent fighting the charges though resulted in his Vietnam orders being rescinded and instead he was dispatched to a remote communications outpost in England. In October 1970, he was sent to one of the numerous US military installations around Mannheim, Germany, a hub for military intelligence operations. A few months later, in January 1971, he was honorably discharged after serving his country for nearly three-and-a-half years.

In late April 1971, shortly after his discharge, Copeland incongruously decided to join a week-long protest organized by the group Vietnam Veterans Against the War. Given his own history and his family history, readers are excused for questioning whether his sudden misgivings about the war were sincere or whether he was in fact working to infiltrate the dissident group. A clue can perhaps be found in the fact that, not long after joining the protest, Ian answered an ad seeking Vietnam veterans who would be willing to sign up to fight as mercenaries in the Congo.

Copeland never made it to the Congo though; instead he went to work for big brother Miles. By 1979, Ian had founded Frontier Booking International, better known by the acronym FBI, which quickly became the go-to booking agency for "new wave" acts, a term that Ian Copeland claims to have coined. Soon he was booking all of brother Miles' acts and many more as well. Between the two of them, Miles and Ian signed, managed, booked, recorded, produced or otherwise handled a remarkably high percentage of the big name acts that emerged from the new music scene.*

The youngest and best known of the Copeland brothers, Stewart, also opted to venture into the emerging punk/new wave scene, but he did so by forming his own 'punk' band. Before actually recruiting any musicians, he quickly came up with a band name, the Police, and designed the band's logo and an album cover. The band that he would then assemble, featuring himself on drums, Gordon Thomas Matthew "Sting" Sumner on bass and lead vocals, and Andrew James Summers on guitar, would soon become arguably the most critically acclaimed and commercially successful of the new bands. The initial success of the Police in the US is what largely opened the floodgates for a new British invasion of punk and new wave bands. And that was in spite of the fact that the band was in no way a punk band and didn't really even qualify as a new wave band. As the British press pointed out, band members were much too professional, and a bit too old, to really fit into the new scene.

In 2002, Stewart Copeland played briefly in a reconstituted version of the Doors, alongside founding members Ray Manzarek and Robby Krieger. Copeland's former bandmate, Andy Summers, who was a decade older than Stewart and Sting, had been on the Laurel Canyon scene back when the original Doors were playing the Sunset Strip. As he wrote in *Rolling Stone* in July 2007, in 1968 he "was living in Laurel Canyon and going to Sunset Strip every night." Briefly a member of Eric Burden and the Animals at that time, Summers had been one of the regulars at the Log Cabin.

And the beat goes on...

* Ian Copeland was also in a three-year relationship with actress Courteney Cox, who famously made her debut dancing with rocker Bruce Springsteen in a music video. Cox, as it turns out, was partially raised by and is the step-daughter of Hunter Copeland, brother of Miles Axe Copeland, Jr. and an uncle of the three boys. Hunter Copeland had been a decorated WWII officer, returning home with a Silver Star, four Bronze Stars, and a Purple Heart.

EPILOGUE

"For whatever reason—it's still not understood by criminologists—California in the 1970s was ground zero for serial killers."
Stella Sands, writing in The Dating Game Killer

ONE THING THAT HAS BECOME VERY CLEAR WHILE RESEARCHING THIS BOOK is that there are disturbing parallels between the Laurel Canyon saga and my previous research on the phenomenon of serial killers—research that led to my earlier book, *Programmed to Kill*. Nowhere is that more true than in the details of the curious case of Rodney Alcala, otherwise known as the Dating Game Killer, who is said to be one of the country's most prolific serial killers. He has been convicted of seven murders, accused of several more, and some law enforcement officials have claimed, rather ludicrously, that he could be responsible for as many as 130 murders. It is only in recent years though that he has been identified as a serial killer, despite the fact that all the crimes he is accused of were committed in the 1970s.

In addition to being an alleged serial killer himself, Alcala allegedly operated on the same turf as a few other, more high-profile serial killers. And as fate would have it, he also had a number of connections to the Laurel Canyon scene and some of the key people and places that made up that scene. In other words, Alcala's story seems to provide a bridge between the seemingly idyllic Laurel Canyon scene and the brutal world of serial murder.

In the opening chapter of Stella Sands' *The Dating Game Killer*, that connection is hinted at:

"As cars cruised up and down Hollywood Boulevard and the Sunset Strip, radios blared edgier, angrier rock and roll: Masters Of War by Bob Dylan, What's Going On? by Marvin Gaye, Eve Of Destruction by Barry McGuire. Musicians from bands like the Doors, the Byrds, Cream, and the Animals played the Whiskey-a-Go-Go [sic] on the Sunset Strip—and partied with wild abandon at the Chateau Marmont Hotel up the street... Amidst all this turmoil and social upheaval in 1968, an event occurred that is not well documented by the era's historians: 'Tali S.,' age eight, was abducted on her way to school."

This story begins though in 1943, in San Antonio, Texas, with the birth on August 23 of one Rodrigo Jacques Alcala-Buquor. Growing up, young Rodrigo (known as Rodney) attended mostly private Catholic schools where he got excellent grades and never showed any signs of being a problem child. In 1951, when he was about eight, he and his family moved to Mexico where he attended the American School. Not long after relocating, Rodney's father left the family and returned to the States alone. In 1954, after a few years in Mexico, Rodney and his mom and siblings relocated once again, this time to Los Angeles, California. By 1956, he was enrolled at the private Cantwell High School for boys, which later merged with Sacred Heart of Mary High School for girls to become the Cantwell-Sacred Heart of Mary High School, owned and operated by the LA Archdiocese.

Alcala finished out his senior year at Montebello High School, graduating in 1960. According to various reports, he had a wide circle of friends and never had any trouble lining up dates during his high school years. In addition to being an excellent student and talented athlete, he was on the yearbook planning committee and he took piano lessons. He was, in other words, a well-rounded and popular kid—the kind of young man you would expect to see voted "most likely to succeed" by his high school classmates.

On June 19, 1961, Rodney Alcala enlisted in the US Army. His older brother was at the time attending prestigious West Point Military Academy, which generally requires a nomination from a US Senator or a member of the House of Representatives. There is no explanation in the available literature as to how the Alcala family had either the financial means or the political connections to secure such an appointment.

Rodney meanwhile entered a program in North Carolina to become a paratrooper but instead served as a clerk, if his service records are to be believed. He was stationed, interestingly enough, at Fort Bragg, which had become, with the creation of the Psychological Warfare Center in 1952, a hotbed of research on 'unconventional warfare.' Fort Bragg is also the longtime home of US Special Forces.

After two years of military service, Alcala unexpectedly showed up at his mother's Montebello home after having gone AWOL. He was quickly hospitalized and informed that he was in immediate need of psychiatric treatment. Taken first to San Francisco, he soon found himself at a military hospital at the Marine Corps Air Station at El Toro, near Irvine, California. He remained there for an unspecified length of time.

Following his release, he returned to his mother's home in Montebello and shortly thereafter enrolled in UCLA's College of Fine Arts, from where he earned a degree in 1968. During his first year there, another young student who had just moved out from Florida—a guy by the name of Jim Morrison—likewise enrolled in UCLA's College of Fine Arts. Both young men displayed a passion for making student films. According to Morrison biographers Jerry Hopkins and Danny Sugerman, during Jim and Rodney's time at the College of Fine Arts, a fellow student cut his girlfriend's heart out.

On September 25, 1968, an eight-year-old girl later identified as Tali Shapiro was abducted while on her way to the Gardner Street Elementary School in Hollywood. At the time, according to Sands, Shapiro was "living temporarily at the Chateau Marmont Hotel in West Hollywood with her brother, sister, mother, and music-industry father." The family was temporarily rubbing elbows with the likes of Jim Morrison and Janis Joplin because, as it turns out, "their home had recently burned down in a fire." As Gary Valentine Lachman has written, the hotel during that era was widely rumored to offer a decidedly unhealthy environment in which to raise a young girl: "Tales of pacts with the Devil followed [Led] Zeppelin throughout their career, and stories of orgies, black masses and satanic rites were commonplace, mostly centered around the infamous Chateau Marmont off the Sunset Strip."

On the morning of her abduction, Shapiro is said to have woken early and, without informing her parents, decided on her own to walk to school rather than taking the bus—which seems difficult to believe given her young age and the fact that the school was a little over a mile away down seedy Sunset Boulevard. As the story goes, Alcala was spotted luring Shapiro into his vehicle by a good samaritan, who then followed Alcala back to his apartment where he called police from a nearby phone. The police though apparently didn't rush over, giving Alcala time to strip, viciously rape and then bludgeon the young girl nearly to death. She was so thoroughly battered, with her head bashed open and a heavy bar placed across her throat, that the responding officer initially thought she was dead.

Upon arrival, the officer knocked on the suspect's front door and was greeted through the window by a partially naked man who claimed he had just gotten out of the shower and would need a minute to get dressed. Despite the fact that the officer was responding to a report of an abducted child (with the witness on the scene) and had just encountered the presumed suspect, he nevertheless allowed that suspect time to get dressed and escape. According to Sands, "In the short time it had taken to kick in the door, the perpetrator—the *monster*—had slipped out the back." The *LA Weekly* concurred, claiming that Alcala "escaped through a backdoor." Not many apartment units, it should probably be noted, come equipped with a back door.

In any event, the apartment was found to be full of photographic equipment and stacks of photographs of young girls. The suspect, however, was nowhere to be found. The case was assigned to, of all people, LAPD detective Steve Hodel, brother of Michelle Phillips' surrogate mom, Tamar Hodel, and son of accused Black Dahlia killer George Hodel. According to a January 21, 2010, article in the *LA Weekly*, Hodel was at the time a "newbie detective working juvenile crimes." The Shapiro family, meanwhile, abruptly decided to relocate to Mexico, a move that is routinely cited as the reason the crime was never prosecuted.

Following his unlikely escape, Alcala immediately relocated to New York and, using the name John Berger, applied for admission to the prestigious New York University School of the Arts. Although the semester had already begun at the notoriously selective school, Berger/Alcala was nevertheless admitted. He attended for three years, working at times as a security guard and, during the summers of 1969, 1970 and 1971, as an arts counselor. One of Alcala's instructors at the school was a guy who during those same years had a slaughter perpetrated at his home, and who Pamela Des Barres once described as being "definitely *not* normal," Mr. Roman Polanski.

In June of 1971, Cornelia Crilley, a TWA stewardess who lived with her family across from the sprawling Cavalry Cemetary, was found dead. She had been in a two-year relationship with a Leon Borstein, then an assistant district attorney for Brooklyn who later became the chief special prosecutor for New York City. Borstein, who claimed that Crilley was the love of his life but who nevertheless married just a year after her murder, was initially the prime suspect. The crime appeared to have nothing whatsoever to do with Rodney Alcala—but a full four decades later, in 2011, he would be indicted for her murder.

By the time of Crilley's murder, Sands notes, "detective Steve Hodel and his LAPD team had been trying to locate Alcala for nearly three years." They finally got a break when Alcala was added to the FBI's Ten Most Wanted list and was subsequently recognized by a couple of the teens at the camp where he served as a counselor. Upon his arrest and return to Los Angeles, Alcala was facing very serious charges of kidnapping, rape and attempted murder, yet he was allowed to cop a guilty plea to a single count of child molestation, for which he received a sentence of one to ten years. He ultimately served less than three years, with much of that time spent at the notorious California Medical Facility at Vacaville. Also housed at Vacaville during that time was Donald DeFreeze, who would soon emerge as Cinque, leader of the so-called Symbionese Liberation Army. According to Dr. Colin Ross, during that same time period, "the CIA was conducting mind control experiments [at Vacaville] under MKSEARCH Subproject 3."

In August 1974, a prison psychiatrist recommended that Alcala be released and he was paroled to LA County and required to register with the local police as a sex offender. Within just weeks of gaining his freedom though, Alcala kidnapped a thirteen-year-old girl and was promptly arrested once again. He again caught a lucky break and was found guilty only of violating his parole and of furnishing drugs to a minor, escaping far more serious charges. He served about two-and-a-half years and was paroled on June 16, 1977. Just days after being released, he asked his parole officer for permission to take a trip to New York City, and, since he had behaved himself so well the last time he was on parole, his request was granted.

Alcala remained in New York for a little over a month, ostensibly to visit relatives. During his time there, a woman by the name of Ellen Jane Hover went missing. Being the small world that it is, Ellen just happened to be the daughter of Herman Hover, who had been the longtime owner of Ciro's on the Sunset Strip, the club that famously launched the career of the Byrds. She was also the goddaughter of Sammy Davis, Jr. For reasons that were never explained, the FBI took a keen interest in Hover's disappearance, which happened to come at a time when New York City was gripped by intense fear. It was, after all, the infamous 'Summer of Sam' and Hover's disappearance on July 15, 1977, was sandwiched between two Son of Sam attacks, one on June 26 and another on July 31.

Hover remained missing for almost a full year, until her skeletal remains were discovered in June of 1978, in a shallow grave on, of all places, the Rockefeller estate in Westchester County. It would be over three decades later that Rodney Alcala would be charged with her murder.

Upon his return from New York, Alcala applied for a job as a typesetter at the *Los Angeles Times*. He applied using his real name and was promptly hired, despite having been twice convicted for felony offenses, having served time for crimes committed against children, being a registered sex offender, being on parole, and holding the distinction of once numbering among the FBI's Ten Most Wanted. A coworker would later say, perhaps tellingly, that Alcala seemed like he knew a lot of famous people.

On November 10, 1977, the nude, brutalized body of eighteen-year-old Jill Barcomb was found posed on a side road adjacent to, and in full view of, the Marlon Brando estate overlooking Laurel Canyon. The murder was investigated by LAPD detective Phillip Vannatter, who would later famously tote a vial of blood around with him while investigating the murders of Nicole Brown Simpson and Ron Goldman. For many, many years, Barcomb's death was credited to the Hillside Strangler team of Angelo Buono and Kenneth Bianchi. Like the Strangler victims, Jill was found nude, strangled, tortured, sexually assaulted, bound and posed on a hillside. And her death occurred amidst a string of Strangler killings—Judith Miller on October 31, Lissa Kastin on November 6, Barcomb on November 10, Kathleen Robinson on November 18, and Kristina Weckler, Delores Cepeda, and Sonja Johnson all found dead on November 20. In addition, Barcomb knew Strangler victim Miller. Nevertheless, the murder would eventually be credited to Alcala, but not for nearly forty years.

According to the official version of events then, Judith Miller, chosen at random, was killed on Halloween by a pair of serial killers. And then a mere ten days later, in an officially unrelated event, her friend Jill Barcomb, also chosen at random, was killed by a different serial killer who, despite being unconnected to the other two serial killers, nevertheless killed and posed Barcomb in a manner remarkably similar to the way Miller was killed and posed. One has to wonder what the odds of that actually happening would be.

In any event, Jill Barcomb, found not far from where Marina Habe had been found nearly a decade earlier, is yet another tragic addition to the Laurel Canyon Death List. As is, I suppose, Ellen Jane Hover. Tali Shapiro narrowly avoided making the list.

At the request of the FBI, Alcala was brought down to the LAPD's Parker Center in December 1977 for questioning concerning the still-missing Ellen Hover. He admitted knowing Hover and even acknowledged being with her on the day she vanished, but he claimed to know nothing about her disappearance. That same month, twenty-eight-year-old nurse Georgia Wixted was found brutally murdered in her Malibu, California, bedroom. For nearly thirty years, there would be absolutely nothing linking Rodney Alcala to the crime or the crime scene.

In early 1978, Alcala was questioned by the Hillside Strangler Task Force, which was composed of members of the LAPD, the LA Sheriff's Department and the Glendale Police Department. He was arrested at that time, though only for the benign offense of being in the possession of marijuana, for which he served a brief jail sentence. For a time though, he was considered a "person of interest" to the task force. On June 23, 1978, just after Alcala's release from that brief jail stint, the savaged body of thirty-two-year-old legal secretary Charlotte Lamb was discovered on the floor of an apartment laundry room in El Segundo, California. Once again, there was no evidence linking Alcala to either the crime, the victim, or the crime scene, and he would not be named as a suspect for some twenty-five years.

On September 13 of that same year, Alcala infamously appeared as Bachelor #1 on television's *The Dating Game*. Despite his criminal history and sex offender status, which surely would have been discovered during the show's screening process, he was presented to women across the country as one of the nation's most eligible and desirable bachelors. The guy doing that presenting was *Dating Game* producer Chuck Barris, who has stated publicly that he was a CIA asset at the time the show was in production and that the show itself was essentially an elaborate CIA front designed to provide cover for Barris' own travels and activities. Mr. Barris was also, according to some reports, a onetime resident of everyone's favorite canyon.

On February 13 of the following year, Alcala picked up a fifteen-year-old hitchhiker by the name of Monique Hoyt, who voluntarily spent that night at Alcala's home. The next day, Valentine's Day, thirty-four-year-old Rodney Alcala took fifteen-year-old Monique Hoyt into the woods to shoot nude photos. At some point the situation turned violent and nonconsensual, resulting in yet another arrest for Alcala. Though facing very serious felony charges, including kidnapping, rape, and the production of child pornography, his bail was set at a paltry $10,000. At the end of April, Alcala gave his two-week notice to his superiors at the *LA Times*. How he had managed to keep his job through his jail sentence for marijuana possession and his arrest for kidnapping a young girl is anyone's guess. The *Times* apparently used the same screening service as *The Dating Game*.

On June 14, another young woman, twenty-one-year-old Jill Parentau, turned up dead in her Burbank, California, apartment. Once again, there was no evidence linking Rodney Alcala to the crime and Parentau's murder would remain unsolved for two-and-a-half decades. Six days after her murder, on the eve of the summer solstice, twelve-year-old Robin Samsoe of Huntington Beach, California, went missing after spending time at the beach with her best friend. Officially, her remains were discovered twelve days later in a heavily wooded area allegedly chosen by Rodney Alcala. But the reality appears to be that it is unknown what became of Samsoe. What is known is that from the time of her disappearance, authorities took a much different approach to dealing with Alcala than they had in the past. Before a month had passed, he was back in prison and would never walk free again.

As the story is generally told, Samsoe was strolling the beach with her friend when they were approached by Alcala with a request to take their photos, ostensibly for a student photo contest. A neighbor who happened to be passing by approached the trio, at which time Alcala lowered his head and quickly shuffled off. The girls went about their business without giving the incident much thought and Samsoe soon said goodbye to her friend. Borrowing the friend's bike, she headed off to a ballet class that she never made it to.

On the afternoon of July 2, a worker with the US Forestry Service discovered human skeletal remains in a heavily wooded section of the Angeles National Forest. The area was littered with discarded beer bottles and cigarette butts. The remains appeared to be those of an adult, and investigators, according to a June 1989 article in *Orange Coast Magazine*, believed the death to be "drug-related." The crime scene, according to the same report, "was given only a cursory examination by the Los Angeles Sheriff's Department." Five days later an LA County coroner decided that the remains were actually those of a child. And not just any child, but the missing Robin Samsoe. Unexplained was how the remains of a child could have been mistaken for those of an adult. Also unexplained was how the child could have been reduced to skeletal remains, completely stripped of flesh and hair, in an absurdly short amount of time.

The only thing that would ever tie Rodney Alcala to those scattered remains would be the testimony of one Dana Crappa, a twenty-year-old seasonal firefighter with the Forestry Service. And it is here, with the introduction of Dana Crappa, that this story grows very murky. As *Orange Coast Magazine* noted, "The exact bit of information that first tied Crappa to the disappearance of Robin Samsoe is not known." Indeed, there doesn't appear to be *anything* that initially tied Crappa to Samsoe. But with considerable molding by police, Crappa would emerge as the star witness for the prosecution.

For reasons that have never been adequately explained, Huntington Beach Police called Crappa in for questioning on August 2, 1979, exactly one month after the discovery of the remains. At that time, Crappa was shown photos of Alcala and Samsoe as well as of Alcala's car. She told investigators that she had never seen the man or the girl before, but that the car might resemble one she had seen parked near Mile Marker 11 (near where the remains were discovered) on either June 7 or June 14 at around 9:30–10:00 PM. Seeing as how the dates provided by Crappa were well before Samsoe's disappearance, this information was of no use to police. The time of day was entirely wrong as well.

Pressed by police to state whether it might have been June 20 or June 21 when she saw the vehicle, Crappa responded that it "definitely could not have been."

On August 7, Crappa was again questioned by police. Miraculously, on this occasion she recalled that she had seen the vehicle similar to Alcala's on June 21, and had done so between 8:00 and 8:30 PM! She added that, prior to her discovery of the remains on July 2, she had no awareness of the crime scene. But at preliminary trial proceedings not long after that meeting, Crappa told a different version of her story; she again said that she had seen the car on June 21, but she now claimed that it had been between 10:00–10:30 PM. She added that she had not seen anyone near the parked car. She also added that she had first seen the corpse on June 29, several days earlier than she had previously claimed. And she added that the corpse was already skeletal at that time.

On February 7, 1980, Crappa met with Huntington Beach Police detective Art Droz and a police psychologist named Larry Blum. She had, however, previously stated that she wanted no further interaction with the police so she was deliberately not told that the men she was speaking to were police personnel. Although authorities heatedly deny it, it is painfully obvious that Ms. Crappa was subjected to hypnotic interrogation techniques during that meeting and at future meetings. According to police, at the February 7 meeting she claimed that she had seen the vehicle on June 21 and that she had in fact seen a man by the car after all! She also said that when she had returned on June 29 she had found clothes strewn about the area, a crusty knife, and six .22-caliber bullet casings. For reasons never explained, she also claimed that she had picked up the bullet casings and thrown them away!

By that time, Crappa's testimony was so ridiculously riddled with contradictions and inconsistencies that it should have had no value to prosecutors in any kind of real trial. Police and prosecutors though weren't quite done with her.

On February 11, she once again unknowingly spoke to police investigators. On February 15, she met with a detective and one of the prosecutors on the case. By then she was claiming to have seen the car on June 20 and to have seen a man guiding a young girl away from the car and into the woods! On the day that meeting was held, the presiding judge ruled that Alcala's prior offenses would be allowed into evidence, including the fact that Alcala was suspected of involvement in Hover's death, a crime he had never even been charged with, let alone convicted of. As Sands noted, "The ruling was a momentous victory for the prosecution. Because there was little direct evidence linking Alcala to the Samsoe crime, the prior attacks would lend credence to their case." It was becoming perfectly obvious that Rodney Alcala was not going to get anything resembling a fair trial.

On February 26, Crappa once again met with detectives and prosecutors. Somewhere around that time she reportedly suffered a nervous breakdown and allegedly became suicidal, leading to her being involuntarily institutionalized. That, needless to say, must have greatly facilitated the process of programming the witness. A defense psychiatrist by the name of Albert J. Rosenstein would later describe Crappa in open court as "a Manchurian candidate at a minor level."

As Alcala's trial got underway on March 6, 1980, the defendant was paraded into the courtroom in cuffs and leg shackles in a deliberate attempt to prejudice the jury. But the real "linchpin of the trial," as Sands wrote, "would be the testimony of one Dana Crappa, twenty-one." On the stand, Crappa's demeanor was odd, to say the least. She frequently took long, awkward pauses—when she wasn't staring blankly into space. According to *Orange Coast Magazine*, her demeanor was so bizarre that the trial judge considered ending her testimony prematurely. She did though tell the story prosecutors wanted her to tell—a story that bore no resemblance whatsoever to the story she told when first mysteriously contacted by police.

In court, Crappa claimed that she had seen the suspect's vehicle on June 20. She also said that she had seen a man resembling Alcala guide a young girl who resembled Samsoe into the woods. Although she had found what she allegedly observed disturbing, she acknowledged that she had told no one of the incident. When her curiosity got the best of her, she said, she had returned to the area on June 25 to have a look around. At that time, she had allegedly seen Samsoe's body, decapitated and with part of her face gone. She had, of course, returned by herself and told no one of her supposed discovery. Crappa further told the jury that she had returned a second time on June 29, again alone. On that visit, she claimed, she had observed that Samsoe's body had been reduced to a pile of bones. In just four days! Following that extremely unlikely second visit, she again, of course, told no one. We are apparently to believe then that she was brave enough to return to a remote murder scene alone on two occasions, but not brave enough to report her discoveries, even anonymously.

Crappa's testimony had no credibility whatsoever, and she was not the only seriously dubious witness trotted out by the prosecution. There were also Robert J. Dove and Michael Herrera, a pair of Orange County jail inmates, both of whom testified that Alcala had given them jailhouse confessions. A third OC inmate, however, testified that he, Dove and Herrera had fabricated the confessions to gain favor with authorities. What the jury didn't hear was that all three inmates just happened to be clients of Alcala's first court-appointed attorney. Of the thousands of inmates in the OC jail, Alcala had supposedly chosen to confess his crime only to three guys who happened to be represented by the guy who was supposed to be defending him.

Despite their best efforts, prosecutors were unable to present any physical evidence at all tying Alcala to the murder of Robin Samsoe; there was no fingerprint evidence, no fiber or hair evidence, no blood evidence, and no DNA evidence. There also don't appear to have been many witnesses who weren't delivering brazenly perjured testimony.

After a half-hearted defense that included alibi testimony from Alcala's girlfriend and two of his sisters, followed by closing arguments and jury instructions, deliberations began on April 29, 1980. Jurors returned the next day with a guilty verdict on the charge of first-degree murder. The date was, of course, April 30—because that's just the way these things always seem to work. The penalty phase of the trial was a perfunctory affair with just two witnesses appearing for the prosecution, both of them parole officers to whom Alcala had previously reported. He was quickly sentenced to death.

At Alcala's first appeal hearing, inmate Joseph Drake took the stand to repeat his claim that he, Dove and Herrera had fabricated Alcala's confessions in order to strike an "informer's bargain" with authorities. He was joined by Dove, who freely admitted on the stand that his previous testimony had been perjured. The inmate testimony had been crucial to the prosecution's goal of adding the special circumstance of kidnapping, which was necessary for the imposition of the death penalty. On May 28, 1981, the presiding judge issued an extraordinary ruling stating that there had been no "perjured evidence introduced during the trial, *and that even had there been*, that was not a substantial consideration regarding Alcala's guilt." (emphasis added)

The special circumstance of kidnapping, therefore, would stand and Alcala was returned to Death Row. On August 23, 1984, however, the California Supreme Court ruled that the lower court had erred in allowing into evidence Alcala's prior offenses. Rodney Alcala would be getting a new trial after all. The available literature invariably expresses outrage over this reversal, claiming that the allegedly criminal-coddling 'liberal' courts let him off on "a technicality," though that is far removed from the truth.

In April of 1986, Alcala's second trial for the murder of Robin Samsoe got underway. There was a problem though: Dana Crappa, whose testimony was the only hope the state had of getting a conviction, privately informed the judge that she would not be able to testify because she remembered nothing about the incident. She also told him that she did not remember previously testifying, which isn't surprising considering that she delivered that testimony in an obviously induced mental state. Signaling that this trial was going to be just as much of a sham as the first trial, the judge ruled that he would allow Crappa's previous testimony to be read into the record without Crappa being present. That, of course, deprived the jury of the ability to judge Crappa's demeanor and body language and all the other non-verbal clues that jurors use to gauge someone's honesty and credibility. It also denied the defense the opportunity to cross-examine the witness and confront her with her wildly varying accounts of the incident.

The remainder of the trial largely followed the pattern of Alcala's first trial, with a number of women—including Alcala's mother, two sisters, and a female coworker at the *Times*—providing testimony for the defense. The jury once again returned with a guilty verdict and he was once again sentenced to death, but only after blasting his attorneys in court for being "unprepared and unwilling" to mount a real defense. Some six years later, on December 31, 1992, the California Supreme Court affirmed Alcala's second conviction. And that, for the next decade or so, would be the end of the Rodney Alcala saga.

That all changed on March 30, 2001, when a federal district court set aside Alcala's second conviction based on the wildly improper introduction of Crappa's prior testimony. The court also opined that the defense had been improperly prohibited from introducing evidence that Crappa's testimony had been induced. On June 27, 2003, the Ninth Circuit Court of Appeals upheld the decision of the federal court and vacated Alcala's conviction, additionally citing the failure by police to secure and properly investigate the crime scene.

The stage was now set for Alcala to stand trial for the *third time* for the murder of Robin Samsoe. The state though was facing quite a dilemma: for whatever reason, there was still a very strong desire to have Alcala take the fall for Samsoe's disappearance, but there was no semblance of a case left. There would be no perjured inmate testimony. There would be no induced testimony from Dana Crappa. There would be no inflammatory admission of prior uncharged crimes. There would be no parading of Alcala in handcuffs and leg shackles. And there still was not a shred of physical evidence tying Alcala to the crime or the alleged crime scene.

On October 17, 2003, Alcala filed a motion to act as his own attorney in the coming trial. This was cast by the media as a misguided, narcissistic attempt by Alcala to put himself in the spotlight. In truth, he was undoubtedly aware that he had been sold out twice before and likely would be again. Indeed, in June 2003, the very month that Alcala's conviction had been vacated, DNA evidence had supposedly identified him as the killer of Georgia Wixted. The state was going to be taking a novel approach to railroading Alcala this time.

Alcala would soon allegedly be linked by DNA evidence to the Lamb, Parentau and Barcomb murders as well. Like Wixted, they were all killed in Los Angeles County, which is under a different court jurisdiction than Orange County, where Alcala had previously stood trial for Samsoe's murder. All five cases were handed off to a grand jury, which, as California grand juries do, met secretly to render a decision. According to Sands, "After hearing all the evidence against Alcala, the grand jury came down with an indictment. Although Lamb, Parenteau, Barcomb, and Wixted had all been murdered in Los Angeles County, the grand jury held open the possibility that prosecutors could consolidate all *five* cases—including that of Robin Samsoe—and try Alcala in Orange County."

After numerous delays, the consolidated trial began in Orange County in early 2010. It was the first time, and to date the last time, that such a cross-county consolidation had been allowed. The state was now going to try to convict Alcala for the Samsoe murder by presenting it as one of a string of murders, with the other four allegedly being open-and-shut, scientifically unimpeachable cases. It appeared that judicial malfeasance had now reached such a level that the state had dusted off four very old murder cases and manufactured evidence linking Alcala to them as a way of garnering a conviction for a fifth murder that was otherwise not prosecutable.

Alcala was by then being widely identified by police and the media as a prolific serial killer who was likely responsible for other, undiscovered murders. Some of the most over-the-top media coverage came from the UK, where a February 2010 headline in the *Telegraph* declared that "US serial killer Rodney Alcala could be 'new Ted Bundy.'" An April 2010 headline in the London *Daily Mail* was even more histrionic: "The 'most prolific' serial killer in US history is sentenced to death as police fear he could be behind 130 murders."

At Alcala's third trial, a fingerprint technician testified that a palm print recovered from the scene of Georgia Wixted's murder thirty-three years earlier was a match for Rodney Alcala. Another technician testified that blood evidence recovered from another of the murder scenes also was a match. Nobody though bothered to explain why Alcala was just then being identified as the perpetrator of these crimes if the evidence linking a known violent sex offender and 'person of interest' to the murders had supposedly been in existence for more than thirty years!

Craig Robison, one of the lead detectives on the Samsoe case, testified that he had arrested Alcala on July 24, 1979, and taken him down to the station while other Huntington Beach officers executed a search warrant on the home. It was at that time, according to Robison, that a Sergeant Jenkins had allegedly discovered a receipt for a Seattle storage locker. Rather then seize the receipt, however, he purportedly left it there and copied down the information on it. The actual receipt was never produced at trial and there is no way of verifying that it ever existed. Following that seriously dubious lead, detectives had discovered a storage unit purportedly filled with photographs and other evidence Alcala had stashed there. Immediately after the discovery of Samsoe's alleged remains, Alcala is said to have driven to Seattle and deposited the items in the unit, after which he stayed overnight and then drove back home. He had, of course, told no one of this alleged trip and no witnesses could place him in Seattle. And there was no explanation for why he would have driven all the way there, to a city he had no known connection to and was not known to have ever visited, to stash the items. Police would later try to connect Alcala to murders previously attributed to Seattle's so-called Green River killer.

Alcala was, needless to say, convicted a third time for the murder of Robin Samsoe, as well as for the murders of Lamb, Wixted, Parentau and Barcomb. On March 2, 2010, the penalty phase of the trial began. A week later, on March 9, the jury returned once again with a recommendation that Alcala be executed. Three weeks later, the presiding judge formally sentenced him to die by lethal injection.

Six months after that third conviction, the television show *48 Hours Mystery* aired *The Killing Game*, a look at the Rodney Alcala case that had been produced by longtime correspondent Harold Dow. The episode was aired posthumously; Dow had died suddenly and unexpectedly a month earlier, on August 21, 2010, just before completing work on the project. It is not beyond the realm of possibility that Dow had discovered something about the Alcala case that those with vested interests did not want aired on national television.

Whether or not Alcala's third conviction in California will stand remains to be seen. Probably as a fallback option in case the convictions are once again overturned, as they certainly should be, Alcala was indicted in 2011 and subsequently convicted in New York for the murders of Crilley and Hover, though it is unclear what evidence those convictions were based on. Over the last several years, authorities have circulated scores of Alcala's photographs in an attempt to link him to additional crimes. To date, not one of those photos has been linked to any known murders or missing persons cases.

So what, at the end of the day, are we to make of Alcala's curious connections to the Laurel Canyon 'peace, love and understanding' scene? If his official bio is to be believed, his first victim, the daughter of a record executive, was snatched from the mouth of the canyon. One of his last victims was left posed at the northern end. And all along the way, such names as Jim Morrison, Roman Polanski, Marlon Brando and Steve Hodel, and such iconic places as Ciros and the Chateau Marmont, unexpectedly pop up in the storyline.

Rodney Alcala's story is a strange one even by serial killer standards. But it is far from being the only serial killer story that the mainstream media got wrong. Interested readers can find a wealth of such stories in my previous book, *Programmed to Kill*.

ACKNOWLEDGMENTS

THOUGH I HAVE A FAIRLY SHORT LIST OF PEOPLE TO THANK HERE, THEIR contributions were invaluable and this book wouldn't have been what it is without them.

First off, my sincerest thanks go to Thomas McGrath of Headpress for, among other things, convincing me to overcome my initial skepticism about working with a publisher to turn this material into a book (it began life as a series of web posts). Thanks go out to Thomas as well for his proofreading and editing skills, and for coming up with the title and epigraph. This book would have never come into being without the salesmanship, and infinite patience, of Mr. McGrath.

Next on the list is David Kerekes, again of Headpress, who also lent his considerable proofreading and editing skills to this work. David was also responsible for the formatting and layout of the book, as well as for coming up with a number of the chapter titles. For all of that and more, I owe a huge 'thank you' to Mr. Kerekes, as I do to Mark Critchell, who perfectly captured the tone of the book with his eye-catching cover art.

Thanks must also be extended to my esteemed colleague, Mr. Nick Bryant, for graciously agreeing to pen the Foreword to this book even though he was working on various projects of his own at the time. And also to my eldest daughter, Alissa McGowan (www.redpenforrent.com), for her irreplaceable editorial advice and assistance.

Lastly, I wish to thank my readers for their invaluable input during the time that this book was a work-in-progress. A good portion of the material in this volume was unearthed only by following links and other tips sent in by alert fans of my website. I can't thank you all individually because there are too many of you, a pretty fair number of whom I know only by email handles, but know that this book would have been considerably shorter and less interesting without your input.

SELECTED BIBLIOGRAPHY & FILMOGRAPHY

Allen, Nick. "US serial killer Rodney Alcala could be 'new Ted Bundy,'" the *Telegraph*, February 26, 2010.

Anderson, Jack. "Secret Study in Behavior Control," *Ocala Star-Banner*, August 4, 1972.

Anderson, Lessley. "Lucifer, Arisen," *San Francisco Weekly*, November 17, 2004.

Anger, Kenneth (dir.). *Scorpio Rising* (1964), Fantoma DVD, 2007.

—— (dir.). *Invocation of My Demon Brother* (1969), Fantoma DVD, 2007.

—— (dir.). *Lucifer Rising* (1981), Fantoma DVD, 2007.

Anon. "'60s: Decade of Tumult and Change, The," *Life Special Double Issue*, December 26, 1969.

——. "Bride Wore Pink, The," *Time*, February 23, 1948.

——. "Mystery of the Greystone Mansion Murders," *New York Social Diary*, August 30, 2007.

Atkins, Susan Denise and Lawrence Schiller. "Witness Tells of that Bloody Night at Tate's," the *Arizona Republic*, December 14, 1969.

Austin, John. *Hollywood's Unsolved Mysteries*, Shapolsky Publishers, 1990.

Bain, Donald. *The Control of Candy Jones*, Playboy Press, 1976.

Barris, Chuck. *Confessions of a Dangerous Mind: An Unauthorized Autobiography*, Miramax Books, 2002.

Bishop, Greg and Joe Oesterle and Mike Marinacci. *Weird California: Your Travel Guide to California's Local Legends and Best Kept Secrets*, Sterling Publishing, 2006.

Black, David. *Acid: The Secret History of LSD*, Vision Paperbacks, 1998.

Blum, William. *Killing Hope: US Military and CIA Interventions Since World War II*, Common Courage Press, 1995.

Boucher, Geoff. "LA Felt the Love of '67," *Los Angeles Times*, August 2, 2007.

Boulware, Jack. "The Rock'n'roll Treehouse," *Mojo*, April 20, 2006.

Bowser, Kenneth (dir.). *Phil Ochs: There But For Fortune* (2010), First Run Features DVD, 2011.

Boyd, Alan (dir.). *Hey Hey We're The Monkees* (1997), Immortal DVD, 2003.

Bugliosi, Vincent with Curt Gentry. *Helter Skelter: The True Story of the Manson Murders*, Bantam Books, 1974.

Burks, John. "Rock & Roll's Worst Day," *Rolling Stone*, February 7, 1970.

Brewer, Jon (dir.). *Legends of the Canyon: Classic Artists* (2009), Image Entertainment DVD, 2010.

The Byrds: Under Review (2007), Sexy Intellectual DVD, 2007.

Captain Beefheart: Under Review (2006), Sexy Intellectual DVD, 2006.

Carey, Timothy (dir.). *The World's Greatest Sinner* (1962), unreleased.

Carlin, Peter Ames. *Catch a Wave: The Rise, Fall and Redemption of The Beach Boys' Brian Wilson*, Rodale, 2006.

Carter, John. *Sex and Rockets: The Occult World of Jack Parsons*, Feral House, 2005.

Childs, Andy. "Lowell George Interview," *Zig Zag: The Rock Magazine*, March 1975.

The Chuck Negron Story: Biography of an Entertainer (2005), Delta Entertainment DVD, 2005.

Cohen, Robert Carl (dir.). *Mondo Hollywood* (1967), CustomFlix DVD, 2006.

Constantine, Alex. *The Covert War Against Rock*, Feral House, 2000.

Copeland, Ian. *Wild Thing: The Backstage, On the Road, In the Studio, Off the Charts Memoir of Ian Copeland*, Simon & Schuster, 1995.

Copeland III, Miles. "Biography of Miles Copeland III, Senior Political Editor," *And Magazine*, www.andmagazine.com/contributors/126_miles_copeland.html.

Corman, Roger (dir.). *The Trip* (1967), MGM DVD, 2003.

Cromelin, Richard. "John Phillips; Singer-Songwriter Led the Mamas and the Papas," *Los Angeles Times*, March 19, 2001.

Crosby, David and Carl Gottlieb. *Long Time Gone: The Autobiography of David Crosby*, Doubleday, 1988.

Des Barres, Pamela. *I'm With The Band: Confessions of a Groupie*, Jove, 1987.

Dow, Harold (prod.). *48 Hours Mystery: The Killing Game*, CBS television, September 2010.

Edelstein, Andrew J. *The Pop Sixties*, Ballantine Books, 1985.

Einarson, John. *Desperados: The Roots of Country Rock*, Cooper Square Press, 2001.

——. *Forever Changes: Arthur Lee and the Book of Love*, Jawbone Press, 2010.

——. *Mr. Tambourine Man: The Life and Legacy of The Byrds' Gene Clark*, Backbeat Books, 2005.

—— and Richie Furay. *For What It's Worth: The Story of Buffalo Springfield*, Cooper Square Press, 2004.

Estabrooks, G.H. *Hypnotism*, Dutton, 1957.

Fong-Torres, Ben. *Hickory Wind: The Life and Times of Gram Parsons*, Pocket Books, 1991.

Forbes, Gordon (dir.). *The Doors: No One Here Gets Out Alive* (1981), Eagle Rock Entertainment DVD, 2002.

Franzoni, Carl. "The Sundazed Interview," www.sundazed.com/scene/exclusives/franzoni_exclusive.html.

Frary, Ihna Thayer. *They Built the Capitol*, Garret and Massie, 1940.

Fricke, David. "Life of a California Dreamer," *Rolling Stone* #867, April 26, 2001.

Frost, Lee (dir.). *Mondo Bizarro* (1966), Image Entertainment DVD, 2012.

Gaines, Steven. *Heroes & Villains: The True Story of The Beach Boys*, Signet, 1986.

Gardner, David. "The 'most prolific' serial killer in US history is sentenced to death as police fear he could be behind 130 murders," London *Daily Mail*, April 1, 2010.

Gilmore, John and Ron Kenner. *Manson: The Unholy Trail of Charlie and the Family* (formerly *The Garbage People*), Amok, 2000.

Goodman, Fred. *The Mansion on the Hill: Dylan, Young, Geffen, Springsteen, and the Head-On Collision of Rock and Commerce*, Vintage, 1998.

Gorightly, Adam. "The Process Church of the Final Judgment and the Manson Family," *Paranoia*, Winter 2007.

Greenfield, Robert. "The King of LSD," *Rolling Stone*, July 12–26, 2007.

Grimes, William. "George S. Morrison, Admiral and Singer's Father, Dies at 89," *New York Times*, December 8, 2008.

Hall, Mark (dir.). *The Mamas and the Papas: Straight Shooter* (1988), Standing Room Only Entertainment DVD, 2010.

Heimbichner, Craig. *Blood On the Altar: The Secret History of the World's Most Dangerous Secret Society*, Independent History and Research, 2005.

Henderson, Richard. *Van Dyke Parks' Song Cycle (33 1/3)*, Continuum, 2008.

Hennig, Gandulf (dir.). *Gram Parsons: Fallen Angel* (2006), Rhino DVD, 2006.

Herken, Gregg. "Dr. Strangelove's Workplace," *Washington Post*, July 6, 2008.

Hiatt, Brian. "High Times in Laurel Canyon and on the Sunset Strip," *Rolling Stone*, July 12–26, 2007.

Hinsche, Billy (dir.). *Dennis Wilson Forever* (2008), Sony Pictures DVD, 2008.

Hopkins, Jerry. *The Lizard King: The Essential Jim Morrison*, Fireside, 1992.

Hopper, Dennis (dir.). *Easy Rider* (1969), Sony Pictures DVD, 1999.

Hoskyns, Barney. *Hotel California: The True-Life Adventures of Crosby, Stills, Nash, Young,*

Mitchell, Taylor, Browne, Ronstadt, Geffen, the Eagles, and Their Many Friends, Wiley, 2006.

——. *Waiting for the Sun: Strange Days, Weird Scenes, and the Sound of Los Angeles*, St. Martin's Griffin, 1996.

Jacobson, Laurie and Marc Wanamaker. *Hollywood Haunted: A Ghostly Tour of Filmland*, Angel City Press, 1994.

Kalush, William and Larry Sloman. *The Secret Life of Houdini: The Making of America's First Superhero*, Atria Books, 2006.

Kamp, David. "Live at the Whisky," *Vanity Fair*, September 4, 2006.

Kay, John and John Einarson. *John Kay: Magic Carpet Ride*, Quarry Press, 1994.

Kelly, Susan. *The Boston Stranglers*, Birch Lane Press, 1995.

Kubernik, Harvey. *Canyon of Dreams: The Magic and the Music of Laurel Canyon*, Sterling, 2009.

Kurtz, Pete. "An Interview With Snoopy Pfisterer," www.60sGarageBands.com.

Labruce, Bruce. "Bijou Phillips Interview," *Index*, 2000.

Lachman, Gary Valentine. *Turn off Your Mind: The Mystic Sixties and the Dark Side of the Age of Aquarius*, Sidgwick & Jackson, 2001.

——. "The Process," *Fortean Times*, May 2000.

Lacy, Susan (dir.). *Joni Mitchell: Woman of Heart and Mind* (2003), Eagle Rock Entertainment DVD, 2003.

Landis, Bill. *Anger: The Unauthorized Biography of Kenneth Anger*, Harper Collins, 1995.

Lawson, Kristan and Anneli Rufus. *California Babylon: A Guide to Sites of Scandal, Mayhem, and Celluloid in the Golden State*, St. Martin's Griffin, 2000.

Lee, Martin and Bruce Shlain. *Acid Dreams: The Complete Social History of LSD: The CIA, the Sixties, and Beyond*, Grove Press, 1985.

Lemons, Stephen. "Return to Wonderland," *Salon*, June 9, 2000.

Lindsell, Alec (prod.). *Frank Zappa and the Mothers of Invention: In the 1960s* (2008), Sexy Intellectual DVD, 2009.

Logan, Dan. "After Extensive Investigation and Two Trials, Huntington Beach Police Finally Put Rodney James Alcala Behind Bars," *Orange Coast*, June 1989.

Longfellow, Matthew (dir.). *Frank Zappa: Apostrophe/Over-Nite Sensation* (2007), Eagle Rock Entertainment DVD, 2007.

Lovett, Anthony R. and Matt Maranian. *LA Bizarro: The Insider's Guide to the Obscure, the Absurd, and the Perverse in Los Angeles*, St. Martin's Press, 1997.

MacDonell, Allan. "In Too Deep," *LA Weekly*, October 3, 2003.

Mank, Gregory William. *Hollywood's Hellfire Club: The Misadventures of John Barrymore, W.C. Fields, Errol Flynn and the Bundy Drive Boys*, Feral House, 2007.

Manzarek, Ray (dir.). *Turtles: Happy Together* (1991), Rhino DVD, 2000.

Mayorquin, Jose (prod.). *Eye on LA: The Legends of Laurel Canyon*, ABC television, 2012.

Maysles, Albert and David Maysles (dir.). *The Rolling Stones: Gimme Shelter* (1970), Criterion DVD, 2000.

McAlester, Keven (dir.). *You're Gonna Miss Me: A Film About Roky Erickson* (2005), Palm Pictures DVD, 2007.

McGowan, David. *Programmed to Kill: The Politics of Serial Murder*, IUniverse, 2004.

——. *Understanding the F-Word: American Fascism and the politics of Illusion*, IUniverse, 2001.

Miles, Barry. *Hippie*, Sterling Publishing, 2004.

——. *Zappa: A Biography*, Grove Press, 2004.

Moench, Doug. *The Big Book of Conspiracies*, Paradox Press, 1995.

Myers, Marc. "Who Else Made More Hit Songs?" *Wall Street Journal*, March 23, 2011.

Nash, Jay Robert. *Bloodletters and Bad Men, Book 3*, Warner Books, 1975.

Neil Young: Under Review: 1966–1975 (1975), Video Music, Inc. DVD, 2007.

Newton, Michael. *Raising Hell: An Encyclopedia of Devil Worship and Satanic Crime*, Avon, 1993.

Norman, Marc. "Hermit Chic" *Los Angeles Business Journal*, May 1, 1992.

O'Casey, Matt (dir.). *Dennis Wilson: The Real Beach Boy*, BBC television, 2008.

O'Neil, Paul. "The Love and Terror Cult," *Life*, December 19, 1969.

Owen, Frank. "The Dark Side of the Summer of Love," *Playboy*, July 2007.

Parkinson, Mike (dir.). *Jimi Hendrix: The Last 24 Hours* (2004), GMVS DVD, 2004.
Pennebaker, D.A. (dir.). *The Complete Monterey Pop Festival* (1967), Criterion DVD, 2002.
Pelisek, Christine. "Rodney Alcala: The Fine Art of Killing," *LA Weekly*, January 21, 2010.
Phillips, Graham and Martin Keatman. *The Shakespeare Conspiracy*, Century, 1994.
Phillips, John with Jim Jerome. *Papa John: A Music Legend's Shattering Journey Through Sex, Drugs, and Rock'n'Roll*, Dolphin Books, 1986.
Pierson, Jim (prod.). *California Dreamin'—The Songs of the Mamas and the Papas* (1994), Hip-O Records DVD, 2005.
Priore, Domenic and Arthur Lee. *Riot on the Sunset Strip: Rock'n'Roll's Last Stand in Hollywood*, Jawbone Press, 2003.
Rafelson, Bob (dir.). *Head: The Monkees* (1968), Rhino DVD, 1998.
Rasmussen, Cecelia. "Rustic Canyon Ruin May Be a Former Nazi Compound," *Los Angeles Times*, September 4, 2005.
Reda, Scott (dir.). *Hippies*, History Channel television, 2007.
Roeg, Nicholas and Donald Cammell (dir.). *Performance* (1970), Warner Home Video DVD, 2007.
Ross, Colin A. *The CIA Doctors: Human Rights Violations by American Psychiatrists*, Manitou Communications, 2006.
Rubin, Josh (dir.). *Derailroaded: Inside the Mind of Larry Wild Man Fischer* (2005), Ubin Twinz Productions DVD, 2011.
Sanders, Ed. *The Family: The Story of Charles Manson's Dune Buggy Attack Battalion*, Dutton, 1971.
Sands, Stella. *The Dating Game Killer: The True Story of a TV Dating Show, a Violent Sociopath, and a Series of Brutal Murders*, St. Martin's Press, 2011.
Scheinfeld, John (dir.). *Who is Harry Nilsson (And Why is Everybody Talkin' About Him)?* (2006), Lorber Films DVD, 2010.
Schudel, Matt. "Tandyn Almer, Enigmatic Composer of 'Along Comes Mary,' Dies at 70," *Washington Post*, February 16, 2013.
Shreck, Nikolas (dir.). *Charles Manson Superstar* (1989), Screen Edge DVD, 2002.
Seidenbaum, Art. "'Mondo,' Home to Roost," *Los Angeles Times*, October 1, 1967.
Seireeni, Rick. "Early Canyon History," Laurel Canyon Association Website, www.laurelcanyonassoc.com/EarlyHist.html.
Sragow, Michael. "'Gimme Shelter': The True Story," *Salon*, August 10, 2000.
Starr, Martin P. *The Unknown God: W.T. Smith and the Thelemites*, Teitan Press, 2003.
Steinberg, Susan (dir.). *Atlantic Records: The House that Ahmet Built* (2007), Rhino DVD, 2007.
Stuart-Ware, Michael. *Behind the Scenes on the Pegasus Carousel with the Legendary Rock Group Love*, Helter Skelter Publishing, 2003.
Street-Porter, Janet. *Scandal!*, Penguin Books, 1981.
Summers, Andy. "LSD Gave You a Sense of Rightness," *Rolling Stone*, July 12–26, 2007.
Terry, Maury. *The Ultimate Evil: The Truth About the Cult Murders: Son of Sam and Beyond*, Barnes and Noble Books, 1999.
Trubee, John. "Last of the Freaks: The Carl Franzoni Story," www.united-mutations.com/f/last_of_the_freaks.htm.
Unterberger, Richie. *Eight Miles High: Folk Rock's Flight from Haight-Ashbury to Woodstock*, Backbeat Books, 2003.
——. *Turn! Turn! Turn!: The sixties Folk Rock Revolution*, Backbeat Books, 2002.
Walker, Michael. *Laurel Canyon: The Inside Story of Rock-and-Roll's Legendary Neighborhood*, Faber and Faber, 2006.
Weller, Sheila. "California Dreamgirl," Vanity Fair, December 2007.
Wick, Steve. *Bad Company: Drugs, Hollywood, and the Cotton Club Murder*, St. Martin's, 1990.
Wilson, Chris (dir.). *Hotel California: LA from the Byrds to the Eagles*, BBC television, 2012.
Young, Paul. *LA Exposed: Strange Myths and Curious Legends in the City of Angels*, St. Martin's Griffin, 2002.

INDEX

INDEX

INDEX

INDEX

ABOUT THE AUTHOR

McGowan was born and raised in Torrance, California, just twenty miles south of Laurel Canyon. He graduated from UCLA with a degree in psychology in 1983, and he ran a small business in the greater Los Angeles area from 1990 until his death in 2015. He was the proud father of three adult daughters. He was also a lifelong music fan who frequently kept his radio tuned to classic rock stations. McGowan's previous books include *Programmed to Kill: The Politics of Serial Murder* and *Understanding the F-Word: American Fascism and the Politics of Illusion* (second edition forthcoming). McGowan's work and website <www.centerforaninformedamerica.com> are now maintained by his eldest daughter. She can be reached at <alissa@centerforaninformedamerica.com>.

A HEADPRESS BOOK
First published by Headpress in 2014

[*w*] www.worldheadpress.com [*e*] headoffice@headpress.com

WEIRD SCENES INSIDE THE CANYON
Laurel Canyon, Covert Ops & The Dark Heart of the Hippie Dream

Cover design: Mark Critchell <mark.critchell@googlemail.com>
Layout: David Kerekes
Headpress Diaspora: Thomas Campbell, Caleb Selah, Giuseppe, Dave T.

A CIP catalog record for this book is available from the British Library

ISBN 978-1-909394-12-4 (pbk)
ISBN 978-1-909394-13-1 (ebk)
NO-ISBN (hbk)

Headpress. The gospel according to unpopular culture.

Headpress NO-ISBN special editions are exclusive to World Headpress and can only be obtained at

WWW.HEADPRESS.COM